PACE ten years on: a review of the research

by
David Brown

D1610149

A Research and Statistics Directorate Report

Home Office
Research and
Statistics
Directorate

London: Home Office

Home Office Research Studies

The Home Office Research Studies are reports on research undertaken by or on behalf of the Home Office. They cover the range of subjects for which the Home Secretary has responsibility. Titles in the series are listed at the back of this report (copies are available from the address on the back cover). Other publications produced by the Research and Statistics Directorate include Research Findings, the Research Bulletin, Statistical Bulletins and Statistical Papers.

The Research and Statistics Directorate

The Directorate consists of three Units which deal with research and statistics on Crime and Criminal Justice, Offenders and Corrections, Immigration and General matters; the Programme Development Unit; the Economics Unit; and the Operational Research Unit.

 The Research and Statistics Directorate is an integral part of the Home Office, serving the Ministers and the department itself, its services, Parliament and the public through research, development and statistics. Information and knowledge from these sources informs policy development and the management of programmes; their dissemination improves wider public understanding of matters of Home Office concern.

First published 1997

Application for reproduction should be made to the Information Section, Home Office, Room 278, 50 Queen Anne's Gate, London SW1H 9AT.

Foreword

In the wake of the Royal Commission on Criminal Procedure, which reported in 1981, the Police and Criminal Evidence Act 1984 (PACE) made fundamental changes to many areas of the law relating to the investigation of crime. The Act was intended to establish a satisfactory balance between the rights of the suspect and the public interest in bringing criminals to justice. Following a series of well-publicised miscarriage of justice cases in the late 1980s and early 1990s, the adequacy of the safeguards which the Act provides for the suspect were searchingly scrutinised by a further Royal Commission on Criminal Justice (RCCJ).

In carrying out their work, the RCCJ gathered a range of evidence about the working of PACE, and were particularly conscious of the considerable body of research which had been undertaken on the working of the Act. At their request, the Home Office Research and Statistics Directorate undertook a review of the relevant research findings. In addition, the RCCJ itself initiated a programme of research, covering a number of key areas in which there were gaps in the literature. This work has added further to the available stock of knowledge about the operation of PACE.

In this report, the literature review undertaken for the RCCJ has been updated with the findings of the work carried out for the Commission, as well as in the light of other research completed more recently. Its publication now is particularly timely because it is exactly a decade since the bulk of the PACE provisions were implemented. It will provide a useful source of reference for all those involved in the operation of the criminal justice system or in carrying out research on it. Its publication at the present time is also opportune because it provides a benchmark against which to measure the impact of recent criminal justice initiatives, including the Criminal Justice and Public Order Act and the 1995 revisions to the PACE Codes of Practice.

CHRISTOPHER NUTTALL
Director of Research and Statistics

Acknowledgements

I am very grateful to Karen Larcombe, formerly of the Research and Statistics Directorate, for her assistance in compiling some sections of this review. I am also grateful to the authors of a number of studies, which were unpublished at the time this review was prepared, for allowing me access to their work.

DAVID BROWN

Contents

Summary

The Police and Criminal Evidence Act 1984 (PACE) is the direct outcome of the Royal Commission on Criminal Procedure's (RCCP) recommendations for systematic reform in the investigative process. The provisions of the Act are designed to match up to principles of fairness (for both police and suspect), openness and workability. Overall, they are intended to strike a balance between the public interest in solving crime and the rights and liberties of suspects.

A considerable body of research on the operation of the Act now exists, and this is reviewed in this report. The main areas examined are as follows.

Stop and search: PACE introduced a general power to stop and search persons or vehicles for stolen or prohibited articles. The safeguards include the requirement to keep records and to inform the person stopped of the reasons for police action.

Entry, search and seizure: PACE provides powers to search premises for evidence, to search premises in connection with making an arrest and to seize evidence. Safeguards relate to the level of authority required to search, the keeping of records and provisions of reasons for searches.

Arrest: PACE rationalises police arrest powers. The basis for arrest is reasonable grounds for suspicion. In less serious offences, arrests may only be made where service of a summons is impracticable.

Detention: detention is only permissible where necessary to secure or preserve evidence, or obtain evidence by questioning. Custody officers, independent from the investigation, decide on the necessity of detention and look after the suspect's welfare while in custody. An upper limit of 24 hours is put on detention without charge, other than in a limited group of 'serious arrestable offences'. Officers of inspector rank or above review the need for further detention at specified intervals.

Questioning and treatment of suspects: suspects have statutory rights to legal advice and to have someone informed of their detention under PACE. They may not generally be interviewed until they have received legal advice, if requested. Accurate records of interviews must be made. Juveniles and the mentally disordered or handicapped must not be interviewed in the absence of an 'appropriate adult'. PACE defines circumstances in which interview evidence is liable to be excluded.

Accountability and supervision: PACE emphasises the need for the reviewability of police actions and the importance of internal police supervision. Custody records for each prisoner must record events occurring during detention. Certain decisions – delaying access to legal advice, for example – must be made by senior officers independent from the investigation. External accountability is enhanced through changes to the police complaints procedure, including the formation of the independent Police Complaints Authority, which supervises the investigation of serious allegations. The Act also provides for arrangements to be made to obtain the views of the community about policing.

The main findings of research are summarised below.

Stop and search

- Pre-PACE research points to considerable under-recording of stops and suggests that the decision to stop was often based on hunch or stereotyping, with Afro-Caribbeans more likely to be stopped than white people. Records of stops were rarely inspected by supervisors. Only a small minority of stops led to arrest.

- Frequency of stop and search has increased under PACE, although to some extent this may be an artefact of better recording. Stop/searches occur most frequently in the Metropolitan Police. Around one in eight searches lead to an arrest.

- It is doubtful if stops are always made on the basis of reasonable suspicion. Where the suspect's consent is obtained, this may not always be fully informed.

- Afro-Caribbeans are more likely to be stopped than white people or Asians, more likely to be repeatedly stopped, and more likely to be searched following a stop.

Entry, search and seizure

- Stemming from clearer statutory powers, there has been a rise in the proportion of searches of premises authorised by the police rather than under court warrants. The most frequently used powers are those to search premises upon or after arrest. Around 15 per cent of searches are conducted with the occupant's consent.

- Around three-quarters of searches on warrant and about half of other searches lead to the seizure of property, usually stolen goods. However, it is doubtful whether all searches are conducted on the basis of reasonable suspicion.

- Around half of those whose premises are searched are satisfied with the conduct of the search. Where there is dissatisfaction it is caused by officers' failures to identify themselves, provide a copy of the search warrant or state their search powers.

- PACE powers to obtain access to confidential information are proving a valuable asset, although problems may arise where large volumes of material are sought or where some explanation of the material found is required.

Arrest and detention

- Although PACE was intended to restrict arrest to situations in which it was strictly necessary, suspects are very rarely summonsed instead. However, there are indications of increased police professionalism and that arrests are now made on a firmer evidential basis. Fewer than before are made without independent evidence.

- Black people are arrested at a higher rate than white people, but this does not appear to be because weaker evidence is used to justify their arrest.

- Custody officers rarely scrutinise the necessity for a suspect's detention in any detail and almost all those arrested are detained. Similarly, reviews of detention after 6 and 15 hours are largely routinised procedures lacking any substantial enquiry.

- Under PACE, those arrested for serious offences are generally held for shorter periods than before but in less serious cases several factors (such as waiting for legal advice or the arrival of appropriate adults) have pushed the length of detention up.

- PACE limits on length of detention have not generally created problems for investigating officers.

- There is considerable regional variation in the bailing of suspects after charge, probably reflecting different interpretations of the PACE bail criteria, particularly in relation to the risks of reoffending.

Treatment of suspects

- The effectiveness of custody officers in looking after the suspect's welfare is constrained by pressure of work and lack of direct oversight of some aspects of the detention process. However, they appear able to maintain a viewpoint independent of that of investigating officers.

- Detainees are generally given written and spoken information about their rights, although not always clearly. There is little evidence that rights are systematically denied.

- A large and increasing proportion of suspects are aware of their basic rights although some confusions remain and the written information provided is not always found to be helpful.

- Nearly 20 per cent of detainees ask to have someone informed of their arrest and implementation of requests is rarely formally delayed. Only around 12 per cent of detainees ask to make a telephone call, and only five per cent receive visitors.

- Doctors are called to examine prisoners in about seven per cent of cases (although in the Metropolitan Police this rises to 25 per cent), usually where detainees are believed to be drunk, but also where mental disorder or mental handicap is suspected.

Legal advice

- The great majority of suspects are given information about their right to legal advice. Improved information has been provided since the first revised PACE Codes of Practice were introduced, raising awareness among suspects that legal advice is free. Custody officers may exercise considerable influence over whether legal advice is sought.

- Requests for legal advice have more than doubled under PACE and have increased further since. Nearly 40 per cent of suspects now request advice, although there are large regional variations.

- Over 80 per cent of those who request legal advice eventually receive it. Cancellation of requests often occur where the chosen adviser is unavailable or where the parents of juveniles consider a lawyer unnecessary.

- In around 70 per cent of cases in which legal advice is given, the adviser attends the police station, but in the remainder advice is given solely over the telephone. A significant proportion of advice is provided by non-qualified solicitors' representatives.

- Legal advisers often obtain only sketchy information about cases from the police, either because they do not ask for it or because the police withhold it. Generally, consultations with clients prior to police interviews are brief. The advice given is usually either neutral in character or to co-operate with police questions. Advice to remain silent is given in around a fifth of legal advice cases.

- In most police interviews legal advisers are passive and do not always intervene to curtail oppressive or repetitive questioning or to allow suspects to present their version of events.

- Access to legal advice was occasionally delayed when PACE was first introduced but this now occurs only exceptionally.

Interviews with suspects

- Under PACE, interviews are rarely conducted with those who are unfit to be questioned. Suspects are also interviewed less frequently. Interviews do sometimes occur with those suffering from psychological conditions due to the difficulties in identifying such disorders.

- Securing a confession remains an important aim of interviewing suspects, although this is now probably more to supplement other evidence.

- Interviewing officers continue to use tactics designed to secure a confession, although unacceptable tactics (for example, exploiting police control over bail and charge decisions) are now used less often.

- Some forms of questioning raise concerns about false confessions. These concerns are mitigated – although not entirely removed – by the fact that in over 90 per cent of cases proceeded with by the police independent corroborative evidence is obtained.

- Between 55 and 60 per cent of those interviewed confess – little different from pre-PACE estimates. Confessions are less likely where suspects are legally advised or the evidence is weak; they are more likely in cases involving juveniles or strong evidence.

- Audio-taping of interviews has led to fewer disputes in court about what was said and has improved the flow of questioning. However, there are considerable problems with written records of taped interview prepared by police officers, with up to half suffering from the omission of salient points, prolixity or prosecution bias. Records prepared by civilians are significantly better in terms of quality and cost.

- Video-taping of interviews has raised some technical problems but has proved its value as a supervisory and training tool. It also appears to offer advantages over audio-taping in a significant minority of cases – some very serious – by clarifying what was taking place in the interview room. However, few videos are presently played at court.

- Little supervision or monitoring of interviewing takes place. One reason is that supervisory responsibility often rests with those who conduct interviews; another is supervisors' reluctance to risk injuring the professional pride of interviewing officers.

- Some questioning of suspects occurs outside of formal police station interviews. Up to 10 per cent of suspects are interviewed after arrest and prior to arrival at the station; up to a third of suspects who are charged may have made admissions prior to reaching the station. Once at the station, a certain amount of unregulated questioning by case officers still occurs.

Right of silence

- Research has provided widely varying estimates of the use by suspects of the right of silence but it would appear that, under PACE, initially around five per cent of suspects outside London and up to nine per cent in London refused to answer all questions, while five per cent and seven per cent respectively refused to answer some questions of significance. This represents little change from the pre-PACE situation.

- Data from recent studies (albeit pre-dating the implementation of the Criminal Justice and Public Order Act 1995) suggest that increasing numbers of suspects are staying silent and that 10 per cent are refusing all questions and 13 per cent some significant questions.

- Suspects detained for more serious offences, those with previous convictions and those who have taken legal advice are more likely to refuse police questions. In the latter instance, this a direct result of legal advice in only a minority of cases. More often, advisers either proffer no such advice, go along with their client's wishes or urge the opposite course.

- Some interviewing officers abandon interviews with silent suspects but others have various techniques – such as increasing the pressure by revealing further incriminating information – to elicit answers.

- Police decisions to take no further action are largely unrelated to whether suspects have exercised their right of silence. There also appears to be no link with CPS decisions to discontinue cases.

- Those who plead not guilty at court are more likely to have refused to answer police questions than those who plead guilty. However, those pleading not guilty who have exercised their right of silence are less likely to be acquitted than other defendants.

- Significant minorities of defendants who plead not guilty raise defences not previously mentioned during questioning. However, few such defences genuinely amount to 'ambushes' because, for example, they relate to matters the suspect could not have raised during police interviews.

Juveniles

- Up to a fifth of suspects detained by the police are aged 16 or under. In around two-thirds of cases parents or relatives act as appropriate adults but, in 20 per cent or more, social workers fulfil this function.

- Parents are often not well-equipped to act as appropriate adults because they may know little about police procedures or what is acceptable in police interviews, may be emotionally upset at their child's predicament, or may take sides with or against the police. Their role is often not explained to them by the police. They tend to play little part in police interviews.

- Social workers also often lack training in the appropriate adult's role. The quality of their response is related to the organisation of juvenile justice work in social services departments and the extent to which staff specialise in this area. Like parents, they generally remain passive during police interviews.

- Around 60 per cent of juveniles' time in custody is spent waiting for an appropriate adult to attend. Demands on social services mean that waits are often longer for social workers than relatives. On average, however, juveniles are detained for shorter periods than adults.

- Juveniles are given full information about their rights less often than adults and in some cases information is either not given at all or not until an adult is present. There have been recent improvements in this situation.

- Juveniles are less likely than adults to request legal advice and there is far more variation between areas in request rates than for adults. There is evidence that the police sometimes delay or avoid taking forward requests by juveniles for legal advice.

- There is some evidence that juveniles are more likely than adults to provide admissions, although questioning is not often oppressive. Admissions are most often provided where there is strong evidence, the juvenile has no previous convictions and the offence is less serious.

PACE and the mentally disordered and mentally handicapped

- Up to two per cent of detainees are treated by the police as mentally disordered or mentally handicapped. Up to one-third are brought to the police station as a place of safety rather than on suspicion of committing an offence. Identifying detainees with mental health problems presents difficulties for custody officers and substantially more detainees may in fact need an appropriate adult.

- Custody officers often summon the police surgeon in the first instance and in many cases, acting on the doctor's advice, do not then call for an appropriate adult.

- Ensuring that detainees with mental health problems understand their rights is problematic. Experiments with simplified versions of the notices currently provided to all suspects have had some success in raising levels of understanding.

- The role of the appropriate adult raises a number of problems. Firstly, there is sometimes confusion as to whether social workers are acting in this role or making an assessment under the Mental Health Act. Secondly, custody officers may not always be right in assuming that professionals know what is expected of them as appropriate adults. Thirdly, there is a lack of clarity about the status of information confided in appropriate adults by detainees.

- The interviewing of those with mental health problems raises dangers of generating false confessions and of over-ready compliance, leading to inaccurate replies. Police officers tend to over-estimate the reliability of the information provided.

- Appropriate adults seldom intervene during interviews with mentally disordered or mentally handicapped suspects and may not always constitute an adequate safeguard against the production of unreliable interview evidence.

Supervision and accountability

Supervision

- Detectives receive relatively little training in the supervision of investigations; in consequence, investigative errors or shortcomings may be overlooked.

- Effective supervision of investigations is impeded by the low visibility of much detective work, issues of professional pride (especially in relation to interviewing skills) and an emphasis on quantity rather than quality of clear-ups.

- The bulk of investigations are supervised by lower-ranking officers, who have their own caseloads to cope with, and not by senior officers. This carried the risk that malpractice or incompetence may pass unnoticed.

- There is tighter supervision by senior officers in major inquiries and in special squads. In major inquiries, supervision is more directive, there are quality control procedures and teams are comprised of officers without established loyalties to each other. In special squads, there is rigorous scrutiny of the evidence before offenders are targeted and tight managerial control over dealings with informants.

Complaints

- No recent research has been carried out in this area. Work carried out in 1987 suggested that, at that time, the Police Complaints Authority (PCA) was less likely to select assault cases than others for supervision. Complaints of assault tend to be particularly difficult to prove and this may have had a bearing on the PCA's decision.

- PCA supervision varied from passive, active or directive, depending on how complex and how high profile cases were. Where investigations were supervised, action was more frequently taken against officers, complaints were less often withdrawn, reports were of better quality and investigation was speedier.

- Most complainants were dissatisfied with the outcome of supervised cases, although they were more likely than other complainants to feel their case had been treated seriously and to receive good feedback and less likely to have experienced pressure to withdraw. Investigating officers felt that the PCA had little impact on the outcome of investigations, although its attention to the case put them on their mettle.

- Informal resolution of complaints was generally not popular with officers subject to complaint since they felt that accepting it was seen as admitting guilt. Officers did not view meetings between officer and complainant as productive.

- Where complaints were informally resolved, most complainants accepted this outcome as satisfactory, despite persuasion to take this course in some cases. Complainants were dissatisfied at not meeting officers subject to complaint and with lack of feeedback.

- A third of complainants reported attempts to dissuade them registering a complaint. Of those withdrawing and proceeding, a majority reported attempts to secure a withdrawal.

- Over two-thirds of complainants were dissatisfied with the outcome of their complaint, usually due to the lack of an apology or of an explanation for decisions reached. Those whose complaints were informally resolved were the most satisfied.

- Investigating officers were concerned to be seen by complainants to be taking their grievances seriously, although they accepted that the low chances of substantiation meant that many complainants would ultimately be dissatisfied. The thoroughness of investigations meant that they tended to be slow, and this was the subject of considerable criticism by officers subject to complaint.

- Public attitude surveys show that up to two-thirds of the public know of the PCA, although rather fewer are aware that it is impartial and independent from the police. Levels of awareness are far lower among members of ethnic minority groups.

Police community consultative committees

- Consultation arrangements now exist in most parts of the country. However, there have been difficulties recruiting members representative of local communities, particularly those from minority ethnic groups and younger people. Meetings are infrequent in some areas and, where public, have tended to be poorly attended.

- Agenda are sometimes dominated by police authorities. For their part, the police have not always been willing to share information, especially where it relates to operational matters.

- The effectiveness of consultative groups appears to be constrained by several factors including: lack of formal authority; absence of hard-edged information; ignorance of policing issues; pro-police orientation; and non-representativeness. However, some groups are notably successful in actively involving local people. Others, which contain influential coalitions of representatives from political parties, local government and statutory and voluntary agencies are effective in raising their agendas with the police.

Conclusions

Fairness, openness and workability

- The review concludes that PACE has introduced a greater element of fairness into pre-charge procedures, in that suspects are now more aware of their rights and given the chance to exercise them, although there remain areas in which improvement is required. There are also benefits for the police in terms of clearer and more certain powers, particularly at the station.

- However, both police and suspect may suffer from the lack of clarity in relation to powers outside the station, particularly stop, search and entry powers, while, at the station, the suspect may be at a disadvantage due to the lack of clear delineation of what interview tactics are permissible.

- The extent to which the exercise of police powers outside the police station can be reviewed after the event is limited where officers act with the apparent consent of the suspect. Reviewability of police action, both at the station and outside, is also constrained by dependence on official records, which may be incomplete, unreliable or unverifiable.

- PACE powers are generally more workable than their predecessors, because they provide clarification and certainty, particularly in relation to detention at the station. However, the use of stop and search and entry and search powers remains problematic, and officers often prefer to operate with the subject's consent.

Legal regulation of policing

- Police behaviour appears to be more strongly influenced by PACE rules inside the police station than out. The reason for this difference is probably that insufficient account was taken of the strong informal working rules which determine how the police behave on the street.

* The lessons to be drawn from the experience of implementing PACE are that new legal rules can alter existing working practices provided that: they are clear; their introduction is accompanied by adequate training; there are effective sanctions and supervision; and the public are aware of their rights and of police powers.

Balance in the investigative process

* The review concludes that PACE has not yet produced a system in balance, in the sense that police powers and safeguards for the suspect are generally well matched in key areas.

* In relation to the exercise of stop and search and entry and search powers and the treatment of at risk groups, suspects may be at a relative disadvantage. However, at the police station suspects may be benefiting considerably from the availability of legal advice and use of the right of silence, to the detriment of the public interest in bringing criminals to account.

* The picture is a shifting one, and current initiatives in the criminal justice field may go some way towards producing a balanced pre-charge process.

1 Introduction

The Police and Criminal Evidence Act 1984 (PACE) fundamentally reformed the law relating to the investigation of crime. The background is well summarised in the introduction to the report of the Royal Commission on Criminal Procedure (RCCP, 1981: 2-3), where it is noted that, although there had been previous reforms in criminal procedure, the approach had been piecemeal and there had been no complete review since the beginning of the century. Several factors underlay the need for a more thorough look, one being general public anxiety about rising crime and concern that the police lacked the necessary powers to deal with it. Equally, however, there were suspicions that the police abused their powers. In this context, the Confait case raised specific concerns about police treatment of juvenile and mentally handicapped suspects.[1]

The RCCP was requested to examine the powers and duties of the police in relation to criminal investigation as well as the rights and duties of suspects. The balance between the needs of the police and the suspect's rights was an essential part of the Commission's remit: they were required to "have regard both to the interests of the community in bringing offenders to justice and to the rights and liberties of persons suspected or accused of crime ..." (RCCP, 1981: iv). PACE, which owed a great deal to the work of the RCCP, echoed their call for balance in the investigative process. The Act's provisions were also designed to match up to three vital criteria – fairness, openness and workability – which the Commission considered to be singularly lacking from many areas of the law relating to suspects' rights and police powers.

Fairness, openness and workability

Fairness was taken to apply to both suspect and police officer (RCCP, 1981: 20-21). Where suspects have particular rights, they should be made aware of them and given the opportunity to exercise them. If rights are to be withheld, the suspect should be told that this is being done and why. Where police powers are exercised, the suspect should be told the basis for police actions. Rules should also be equitably applied, without variation between

---

1   For a full account see Price and Caplan (1976) and the Fisher report (1977).

different groups of people or in different parts of the country. For the police, fairness means that rules should be part of a clear and understandable framework, and not liable to arbitrary reinterpretation at a later stage.

Openness means not only that what is happening should be clear to the suspect, but also reviewable by others. Decisions should be explained to the suspect, and written down so that supervisory officers, legal advisers and the courts may have access to them later. This is particularly important in relation to what happens at the police station out of public view.

Workability, like fairness, is a double-edged standard. For the police, it means that their powers should be: sufficient to fulfil their duty to detect and investigate crime; clear and certain; and able to take account of the practical circumstances in which the police operate. At the same time, the rules should enable the police to respect the rights of the suspect.

The Police and Criminal Evidence Act 1984

The main PACE provisions covered by this review are outlined below,[2] together with an indication of how the legislation was intended to improve on existing law and embody the principles described. Fuller references to specific parts of the Act or the five accompanying Codes of Practice are provided at various points in the review where relevant.

Stop and search

Pre-PACE stop and search powers suffered from the defects that they varied considerably around the country, were in some respects inadequate, and were unclear. There was evidence that stops were conducted randomly rather than on the basis of sound evidence (RCCP, 1981; Smith and Gray, 1985). PACE introduced a general power to stop and search persons or vehicles for stolen or prohibited articles on reasonable suspicion. There are safeguards against abuse: the person to be searched must be told the grounds for making the search and the officer's name and station; a written record must be made and the person searched has the right to a copy; and guidance is given about the circumstances in which voluntary searches, outside the ambit of the Act, are permissible. A Code of Practice (Code A) provides detailed rules on the conduct of stops and searches.

---

2   For a more detailed account of the Act, see Zander (1995).

Entry, search and seizure

The law here was also unclear and there were notable omissions in the powers that the police claimed they needed. It was held in 1982, for example, that there was no power to search the house of arrested persons for evidence connected with crimes for which they had been arrested.[3] The Act distinguishes entry according to whether it relates to a search for evidence or whether it is in conjunction with arrest. In the former case, the level of authority (magistrate or circuit judge) needed to search depends on the nature and confidentiality of the material named in the search warrant. In the latter, PACE provides widely drawn powers for the police to enter and search premises in connection with making an arrest or to enter and search premises occupied or controlled by someone under arrest for an arrestable offence. The Act also provides a broadly drawn power to seize anything reasonably believed to be evidence of the offence being investigated or any other offence. Safeguards against abuse of these powers are found in the Act itself and a Code of Practice (Code B). Principally these relate to: the need to seek higher authority for searches and to provide information to justify them; record-keeping requirements; the provision of information about the search to the occupant or controller of premises; and general rules in the Code about police conduct of searches.

Arrest

The pre-existing law suffered from a confusing array of common law and statutory powers of arrest. The RCCP proposed simplifying arrest powers and limiting the circumstances in which people might be deprived of liberty. In response, PACE repealed most statutory powers of arrest without warrant and replaced them with one power of arrest for offences categorised as arrestable.[4] Other than where a suspect is caught in the act, or is known to have committed or is about to commit such an offence, arrest must be made on the basis of reasonable grounds for suspicion. For offences not classed as arrestable, there is again the requirement of reasonable suspicion, but PACE restricts arrest to cases where service of a summons is impracticable (the necessity principle): for example, the suspect's name or address cannot be ascertained. The Act also makes it clear that suspects should be in no doubt about their status: if someone voluntarily accompanies a police officer to the police station, they should be told at once if a decision to arrest them is taken.

---

3   McLoric v. Oxford (1982) Q.B. 1290.
4   Arrestable offences are defined in s. 24 of PACE. Powers of summary arrest apply to: (a) offences for which the sentence is fixed by law; (b) offences for which a person of 21 years of age or over (not previously convicted) may be sentenced to imprisonment for a term of five years; and (c) a range of other specified offences, such as taking a motor vehicle or other conveyance without authority.

Detention

The RCCP considered the existing law inadequate to regulate the time suspects spend in custody. And, while police forces had generally made arrangements for looking after the interests of the detainee, these varied widely. PACE now clearly states the basis on which suspects may be held without charge: to secure or preserve evidence relating to an offence for which someone is under arrest or obtain such evidence by questioning. If sufficient evidence is available, the suspect must be charged; otherwise, if detention is not necessary the person must be released. The Act creates the key post of custody officer, the holder of which is independent from the investigation of any offence and has responsibility for the care of suspects while they are held at the police station. A ceiling of 24 hours is placed on detention without charge, other than in 'serious arrestable offences', in which detention may extend to 36 hours on the authority of an officer of at least superintendent rank and, at most, 96 hours under warrants of further detention issued by magistrates' courts. At regular intervals, review officers (of inspector rank or above) not directly involved in the investigation must examine the need for detention to continue.

Questioning and treatment of suspects

Rules on the questioning and treatment of suspects were deficient in several respects. Suspects had the right to legal advice, but the police did not have to tell them about it. Few requested solicitors and the police often turned down requests that were made. There was little guidance to the police on how to conduct interviews or provision for independent monitoring. Interviews with juveniles were sometimes conducted without an adult present, running the risk that admissions might be deemed unreliable. The police sometimes lacked necessary powers: for example, there was no statutory basis for searches of suspects at the station (although they were routine). And the police had no power (without applying to a magistrates' court) to take suspects' fingerprints without consent, even though this might be crucial to the investigation.

PACE and two associated Codes of Practice address these shortcomings. The right to legal advice is put on a statutory footing and custody officers are required to inform suspects of it. Suspects may choose their own solicitor or a duty solicitor from a scheme set up under the Act, and may not (except in urgent circumstances) be interviewed until they have received legal advice. Access to a lawyer may only be delayed in serious arrestable offences[5] in

---

5   Serious arrestable offences are defined and listed in s.116 and Schedule 5, Part 1 of PACE. There are three types of arrestable offence (SAO): (a) those that are always SAOs (e.g. treason, murder); (b) those that are only SAOs for the purpose of the provisions on delaying access to a solicitor or notification of arrest (e.g. terrorist offences); and (c) those which are only SAOs in certain circumstances (e.g. their commission has led or is intended or is likely to lead to serious consequences such as interference with the administration of justice or with the investigation of offences or of a particular offence).

specified circumstances. Accurate records of interviews must be made whilst they are in progress.[6] Code C addresses the way in which interviews are to be conducted and the physical conditions of interview rooms. The procedure in tape-recorded interviews is covered additionally by Code E. Juveniles and the mentally disordered or mentally handicapped are not to be interviewed in the absence of an 'appropriate' adult.

Fingerprints may be taken in specified circumstances on the authority of a superintendent if the suspect refuses consent. Searches of suspects are also put on a statutory footing; however, they are not necessarily to be routine and searches of intimate parts of the body may only be carried out on a superintendent's authority to look for Class A drugs or items that might be used to cause injury.

In addition to these provisions, PACE and Code C cover outside contacts by the suspect. This issue had not been considered problematic by the RCCP, since intimation of arrest was already covered by the Criminal Law Act 1977. The right to have someone informed and to make a telephone call are now spelt out in more detail. The rights of foreign nationals to contact diplomats are also covered.

Confession evidence

PACE made major changes to the law on confessions and their admissibility. While this review does not deal with the treatment of confession evidence by the courts, it does deal with the conduct of police interviews and, hence, on practices which raise issues of admissibility of evidence. The pre-existing common law position was that a confession was only admissible if the prosecution could show it to be voluntary. This meant that it had not been obtained by "fear of prejudice or hope of advantage exercised or held out by a person in authority" or by oppression. This rule was criticised on the basis that it was hard to assess whether a confession was truly voluntary. The test applied in PACE is partly one of reliability: was the confession obtained in consequence of anything said or done which was likely in the circumstances existing at the time to render it unreliable? The other test is whether the confession was obtained by oppression of the person who made it. In either circumstance, the court must not allow the confession to be given in evidence (unless the prosecution proves beyond reasonable doubt that the confession was not obtained in this way). Quite apart from the provisions relating specifically to confessions, the Act incorporates a general test of fairness for the admissibility of evidence. This may, however, be applied to confession evidence.

---

6   When PACE was first introduced, written contemporaneous notes of interviews were made. Most interviews are now tape-recorded. In a few areas they are also video-taped.

Accountability and supervision

Following from the RCCP's disquiet about the secrecy of many police actions and decisions, PACE seeks to increase the scope for review by supervisors and others. There are many requirements for detailed record-keeping. A custody record, that must be kept for every prisoner, records all events during a period of detention. Searches of premises, vehicles and persons are also accompanied by recording requirements.

Police accountability is both internal and external in nature. Internally, supervisory officers may scrutinise records to check correct procedure has been observed. Breaches of provisions of the Codes of Practice amount to infractions of the police disciplinary code and may attract disciplinary action. Senior officers not involved in the investigation are also responsible for various review functions: for example, assessing the need for further detention or decisions about delaying access to legal advice. External accountability is provided through several mechanisms: first, through a new complaints procedure. At the lower end of the scale, complaints may be informally resolved if the complainant agrees. If this is inappropriate or the complainant does not consent, the complaint is investigated. Decisions about discipline are made by chief officers, but they are reviewed by a new body independent from the police, the Police Complaints Authority. Ultimately, the Authority may direct that disciplinary charges may be brought if it disagrees with a chief officer's decision. In more serious cases, the Authority may, or in certain cases must, supervise the investigation of the complaint.

A second avenue of accountability is provided through the exclusion of evidence by the courts. Confession evidence obtained in breach of the Act's provisions (see above) or evidence generally that would have an adverse effect on the fairness of proceedings may, at the court's discretion, be excluded.

A third, broader, form of accountability is provided by a new requirement for arrangements to be made in each force to obtain the views of the community about matters concerning policing in the area. This provision arises from the Scarman report on the Brixton disorders, which pointed to the inadequacy of communication between police and public (Scarman, 1981).

Assessing PACE

This report considers to what extent the underlying aims of the legislation have been achieved. This is done principally by examining the operation of constituent parts of the Act and Codes. This shadows the approach adopted by most research: clearly, examining the effects of PACE as a whole is beyond the scope of individual studies. However, from this examination the report draws some general conclusions about the broader effects of PACE. These relate, first, to the prospects for formal rule-making to influence police practice. A certain amount of pessimism in this regard has been expressed by various researchers and commentators (see, for example, Baldwin and Kinsey, 1982; Reiner, 1985; Smith and Gray, 1985; Smith, 1986; McConville *et al*, 1991). Secondly, by taking a broader view, the review seeks to assess whether there is any evidence that the criminal process now incorporates the degree of balance which the RCCP felt to be so desirable.

In examining the impact of PACE, it must be kept in mind that the Act has not been implemented over the past ten years against a static background. There have been changes, for example, in patterns of criminal activity, in the response of suspects to the condition of being in custody, and in the organisation of criminal legal advice work. It follows, therefore, that the effect of particular provisions of the Act may well not be a constant but may change over time. This process of change can be charted where a number of studies covering the same topic have been carried out during the life of the Act. It is possible, for example, to point to trends in requests for legal advice among suspects. Generally, however, there has not been sufficient research to have generated a sequence of studies on each aspect of PACE. It must also be remembered that the rules under which the police operate have not remained the same. Thus, the Codes of Practice issued under PACE by the Home Secretary to regulate practice in several important areas, such as the exercise of stop and search powers and the detention of suspects have been revised twice since their original introduction, first in April 1991 and again in April 1995. There have also been important legislative changes impinging upon police work, among the most significant of which have been the provisions of the Criminal Justice and Public Order Act 1995 relating to the suspect's right of silence. In time, further research will be carried out to examine the impact of such changes. The present review provides an important benchmark of previous practice against which comparisons may be made when this research is undertaken.

2 Stop and search

The bulk of crime is brought to police notice and cleared up as a result of information provided by members of the public (Reiss, 1971; Mawby, 1979; Steer, 1980; Bottomley and Coleman, 1981). Proactive police tactics are responsible for bringing relatively few offences to notice. However, such tactics have attracted a disproportionate amount of attention in recent years, not least because they have impacted heavily on specific sections of the community. Police stop and search powers have perhaps generated the most debate (Willis, 1983; Reiner, 1992; Young, 1994).

Pre-PACE stop and search powers were contained in a variety of national and local legislation. There were, for example, general powers to stop and search for firearms and controlled drugs. However, powers to stop and search for stolen goods were only to be found in local legislation, as was the case in the capital. A study by Willis (1983) of the use of such pre-PACE powers found considerable under-recording of stops. Although the various legislation usually had some requirement of reasonable suspicion, she found that there appeared to be a large element of hunch or stereotyping behind the decision to stop and search. Black people particularly were more likely to be stopped than whites. Some types of stop were much more likely to result in an arrest than others. She also found that records of stops were rarely inspected by supervisors.

Further evidence of the unsatisfactory state of the law on stop and search was revealed by the Policy Studies Institute's research on policing in London (Smith and Gray, 1985) and by data collated for the RCCP (1981a). Smith and Gray found that the criterion of reasonable suspicion was not an important determinant of decisions to stop and, as Willis had noted, that black people were far more frequently the subject of stops than white people. Only about one in twelve stops led to an arrest or report for summons. The RCCP evidence pointed to a similarly low success rate.

In framing the PACE provisions in this area, the defects of the pre-existing stop and search powers were taken into account. The new powers, which apply to the stop and search of persons and vehicles for stolen or prohibited articles, are designed to be clear and to apply nationally. They incorporate safeguards, including the requirement of reasonable suspicion, the provision of reasons for police actions and completion of a written record. The record is also intended to aid third parties to review police use of these powers. A variety of other powers to stop and search are preserved. The manner in which all stop and search powers are to be used is regulated by PACE Code of Practice A.

The most wide-ranging study to examine the operation of the PACE stop and search provisions was conducted by Hull University Centre for Criminology and Criminal Justice in a force in the North of England. The findings are based on an examination of over 200 stop and search records drawn from 1986 and 1987, observation of street policing, and interviews with police officers. Several crime surveys have also touched on the PACE stop and search provisions. These include: the 1988 British Crime Survey (BCS) (Skogan, 1990; Skogan, 1994); the Hammersmith and Fulham Crime Survey (HFCS) (Painter et al, 1989); the Second Islington Crime Survey (SICS) (Crawford et al, 1990); and a recent survey in North London (Young, 1994). Home Office Statistical Bulletins (Home Office, various years) collate national data on the frequency of searches under the PACE powers, their purpose and outcome.

Frequency of stop and search

Since the PACE provisions were designed to eliminate arbitrariness in the use of stop and search, fewer searches or an increase in their productivity (or both) might be expected if this aim is being achieved. However, there are methodological problems in making comparisons between pre-PACE and present day statistics. The quality of pre-PACE statistics varies considerably, and they are spread across a range of different powers, only some of which are comparable with those existing now. Some were only available in specific areas of the country. There was only a statutory recording requirement in relation to stop/searches under the Misuse of Drugs Act 1971. Furthermore, stops rather than searches were sometimes used as the basis for analysis; and outcomes were variously expressed in terms of arrests, prosecutions and the finding of prohibited items. The extent of under-recording of searches made under statutory powers is also unknown. Although victim surveys – notably the BCS (see Skogan, 1990; 1994) – provide some indication of the true level of stop/searches, they are an inaccurate tool to distinguish whether the stop was made with consent or under the exercise of a particular power and, if so, which.

Official statistics on stop/searches under Section 1 of PACE published by the Home Office Statistical Department (Home Office, various years) show a steady rise year on year in the number of searches recorded by the police: in 1986, there were nearly 110,000; by 1990 this had risen to almost 257,000; while the most recent figures, for 1994, show 576,111. The rise in stop/searches probably reflects both an increase in police activity in the face of rising crime and more comprehensive recording of voluntary searches (see below). Variations in these respects undoubtedly contribute to the large differences found between forces in recorded stop/searches. The Metropolitan Police have consistently dominated the statistics: the most recent data show that 52 per cent of recorded stops and searches were made in the capital (Home Office, 1995).

No comprehensive pre-PACE figures are available. However, Bottomley *et al* (1989) compared the level of drugs searches under the Misuse of Drugs Act 1971 with PACE drugs searches. They found that the number of recorded searches doubled. They do not necessarily take this to mean that the require-ment of reasonable grounds for suspicion has had no impact but consider that recording may have increased with the introduction of standard forms readily available to all officers.

Victim surveys suggest little change in the real level of stops (c.f. searches) between pre-PACE years and the early days of the legislation. The 1988 BCS, which was able to provide a comparison with the 1982 sweep of the survey, pointed to a marginal decrease in foot stops and no change in vehicle stops (Skogan, 1990). The report notes that this apparent stability may be the product of competing influences, some – particularly the standard of suspi-cion required – depressing the level of stops and others – such as the national availability of the stop and search power – pushing that level up. The SICS also found no change in the level of foot stops since the first survey, conducted in 1985 (Crawford *et al*, 1990). However, the overall rate of stops in this survey, as well as in the HFCS (which did not include pre-PACE data: see Painter *et al*, 1989) and Young's (1994) North London survey was over twice as high as that found by the BCS, reflecting higher use of stop and search powers in inner-city areas.

The most recently available BCS data (from the 1992 sweep) show a rise in the real level of stops, both in England and Wales as a whole and in London. The increase is confined to vehicle stops, with 16 per cent of respondents reporting such stops in 1992 compared with 12 per cent in 1988[1] (Skogan, 1994). What might the expected effect be on searches? It may be inferred from the BCS data that the number of searches following stops would not be expected to have changed substantially. The 1992 BCS shows that the search rate following foot stops has remained at 22 per cent since the 1988 survey. The rate at which pedestrians are stopped has also not changed. And, although there are more vehicle stops, the search rate has declined from 10 per cent in 1988 to seven per cent in 1992 (Skogan, *ibid*), virtually cancelling out the effect of the increase in stops on the level of searches. In contrast, the

---

1   In 1982, 1988 and 1992 three per cent of respondents stated that they had been stopped on foot (Skogan, 1994).

official statistics actually show a 135 per cent increase between 1988 and 1992 in the number of searches recorded following foot and vehicle stops (Home Office, 1989d; 1993). One possible inference that may be drawn from the differing trends in the official and BCS estimates is that an increasing number of searches are now being officially recorded. There is, as yet, little firm evidence of this. Roughly similar numbers of respondents in both the 1988 and 1992 sweeps of the BCS recalled officers filling out an 'official report' of the incident (Skogan, 1994). However, it may be that respondents' memories are unreliable in this respect and that this is not necessarily evidence which refutes a rise in official recording.

One effect of PACE may be to have reduced the number of stops which lead to searches. There is evidence on this score from both the BCS and the SICS. The latter provides the more striking illustration of this in relation to foot stops, with the proportion searched falling by half from 50 per cent to 25 per cent (Crawford *et al*, 1990). The fall shown by the BCS is smaller – 29 per cent down to 22 per cent; however, the most recent survey does show a marked reduction in vehicle stops leading to searches, down from 13 per cent to seven per cent (Skogan, 1994). These figures might be taken to suggest that the requirement of reasonable suspicion to undertake a search has had some impact, particularly in areas where stop rates are high and pre-PACE searches may sometimes have been conducted with a degree of arbitrariness (Smith and Gray, 1985). However, recent evidence from Young's (1994) survey in North London, suggests that the search rate in some areas may be far higher: apparently, three-quarters of those stopped on foot in this area were searched.

It is difficult to account for such a wide disparity in the search rate. It may reflect that stops in some areas are made on a firmer basis of suspicion, and searches are therefore more often justified. Young (*ibid*), for example, suggests that in high crime areas, where law-abiding members of the public avoid certain areas at specific times, the catchment population for stop and search is highly structured. The police may therefore be more likely to be successful in singling out those engaged in criminal activity. On the other hand, it may be that police perceptions of particular areas as high crime ones may lead them to make more searches of those stopped, in the belief that they are likely to be involved in crime.

Measuring the 'success' of stop and search

The only nationally available measure of the 'success' rate of searches is the proportion leading to arrest. This has declined very gradually since the introduction of the PACE powers from 17 per cent in 1986 to 12 per cent in 1994 (Home Office, various years). These figures do not, however, take account of searches that lead to proceedings by way of summons or to a formal police caution. Local surveys have produced figures not greatly at variance with the official statistics: for example, Young's (1994) North London survey showed an arrest rate of 18 per cent.

The arrest rate varies according to the reason for the search. The most recent figures show that searches for offensive weapons and drugs are most likely to lead to arrest (in 14% of cases) and those for going equipped least likely (in 7% of cases). Searches for stolen property and for firearms lead to arrests in 11 per cent and eight per cent of cases respectively (Home Office, 1995). No comparable, national, pre-PACE figures on arrest rates are available. Metropolitan Police figures exist, but are based on stops rather than searches. Willis (1983) found that nine per cent of recorded stops in London led to an arrest in 1981. While it is known that around one in four pre-PACE stops led to a search, stops leading to an arrest are not always preceded by a search. Pre-PACE figures were collected on stop/searches in drugs cases although the outcome was measured in terms of drugs found rather than arrest. In 1979, 22 per cent of those searched were found in illegal possession of drugs (RCCP, 1981a); in 1994, arrests for drugs as a percentage of PACE searches for drugs came to 14 per cent (Home Office, 1995). Bottomley *et al* found a comparable pattern in their Hull study. The apparent decline in the success rate may, they suggest, reflect more comprehensive recording of unproductive searches.

Arrest rates vary widely between forces, ranging from seven per cent in Bedfordshire and nine per cent in Derbyshire up to 21 per cent in Kent and 22 per cent in Humberside (Home Office, 1995). Possibly, this may be yet another reflection of varying practices in recording searches, although it also raises the as yet unanswered question of whether different levels of suspicion are used to justify searches. Another possibility to be considered is that the outcome of stop and search may vary according to the state of police relations with the public in particular areas. Where relations are good, it is probable that the great majority of stops and searches are carried out in a non-conflictual manner. In an observational study in two areas of Surrey and the Metropolitan Police area, Norris *et al* (1993) found this to be the case in the great majority of over 300 stops which they observed. However, they noted that the demeanour of the person stopped had an important bearing on the outcome. It is reasonable to suggest that, where police relations with the public are not always good, encounters between the two are more likely to lead to confrontation and a possible arrest.

Stop/searches may also be looked at in terms of the extent to which they contribute to the prevention or the detection of crime. Judged in these terms, the emphasis is primarily on the detection of offences. The most recent Home Office figures show that nearly 70 per cent of stop/searches were for stolen property or drugs (Home Office, 1995). In contrast, less than a third can be said to have had a preventive objective: for example, searches for items to be used in the course of burglary or theft (18%) or for offensive weapons (5%). Moreover, not only are preventive searches less frequent but they are generally less successful (see above). Thus, arrests of those searched on suspicion of 'going equipped' run at a considerably lower rate than is the case for those suspected of carrying stolen property or drugs.

Another aspect to the success of stop/searches is their contribution to arrests and crime clearance. Young (1994), in a study based in selected areas of London, found that nearly eight per cent of all arrests followed a stop/search. In a more broadly based study, set in seven police forces (including the Metropolitan Police), Phillips and Brown (forthcoming) found a slightly higher proportion of 11 per cent. Young (1994) assesses the contribution of stop and search to arrests as 'minor', and argues that it must be put in the context of the potential damage done to police/public relations by the preponderance of unjustified stop/searches. Whether this contention can be sustained is debatable, however, for evidence from the BCS suggests that the great majority of those stopped by the police are satisfied with the way the encounter is dealt with (Skogan, 1990; 1994).

In terms of their contribution to crime clearance, it would seem that, broadly speaking, arrests following stop/searches are as effective as arrests arising in other circumstances. Phillips and Brown (forthcoming) found that 67 per cent of those arrested following a stop/search were charged or cautioned, little different than the figure of 69 per cent for those arrested otherwise. It may be deduced, therefore, that stop/searches contribute up to 11 per cent of primary clearances (i.e. by way of charge or caution). However, Phillips and Brown found marked differences in the rate at which different kinds of stop/search led to a charge or caution. Thus, only 51 per cent of those arrested following a search for stolen property were charged or cautioned compared with 73 per cent of those arrested following a drugs search. They argue that this suggests that the police may be prone to arresting suspects in some kinds of situation in which the threshold of reasonable suspicion has not been reached.

The study by Young (1994) in North London is the only one to have evaluated stops and searches in terms of the eventual court outcome of the case. He found that only 40 per cent of arrests following a stop/search led to a finding of guilt. However, he gives no figures for cautions. Since nearly half of arrests in his sample were for drugs offences, largely possession of cannabis, it is probable that a significant number of these received a police caution.

Impact of PACE on stop and search practices

A key aim of the PACE stop and search provisions was to structure the use of police discretion: for example, by specifying what level of suspicion was required to trigger the powers and by requiring records to be kept. In examining this aspect of PACE, Bottomley *et al* (1989) observe in their Hull study that PACE's success is dependent upon: (i) officers understanding and internalising the relevant rules contained in PACE and Code of Practice A; (ii) being willing and able to follow them; (iii) diligently and accurately recording the details of events; and (iv) supervisors being willing and able to monitor records and impose sanctions where appropriate.

Various commentators, *a priori*, expressed scepticism about the provisions. Stone (1986) suggested that the procedures required by PACE and the Codes may be more an administrative nuisance for the police than a benefit to the suspect, while Curtis (1986) argued that they are out of touch with the reality of street policing. Doubt was expressed as to whether the concept of reasonable suspicion could be used as an effective constraint on police actions (Smith, 1986). The original version of Code A attempted to define it at some length (Code A, Annex B), noting that it went beyond mere suspicion, and involved some concrete basis for suspicion against a particular individual that could be considered and evaluated by an objective third person. It was no less than the degree of suspicion needed to arrest for offences to which the stop and search powers related.[2]

Bottomley *et al* (1989) raise too the issue of searches with the consent of the suspect. The original version of Code A said little about consensual searches, although Home Office Circular 88/1985 advised that "[v]oluntary search must not be used as a device for circumventing the safeguards established in Part 1 [of PACE]" (Home Office, 1985b). In some situations there may be no power to search, in which case officers must rely on securing consent and PACE recording requirements do not apply. It is less clear what should be done where a power to search exists, but the suspect consents to the search. Dixon *et al* (1990a) argue that, although the power is available in these circumstances, it could be said that it is not exercised because consent is given. This would mean that completion of a formal record would not be needed.

---

2   The revised Codes, brought into effect in April 1991, clarify and simplify the definition of reasonable suspicion. The distinction between mere and reasonable suspicion is no longer included, nor the requirement that the level of suspicion must be equivalent to that necessary to arrest.

Reasonable suspicion

From their examination of stop and search records, Bottomley *et al* (1989) argue that it is doubtful in some cases whether the standard of reasonable suspicion is reached. Rather, they note that officers may have directed their minds to issues other than the level of suspicion in deciding whether to undertake a search as a PACE search. What occurred during or even after the search may have been important. Thus, whether a suspect co-operated could be important; so could the possibility of later repercussions. The preference of some officers appeared to be to evade PACE requirements, either by obtaining the suspect's consent, wherever possible, or arresting. Generally, the researchers conclude that the majority of officers did not feel that they had been unduly affected by the introduction of a more restricted concept of reasonable suspicion.

The apparent failure to regulate police conduct by the requirement of reasonable suspicion has not been greeted with surprise by those who have written on this aspect of policing. Bottomley *et al* (ibid.) themselves question whether officers on the street can be expected to make the required distinctions between levels of suspicion when confronted with practical situations. Dixon *et al* (1989) point to major difficulties for officers in operating on the basis of individualised suspicion where, for example, someone is stopped late at night in an area in which burglaries are common, although there has at the time been no report of a specific burglary that night. Young (1994) also notes that the police have to exercise considerable discretion in making stops for, among the plethora of incidents that confront them every day, the obvious suspects are in the minority.

Dixon *et al* (1989) and McConville *et al* (1991) have underlined how attempts at regulation may conflict head-on with traditional working practices. The former note that working rules are historical products deeply engrained in police culture. The latter argue that the lack of clarity in the definition of reasonable suspicion makes it inevitable that the police will fall back on informal methods of working. The result is that decisions about whether to stop and search may depend on whether a person is known to the police or on hunches about the 'suspiciousness' of particular classes of person in specific locations at specific times. Supporting this view are the findings of various surveys which have drawn attention to the way in which stop and search is heavily patterned according to age, class, gender, race[3] and area (see, for example, Skogan, 1990, 1994; Jefferson and Walker, 1992; Young, 1994).

Young (1994) acknowledges that this patterning suggests that the police act on the basis of stereotyping rather than of reasonable suspicion. However,

---

3   The issue of race in relation to stop and search is discussed further on.

he argues that other possible ways of proceeding present difficulties. One alternative, acting on what he terms 'democratic' suspicion, according to which the police regard all members of the public with equal suspicion, would produce few arrests because those suspicions would generally prove to be unfounded. Another possibility, that searches should be based on firm evidence, is often not available because the police depend heavily on information from the public. For some of the kinds of crime for which stops and searches are made (for example, drugs offences and going equipped), it is unlikely that members of the public are in possession of relevant information or are are willing to help. Confronted with these difficulties, Young argues that there is a certain rationality in the police focusing on those whom their experience suggests are most involved in crime (particularly, young, working class males), for this will bring the greatest marginal yield with limited resources. Even so, the bulk of such stops will still be unproductive.

Searches with consent

By no means all searches are carried out under the PACE section 1 power, but are conducted with the consent of the person stopped. However, Bottomley *et al* (1989) found considerable confusion surrounding this issue. One difficulty relates to the question of what amounts to consent. Home Office Circular 88/1985 emphasises that co-operation alone should not be taken as implying consent (Home Office, 1985b). In effect, consent should be informed by an awareness of rights and police powers. Dixon *et al* (1990a) suggest, however, that the bulk of searches in the Hull research were carried out on the basis of consent that amounted to "acquiescence based on ignorance". Few officers reported that suspects appeared aware of their rights under PACE.

The result of the use of consent is the large-scale under-recording of stops and searches. In the Hull study, in a force of 2,000 officers, only around 700 stop/searches were recorded in 1986 and 1987, and less than 600 in 1988; in contrast, officers reported that they might carry out up to four or five stop/searches during a late shift. Dixon *et al* (1990a) suggest that national figures on stop and search, which show less than one stop/search per officer a year, also imply under-recording due to the use of consensual stop/searches. A comparison of BCS data and official statistics also points to the same conclusion, although there may be an increasing tendency towards official recording (see above). According to Dixon *et al* (ibid.), the police view appears to be that, if consent is given, a power is not being exercised even though the power exists. In their research force (through revised Standing Orders) and nationally, through a Home Office Circular, moves have now been made to ensure that all searches made under PACE powers are recorded, irrespective of whether consent is given. Bottomley *et al* (1989) suggest that this may create difficulties. Firstly, searches with consent do not necessarily require reasonable suspicion; if they are then recorded in accordance with PACE it may be impossible to record satisfactory grounds for the search. Secondly, the official statistics will tend to show greater use of coercive police powers than is actually the case.

Dixon *et al* (1990a) suggest that, whatever the modifications to the rules, they may only have limited effect because this is an area in which formal rules have relatively little impact on what takes place on the ground. Non-recording stems from the irrelevance of PACE requirements in practical policing situations. They argue that police powers are typically applied to low-status, marginal members of society and concepts such as rights and informed consent sit uneasily with police views of such persons. Bottomley *et al* (1989) suggest too that some officers feel the requirement of reasonable suspicion acts as a constraint and prefer to obtain consent rather than raise the possibility of having to justify their suspicions later. They also point out that such suspicion is not a quality that is either present or absent from an encounter but may emerge as it proceeds. This is in contrast to the presumption apparently underlying the PACE power. Officers may therefore prefer to proceed by way of consent. Dixon *et al* (1989) also point out that consent may be a preferable option where, as may often be the case, the purpose of the stop is more to collect information than investigate a possible offence.

Bottomley *et al* (1989) argue that whether searches are formally recorded may be attributable more to a variety of contingent factors than to legal requirements: for example, failure to negotiate consent to a search, the need for officers to safeguard themselves where a search leads to an arrest, or the recording of searches for intelligence purposes. They conclude that there is a large grey area between exercise of the PACE stop/search powers and true consensual searches, in which searches are done outside of PACE procedures with the co-operation of the suspect but without informed consent. There is a threat to the safeguards for the suspect in such cases: since the principles under which the PACE rules are applied are unclear and uncertain (despite the aims of the legislation), it is unlikely that a set of 'correct' rules will be internalised and implemented by officers.

Record-keeping and supervision

PACE places emphasis on maintenance of records, which may be scrutinised by supervisors and others, as a safeguard for the suspect. However, it would appear that police practices in compiling such records are patchy. Respondents to the BCS indicated that no written record had been made in 69 per cent of vehicle stops and 79 per cent of pedestrian stops (Skogan, 1994). Two other surveys, the SICS and HFCS, reported that no written record had been made in 61 per cent and 47 per cent respectively of cases in which stops and searches had been carried out (Crawford *et al*, 1990; Painter *et al*, 1989).

Bottomley *et al* (1989) found that, where records were completed, it was frequently not possible to say from the information provided whether a search had been made on the basis of reasonable suspicion. Their value for monitoring purposes is therefore limited. This they attribute to unrealistically high expectations of record-keeping as a means of regulating police conduct. However, they also point out that the guidance to officers on reasonable suspicion is unclear and not always easy to apply (it has since been clarified in revised Code of Practice A). Better training might lead to adequate completion of records. More practically, they note that the form provided is small and leaves little scope for outlining the grounds for suspicion, which may be complex.

Inadequate completion of forms may reflect that officers have little expectation that records will be examined by supervisors. Less than a quarter of officers interviewed in the Hull study referred to checking of stop and search records as a mode of supervision. Supervisors themselves mentioned that they did this rarely and the majority felt oversight of stop and search largely ineffective. While it is true that street policing is of low visibility to supervisors (Chatterton, 1987), Bottomley *et al* (1989) conclude that there is potential for supervision to influence practice on the streets to a greater extent. This required supervisors to be made more aware of the value of records as an aid to supervision, for beat officers to receive better guidance in the completion of records, and for the expectations of both to be raised that records will routinely be inspected.

Stop and search of ethnic minority groups

The extent to which members of different ethnic groups are disproportionately stopped and searched and the reasons for any disparities have generated considerable debate. Arguments about the frequency with which those from the ethnic minorities are stopped and searched may be expected to diminish with the introduction of nationwide ethnic monitoring of stop and search from April 1996.[4] It is unlikely, however, that the debate about the reasons for differential rates of stop and search will fade away.

---

[4]   Her Majesty's Inspectorate of Constabulary have required all forces in England and Wales to divide stops and searches into those of white and non-white persons since 1993. However, from April 1996 the Home Office has required a more detailed breakdown using the four point classification of White, Black, Asian and Other.

Stops of Afro-Caribbeans

Both the former and revised PACE Codes of Practice stress that reasonable suspicion can never be justified solely on the basis of factors such as a person's age or colour or 'stereotyped images of certain persons or groups as more likely to be committing offences' (Code A, 1.7). Pre-PACE research suggested that racial stereotyping was responsible for the targeting of particular groups, particularly Afro-Caribbeans (Smith and Gray, 1985). Crime surveys carried out since the introduction of PACE also generally point to a relationship between age, sex, race and class and the likelihood of being stopped and searched. However, they also suggest that there are complex interrelationships between these variables, as well as variation in police stop and search practice between areas, which make it difficult to reach conclusions about the existence or extent of discriminatory policing (FitzGerald, 1993; Jefferson, 1993; Reiner, 1993).

Pre-PACE studies suggested that Afro-Caribbeans were much more likely to be stopped than white people (Willis, 1983; Smith and Gray, 1985; Southgate and Ekblom, 1984; Jones et al, 1986). The weight of evidence from a number of post-PACE studies, both with regard to foot and vehicle stops, is to similar effect (Skogan, 1990 and 1994; Crawford et al, 1990; Norris et al, 1993; Young, 1994). In considering the significance of these findings it is necessary to bear in mind that the black and white populations have different age and class structures (FitzGerald, 1993). In particular, the Afro-Caribbean population has a high concentration of young people and is predominantly drawn from the working class. Several commentators have pointed out that, because large-scale surveys cover members of all classes, they will inevitably find 'discrimination' because they are covering dissimilar black and white populations (Walker et al, 1990; Jefferson, 1993; Reiner, 1993). When socio-demographic factors are controlled for in large-scale surveys this considerably narrows – although it does not remove – differences in the rate at which black and white people are stopped. Thus, in the BCS, young Afro-Caribbean males were only slightly more likely than their white counterparts to be stopped (Skogan, 1990). And, on re-analysing the SICS data, Young (1994) found that young, black, working class males were only marginally more likely to be stopped than whites.

Tuck and Southgate (1981) have emphasised the importance of comparing similar black and white populations if research is to have any chance of detecting possible discrimination in the application of stop and search powers. For this reason, they advocate research in small and homogenous areas. Their own pre-PACE study in districts of Manchester found no difference between stops, searches and arrests of young white and Afro-Caribbean men. The post-PACE HFCS also showed little difference in stop rates between black and white people (Painter et al, 1989). Other recent studies, which have singled out small areas, have not replicated this finding. However, as will be noted, there are difficulties with this 'small area' approach in identifying areas which are genuinely homogenous in terms of the age and class of the population. Furthermore, the extent to which the police use stop and search may vary considerably, both within one force and around the country, and this may have considerable implications for the results of surveys which deal with respondents' experiences of stop and search.

In one recent local survey, in the Finsbury Park area of North London, Young (1994) found substantial differences in adjacent areas between the relative stop rates of black and white people, with the former being around three times more likely to be stopped in one area, but only slightly more likely in the other. The variations were apparently not satisfactorily explained by differences in the age and social class of black and white populations in the two districts. Young suggests that the similarity in stop rates for black and white people in one area could be related to the relative homogeneity of the black and white populations in terms of social class. In the other area, where black people were far more likely to be stopped, he suggests that the mixed class composition of the local population is relevant. In support of this argument he points out that, while black and white members of the working class were stopped at roughly similar rates, black members of the lower middle class were four times as likely to be stopped as their white counterparts. However, Young's failure to provide any satisfactory data on the class composition of the areas studied or on any class differences between ethnic groups rather weakens his conclusions. Also, the figures on which his analysis are based and particularly the numbers of black people stopped are probably too small to be reliable.[5]

Findings which do not easily fit the 'race and class' thesis were also discovered in a survey carried out in Leeds (Walker et al,1990; Jefferson, 1993). They found that, in poorer areas where the majority of black people lived, they were less likely than white people to be stopped, but in areas where relatively few black people lived they were more likely to be stopped. This study is open to some criticism. FitzGerald (personal communication) has noted that stop and search is used relatively little in Leeds, particularly compared with London, and the rates given for blacks in areas with small black populations are likely to be unreliable. The benchmark data on ethnic minority populations that was used was also considerably out of date. Furthermore, the study did not differentiate Afro-Caribbeans but included them with Asians in an all-embracing 'black' category. She also notes that the white population that was more likely to be stopped in areas with 'high' black populations was atypical,

---

5   A general criticism of the report of this study is that considerable use is made of percentages and rates (e.g. stop rates) but that base figures are rarely provided. Where they are given or can be deduced, it is often the case that cell sizes are very small.

being disproportionately young and living in rented accommodation. Most were probably students living in bedsitters in mainly Asian areas.

The attempts made in the studies described above to establish whether particular groups are over-represented in the stop and search statistics and whether this could be considered to amount to unjustified discrimination have been viewed sceptically by Reiner (1993). He points to the limitations of statistical analysis and the difficulty in examining the treatment of different racial groups, of controlling for any more than a few 'legally relevant' variables. Any variation in treatment that is found could be due as much to the effect of other variables that could not be controlled for as to discrimination. For this reason, he argues that it is inconceivable that this approach could ever conclusively establish racial discrimination.

Young (1994) also makes the pertinent that not all sections of the community commit crimes equally. He suggests that police decisions about who to stop may therefore be influenced by an awareness of which groups are most likely to commit certain kinds of offence.[6]

Stops of Asians

Most crime surveys have also examined the experiences of Asians. It would appear that the likelihood of their being stopped tends to be similar to or lower than that for white people (see, for example, Skogan, 1990 and 1994; Walker *et al*, 1990; Young, 1994). Jefferson (1993) suggests that the reasons for this are complex but are partly related to socio-demographic differences in the Asian population in terms of class and education. He also argues that racial stereotypes of Asians held by the police and others, key elements of which are conformity and subjection to familial and community ties, are important. These militate against their being perceived as potentially or actually 'criminal' and this is reflected in lower rates of stop and search (as well as in differential action at later stages of the criminal process).

Frequency of searches

Few studies have examined the incidence of searches relative to stops. From those which have done so, there is some evidence of racial differences in the proportion of those stopped who are then searched. Both the BCS and HFCS show that, even when other factors are taken into account, Afro-Caribbeans are far more likely than white people to be searched (Skogan, 1990 and 1994;

---

6   The question of the relative involvement of different ethnic minority groups in crime has engendered considerable debate which it is beyond the scope of this review to explore. Readers are referred to FitzGerald (1993) for an examination of the evidence.

Painter *et al*, 1989). The 1988 BCS found this tendency was more pronounced in vehicle stops (Skogan, 1990); however, this trend appears to have altered in the 1992 BCS, with Afro-Caribbeans and Asians being more likely to be searched in pedestrian stops (Skogan, 1994). The HFCS also examined subsequent police action and found a far greater likelihood that Afro-Caribbeans would be taken to the police station and subsequently charged with an offence.

On the one hand these findings could be taken to mean that an element of racial stereotyping is at work. On the other hand, it may be contended that they show that the police are now more cautious about stopping Afro-Caribbeans and, because their suspicions are better-founded, stops are more likely to result in a search and an arrest. Yet another interpretation is suggested by Norris *et al* (1993). They argue that race does not have an important bearing on whether those stopped are searched. Basing their findings on direct observation of the stopping of over 319 persons in the Metropolitan and Surrey police areas, they conclude that the demeanour of the person stopped had an important bearing on the outcome. Also important were age and the class of the person stopped (as gauged by their manner of speech). Those who were agitated or antagonistic were more likely to be subjected to a search. Generally, the authors argue that the dynamics of police encounters with those stopped are strongly determined by a person's demeanour. This in turn may be linked with race, but it may not be race in itself which determines the course of events.[7] However, they do not dispute that race is a significant determinant of who is stopped in the first place. It is submitted that their contentions have some weight. As others have noted, police officers view maintaining respect for the uniform as a significant goal in adversarial contacts with the public (Brown and Ellis, 1994). Furthermore, large-scale surveys have not involved first-hand observation of stops and have been unable to take account of the interpersonal dynamics of police/public encounters. This line of research may merit replication in a wider range of areas with different ethnic breakdowns.

Multiple stops

Crime surveys, unlike official statistics, provide an indication of the extent to which individuals are stopped repeatedly by the police. In common, these surveys suggest that a proportion of those stopped and searched are likely to undergo this experience repeatedly, although estimates vary between surveys. This may reflect differences in police practice from area to area. At the lower end of the scale, Painter *et al* (1989) found that 35 per cent of their sample in Hammersmith and Fulham had been stopped and searched more than once during the past year. In contrast, Young (1994) cites a figure

---

7   See too Jefferson (1993), who reaches rather similar conclusions.

of 63 per cent in his Finsbury Park survey. Sixteen per cent of respondents claimed to have been stopped and searched more than ten times. The average number of stops and searches per person ranges from two in the SICS (Crawford *et al*, 1990) to six in Young's (1994) survey.

The pre-PACE PSI study found that it was significantly more likely that Afro-Caribbeans would be the subject of multiple stops by the police (Smith and Gray, 1985). The largest-scale survey since PACE, the BCS, continues to show that Afro-Caribbeans are more likely than whites to be subjected to multiple stops, although, in the 1988 sweep of the survey, the difference between the two groups did not reach statistical significance. Twelve per cent of white people who were stopped recalled being stopped more than once, while the comparable figure for Afro-Caribbeans was 19 per cent (Skogan, 1990). In the 1992 sweep, 15 per cent of Afro-Caribbeans recalled three or more stops during the past year compared with three per cent of the population as a whole (Skogan 1994)[8]. There is further evidence on this score from locally based crime surveys. Thus, in North London Young (1994) found that members of the black community who were stopped were, on average, stopped eight times during the course of the past year, compared with five times for white people. The number of stops and searches per 100 of the black population was 78 compared with 22 for white people. (See too the HFCS's findings: Painter *et al*, 1989.)

Both the BCS and locally-based crime surveys are in agreement that Asians are less likely than white people to be subject to multiple stops (Skogan, 1990 and 1994; Painter *et al*, 1989; Crawford *et al*, 1990; Young, 1994).

Conclusions

The pessimistic conclusion drawn by Bottomley *et al* (1989) is that PACE has not changed the way in which the majority of police officers conduct stops and searches. At face value, this finding may be taken as supporting the view, most trenchantly expressed by Smith (1986), that stop and search typifies those aspects of police practice which cannot effectively be controlled by legal rules. He has argued that there is no way in which a vague criterion such as 'reasonable suspicion' can be made into an effective constraint. According to this view, the PACE rules in this area are a presentational gloss, which exist mainly to put an acceptable face on the practices of the police on the street. Smith places faith in administrative, rather than legal, means of controlling police actions: for example, through the construction of appropriate performance indicators which measure the efficiency and yield of stop and search in tackling crime.

---

8   It is not stated whether this difference is significant.

However, other commentators and the Hull researchers themselves have been less pessimistic about the scope for legislation to influence police conduct. Baldwin and Kinsey (1982) argue that the law does have a role to play here, but its limits must be recognised. Firstly, it is necessary to examine the context of police rule-breaking, secondly to identify areas which are amenable to legal definition and control and, thirdly, to see what complementary control systems (e.g. management, supervision and external review) are available. They suggest that a body of legal rules may, at the least, act as a marker of the limits to police behaviour, if not achieving precise control of the detail of it.

The Hull researchers adopt a similar perspective, arguing that the existence of police working rules on stop and search and, particularly on what constitutes adequate suspicion, are not necessarily fatal to legal regulation (Dixon *et al*, 1989). They identify five main shortcomings of the legislation which prevent it being successful and which are all, to varying degrees, remediable. First, the required standard of reasonable suspicion is not expressed clearly enough to be workable. The concept is also too static and individualistic to deal with many practical policing situations. Officers were also unclear about the circumstances in which consensual searches should be conducted.

Second, if PACE was intended to mark a major change in the way police officers use coercive powers, it should have been accompanied by more effective training to counteract existing police culture. In particular, it should not have been taken for granted that police officers are readily able to apply legal criteria to practical situations requiring quick decisions. The research evidence suggests they will tend to apply non-legal criteria.

Thirdly, PACE was introduced amidst political controversy and considerable police discontent. Dixon *et al* (1989) note that the Police Federation, for one, considered that the civil liberties lobby had won the day in relation to the debate over stop and search and that the powers which resulted were too restrictive to be useful in practical policing situations. They were also seen as carrying an inappropriate threat of disciplinary action (for failure to comply with Code A). Dixon *et al* (ibid.) argue that the response of rank and file officers may have been to view the constraints on use of stop and search as something to be got round, if possible.

Fourthly, it is argued that the sanctions for failure to comply with the PACE and Code provisions are inadequate. Few people make official complaints about stops, and external bodies (for example, police consultative committees – see below, Chapter 9) have little influence on police operational matters. Furthermore, supervisors make little use of stop and search records to check on practice, and there are only limited possibilities for active supervision on the street.

Lastly, public knowledge of police powers is limited. This means that it is easy for the police to engineer 'consent' to stop and search.

There may be a need for a more broadly-based replication of the Hull study, which was conducted in one force only. Data were collected at a relatively early stage in PACE's life and some of the uncertainties about consensual and non-consensual searches may now have been resolved. In particular, there appears to have been a particular problem in the research force with conflicting guidance issued by the force itself as to the interpretation of PACE provisions. Other forces may not have experienced similar problems. Experiences may also have differed depending on the pre-PACE stop and search powers that were available. Furthermore, revised Code of Practice A aims to clarify some of the difficulties which were identified in the study. For example, a clearer and simpler definition of reasonable grounds is provided; the distinction between mere and reasonable suspicion is discarded (Code A 1.6 – 1.7). The Code also emphasises the need for officers searching persons on a voluntary basis to make it clear that their co-operation is being sought (Code A 1D, b), so that they are in no doubt that the search is not being carried out under colour of law.

The study also relied considerably on police records for its conclusions. The low visibility of police actions outside the station meant that few searches were observed. The reasons recorded on search records suggest that there were sometimes not reasonable grounds for undertaking searches. However, care must be exercised in interpreting this finding. This may reflect poor completion of forms, given officers' low expectations of their being scruti-nised by others, rather than genuinely inadequate grounds. It is also more likely that recorded, rather than unrecorded, searches were made on valid grounds, given officers' preference for negotiating consent when in doubt as to whether use of the PACE power was justified.

Summary

- Official statistics show a marked increase in the use of PACE stop and search powers. However, crime surveys suggest a more modest increase and that a rise in formal recording may account for the trend shown by official statistics. Use of the PACE powers varies widely between police areas, with the Metropolitan Police being the most frequent user.

- There appears to have been a decrease in the frequency with which searches follow stops, although in some areas the majority of stops lead to a search.

- The proportion of searches leading to an arrest has declined gradually since 1986; currently, around one in eight are 'successful' as judged by this measure. Those searched for stolen goods, offensive weapons or drugs are most likely and those suspected of going equipped least likely to be arrested. Up to 11 per cent of all arrests stem from stop/searches. Around two-thirds of those arrested following stop/searches are charged or cautioned.

- It is doubtful whether the police always carry out stops on the basis of reasonable suspicion. Inadequate completion of stop and search records makes it difficult for supervisors to monitor whether this requirement has been met.

- Many searches are carried out with the consent of the person stopped, although it is likely that such consent is rarely fully informed. Searches carried out with consent are often not officially recorded.

- Afro-Caribbeans are more likely to be stopped than white people or Asians. When age and class are controlled for, the disparity is reduced. There is some evidence from local surveys that stop and search practice varies considerably from one area to another and this makes it difficult to deduce whether there is any clear pattern of discrimination.

- A minority of those stopped are stopped repeatedly. Afro-Caribbeans are more likely than white people to be the subject of repeated stops.

- Afro-Caribbeans who are stopped are far more likely than white people to be searched. There are competing explanations of why this should be so.

- PACE may have had only a limited impact on police stop and search practice due to: difficulties over clarifying the concept of reasonable suspicion; inadequate training; inadequate or inappropriate sanctions for breach of PACE; and lack of public awareness of stop and search powers.

3 Powers of entry, search and seizure

PACE put on a statutory basis and supplemented police powers to enter and search premises and seize evidence, while introducing safeguards against the abuse of these powers. Among the new powers introduced was that of access to personal information relating to a serious arrestable offence, which is innocently held in confidence by a third party.

Relevant research

There are two main sources of information about the operation of the new powers. The first is the Hull research referred to in the previous chapter (Bottomley *et al*, 1989), which paid some attention to this area in a more wide-ranging study of the exercise of police discretionary powers.

The second is a study of search and seizure carried out by Sheffield University (referred to hereafter as the Sheffield study), reported principally in Lidstone and Bevan (nd) and also in Lidstone (1989). This was carried out in two (unnamed) provincial police forces between February 1988 and May 1989. The research focused on two large cities with high crime rates, where it was expected that the full range of PACE powers would be used by the police. The research had four main aims:

(i) to examine the use made of the new search and seizure powers provided by PACE

(ii) to assess the safeguards provided by PACE against abuse of these powers

(iii) to assess the impact of these powers on the people against whom they are exercised

(iv) to consider the impact of the PACE powers in the wider context of police powers of search and seizure existing before PACE and those which survive the Act.

PACE requires the police to maintain a register of all searches (Code B, 8.1) and to record certain key items of information about each search (Code B,

7.1). These records were a primary source of information for the Sheffield research and a total of 861 search records was examined. In addition, the researchers interviewed more than 260 police officers involved in carrying out or authorising searches and over 130 householders of premises searched. A researcher also spent more than a year with police officers and was able to witness a number of searches being conducted.

By way of comparison with the pre-PACE situation, a limited amount of information is available from a survey carried out for the RCCP in ten police forces (RCCP, 1981a).

Before discussing the findings of these studies, some of their limitations need initially to be noted. Both post-PACE studies are of limited value for depicting national patterns in the use of the new search powers. The Sheffield study was carried out in sections of two provincial police forces and the Bottomley study in just one force. Neither study included any detailed examination of practices in the Metropolitan Police.[1] The pre-PACE survey for the RCCP, on the other hand, was heavily skewed towards the Metropolitan Police Service, which contributed nearly one-third of the searches included. A peculiarity of the Metropolitan Police Service was the disproportionately high use of searches under a magistrates' warrant. Another feature of the pre-PACE survey was that a number of stations had specialist squads, notably drugs squads, which biased the survey towards searches for drugs. Neither Bottomley et al nor Lidstone and Bevan comment on whether the activities of such squads may have affected their results.

Frequency with which search powers are used

Bottomley et al (1989) looked at the frequency of searches under all PACE powers during 1986 and 1987 in three sub-divisions of their research force. They found that their use increased by almost two-thirds in the latter year. They attribute this partly to greater recording of searches as officers became more familiar with recording procedures and partly to a genuine increase. The bulk of the increase was found in searches of premises after arrest, a power which the police may have come to find especially attractive (see below).

Both Bottomley et al (ibid.) and Lidstone and Bevan (nd) found similar patterns to the use of the various PACE search powers. The most commonly used were those available under ss.18 and 32 to enter and search premises upon or after arrest (together these accounted for 62% of searches in the

---

1   The Metropolitan Police declined to assist with the main Sheffield study, although they co-operated with an examination of the rather more specialised PACE powers dealing with confidential information (Lidstone and Bevan, nd)

former study and 49% in the latter). The power under s.17 of PACE to enter premises to search for and arrest a person was much less frequently used, accounting for eight per cent and six per cent of cases respectively in the two studies. Searches occurred under magistrates' warrants in 12 per cent of cases in both studies. These figures mark a dramatic decline in searches under warrant, which the RCCP survey found to constitute over one-third of all searches, and a large rise in searches upon or after arrest, which formerly amounted to just over 40 per cent of searches (RCCP, 1981a). Lidstone (1989) attributes the decline in use of warrants and increase in police autho- rised powers to the clarification incorporated in the Act. Clearly, the police will prefer to avoid the inconvenience of an application to a court if an easier option is readily available.

The bulk of non-warrant searches (around 80 per cent) relate to the investi- gation of theft or related offences such as burglary and robbery (Lidstone and Bevan, nd). Drug offences account for around six per cent of searches.

Lidstone and Bevan (nd) suggest that it is highly likely that official records of the use of PACE search powers under-estimate the true level of searches, although by how much is not known. From their interviews with police officers they found that some routinely made no official record other than notes in their pocketbook or the custody record of searches carried out when arresting the occupier of premises. This may account for the fact that only two per cent of non-warranted searches were recorded as being made under s.32(2)(b) of PACE (which authorises the search of premises in which a person was found when arrested). Bottomley *et al* (1989) also found a rela- tively small proportion of searches were made under this section, although their figure (8%) is somewhat higher than that of the Sheffield study. The under-recording may stem from misunderstanding of the PACE requirements or police officers' preference for avoiding formal procedures if at all possible.

Searches under warrant

Grounds for issuing warrants

Among the key safeguards governing warrant searches is the requirement for supporting documentation specifying the grounds on which the application is made, the relevant legislation, the premises to be entered and searched, and the articles or persons sought (PACE s.15(2)). The recording of this information is intended to aid the later reviewability of police actions.

Both the Hull and Sheffield research found that searches under magistrates' warrants were predominantly for drugs under the Misuse of Drugs Act 1971 or for stolen property under the Theft Act 1968, although the latter study also noted that an important minority of searches concerned pornographic material or firearms believed to be possessed illegally (Bottomley *et al*, 1989; Lidstone and Bevan, nd). Very few searches were made under s.8 of PACE, a new provision which authorises magistrates to issue a warrant to search for evidence of a serious arrestable offence. The Sheffield study found just four such warrants were executed in the six-month research period in one city and none in the other (Lidstone and Bevan, ibid.). The advantage of s.8 is that it avoids the police having to apply for multiple warrants to search for different types of item (e.g. firearms and drugs); also, it enables a search to be made for evidence which does not fall under the various other enactments governing searches on warrant (e.g. items of clothing worn by the suspect).

A search warrant may be granted on the basis of the reasonable belief that items sought (e.g. drugs or stolen goods) are to be found on the specified premises. The Sheffield study found that the informations supporting applications for search warrants sometimes outlined the grounds for such beliefs in some depth. For example, in some drugs cases details were given of covert surveillance operations over a considerable period. In other cases, particularly searches for stolen goods, applications often lacked specificity and commonly referred to 'information received' or 'information from a reliable source' without any precise confirmation (Lidstone and Bevan, nd). It is difficult to see how magistrates are able to make informed judgements about whether to grant warrants in such instances. Ultimately, reliable sources are those which the police, in their subjective view, deem to be reliable. The Sheffield study notes that searches carried out on the basis of such 'reliable' information turned out to be fruitless in well over 50 per cent of cases (Lidstone and Bevan, ibid.).

The requirement to specify, as far as is practicable, the items sought is intended to act as a safeguard by preventing 'fishing expeditions' and limiting the search to the extent necessary to discover such articles. Searches which go beyond what it necessary may be unlawful and any evidence discovered in consequence declared inadmissible. The Sheffield study found that, while warrants to search for stolen goods generally specified the property sought reasonably precisely, in a minority of cases it was doubtful whether there was the required level of specificity. For example, warrants which referred simply to 'electrical goods' or 'property believed to be the proceeds of crime' were arguably too broad in their coverage (Lidstone and Bevan, ibid.).

Authorisation of warrant searches

Code B (2.4) requires an officer of at least inspector rank to authorise applications for search warrants. It would appear, from the interviews carried out with police officers for the Sheffield study, that obtaining this authorisation is regarded by officers as a more rigorous hurdle than obtaining a warrant from the magistrates and the enquiries made by inspectors were often quite penetrating and extensive. Nonetheless, permission to apply for a warrant was rarely refused (Lidstone and Bevan, nd). The Hull study found that nearly half of searches were authorised by uniformed inspectors although carried out by CID officers; however, in one sub-division over three-quarters of searches were authorised by senior CID officers (Bottomley *et al*, 1989). In almost half of searches property was seized that was not covered by the warrant. This is permissible if, for example, an officer has reasonable grounds for believing it is evidence of an offence (B 6.1), but reasons for seizure must be recorded (B 7.1) – a safeguard against 'fishing expeditions'. It was found, however, that this was not always done.

Officers interviewed claimed that they had never had an application for a warrant turned down by the magistrates, although there is no way of knowing whether this means that they always had reasonable grounds (or were able to present their grounds as reasonable to the magistrates) or whether magistrates were unable or unwilling to undertake any thorough enquiry into the circumstances. One criticism of warrant searches made to the RCCP was that magistrates tended to 'rubber stamp' police requests.

In this context it is relevant to note that the Sheffield researchers found that at one of their two sites nearly half of all warrants were returned unexecuted (Lidstone and Bevan, nd). Sometimes there were sound reasons why a search under warrant was not necessary: for example, the occupier might have been arrested before the warrant could be executed and a search could then be made under post-arrest search powers. But the study also found evidence that the police sometimes sought search warrants as a pre-emptive measure where they were about to mount surveillance operations in drugs cases. Should drugs be taken onto the premises being watched a search could then be conducted. In fact, the authors argue that this practice is of doubtful legality since the Misuse of Drugs Act 1971 only authorises the issue of a warrant when there are reasonable grounds for suspecting that controlled drugs are 'unlawfully in the possession of a person on any premises'. The fact that warrants are issued in such instances suggests that magistrates do not make any substantial enquiries into the relevant details or that the police presentation of their case is less than frank about the circumstances.

Success rate of search warrants

The Hull study shows that around three-quarters of warrant searches were successful in the sense that they led to the seizure of property (Bottomley *et al*, 1989). The Sheffield study gives a slightly lower figure of two-thirds

(Lidstone and Bevan, nd). Both figures are substantially higher than the 46 per cent found in the Royal Commission survey (Royal Commission, 1981a). It is fairly frequently the case, however, that the property seized in the course of a search is not that specified in the warrant. If a stricter definition of success is used which excludes such seizures, the figures are considerably lower. The Sheffield study found just 42 per cent of warrant searches to be successful in these terms.

Both the Sheffield and Hull studies found that there was a particular likelihood of drugs searches leading instead to the seizure of stolen property. This was the case in one-third of drugs searches in Sheffield, for example (Lidstone and Bevan, nd). The authors of the report on the Sheffield study register surprise at the low success rate of drugs searches – in one of their research cities only 21 per cent led to the seizure of drugs. They argue that drugs operations are often based on covert operations involving surveillance, which could be expected to generate reliable information. Searches for stolen property, on the other hand, are more likely to be based on information from less dependable sources.

Searches upon and after arrest

PACE put police powers in this area on a clear statutory basis, with various safeguards. Formerly, it had been assumed by the police that they possessed the power at common law to enter and search the home of an arrested person for evidence connected with the crime for which they had been arrested. However, the Divisional Court held in the case of McLorie v. Oxford[2] that they did not have this right (Zander, 1990). That the police should have such a power is clearly important in a variety of circumstances: where, for example, they need to search the premises of those arrested for burglary to look for stolen property or tools used to gain entry (Brown, 1991). They now possess the power under s.18 to search premises occupied or controlled by a person under arrest for an arrestable offence. Searches carried out under this power will normally occur after a suspect has been taken to a police station, and must be authorised by an inspector or higher ranking officer. However, it is also possible under s.18(5) for a search to be made before an arrested person is taken to the station, but an inspector must be informed of the search on the suspect's arrival at the police station and the reasons for it recorded in the custody record.

The fact that the bulk of recorded searches of premises are carried out under s.18 reflects its usefulness (Bottomley et al, 1989). Brown (1991) found this power was used particularly in burglary cases, with 17 per cent of arrests

---

2   (1982) Q.B.1290.

leading to a s.18 search. Searches may yield important evidence: in the same study, Brown notes that over two-thirds of those whose premises were searched were charged or cautioned, compared with around half of suspects in cases where no search was carried out. Bottomley *et al* (1989) found that around a third of searches led to property being seized. However, this is slightly lower than the figure of 40 per cent found in the RCCP survey (RCCP, 1981a).

One safeguard associated with this power is that a search may only take place if there are reasonable grounds for suspecting that there is on the premises evidence relating to the offence for which a person is under arrest or a connected or similar offence. Bottomley *et al* (1989) provide anecdotal evidence of searching in relation to unconnected offences. Lidstone and Bevan(nd), basing their conclusions on a large sample of case studies, suggest that there are often no reasonable grounds which would persuade a reasonable person that stolen goods, for example, are to be found on premises to be searched. They note that sometimes the level of suspicion is very generalised. Thus, where a person is caught in the act of breaking into a car, unless they admit to other offences or have a record for similar offences there can only be a generalised suspicion that stolen goods of an unspecified nature from other possible offences might be found. For this reason, officers conducting searches try, where possible, to proceed with the suspect's consent, thereby circumventing the PACE requirements. This course raises separate difficulties (see below).

Another safeguard is the requirement for written authorisation by an inspector; the same study found little evidence of this being refused. Prior authorisation is not required where the presence of the occupier or controller of premises is necessary 'for the effective investigation of an offence' (PACE s.18(5)). Bottomley *et al* (ibid.) found that this exception was used to justify the expedient searching of an arrested person's home without first taking them to the station. They also found some evidence to suggest that this power was used where arrests were made on somewhat speculative grounds to carry out searches which might confirm the basis for arrest. This is the kind of 'fishing expedition' which the legislation was intended to eradicate.

A power is also provided by s.32 to enter and search premises in which a person arrested was found at the time of arrest or immediately prior to arrest. This power is more limited than the s.18 power, applying more or less at the time of arrest only (Zander, 1990). The power of search is also limited to evidence relating to the offence for which a person has been arrested, and depends on there being reasonable grounds for believing that there is evidence of that offence on the premises. Bottomley *et al* (1989) found that very few recorded searches fell under this section. However, officers interviewed admitted that such searches were common practice. The study

suggests that there may be considerable confusion about recording requirements for searches that do not need the authorisation of a senior officer,
probably because the primary legislation does not spell out what is required,
although Code B does.

Entry and search to make an arrest

Under s.17 of PACE, the police possess the power to enter and search
premises to execute an arrest warrant or arrest a person for an arrestable
offence. Both Lidstone and Bevan (nd) and Bottomley *et al* (1989) found this
power was rarely used. The latter study noted that searches mainly appeared
to be recorded where entry had to be forced or damage was caused or
where there might be other repercussions for the officers concerned. As
with the s.32 power, such searches do not require a senior officer's authorisation and it is suggested by the authors of the Hull report that equally there
may be confusion about recording requirements. Well over a third of officers
interviewed (both uniformed and CID) stated that searches to make an arrest
were rarely or never recorded in the official register. There was found to be
considerable variation between areas in understandings about recording
requirements. These aside, Lidstone and Bevan (nd) conclude that the s.17
power has proved to be a useful clarification of a previously confused area.

Searches with consent

The existence of the PACE search powers described above does not preclude
a person from consenting to a search of his or her premises. Indeed, as
Lidstone and Bevan (nd) point out, in some circumstances the police may
have to rely on consent because no power to search exists. In other cases,
however, the police may prefer to proceed with consent as an alternative to
using a PACE power or to invoke a PACE power *and* obtain consent. Before
the introduction of PACE, research by Lidstone (1981) pointed to the importance at that time of consent. Nearly three-quarters of entries to search
premises for stolen property or evidence of an offence were carried out with
the consent of the suspect or occupier. The heavy dependence on consent
was attributed to a mix of uncertainty about the nature of common law
search powers, the ignorance of those with whom the police dealt and
professional pride on the part of the police, who saw their ability to bluff
their way into premises as the mark of a good detective.

Lidstone and Bevan (nd) note that the clarification of police search powers by
PACE and the inclusion in Code of Practice B of provisions designed to ensure
that consent is true and informed would be expected to have reduced
reliance on consent. In fact, they found that consent still figured prominently,

with nearly one-third of searches being thus categorised. Bottomley *et al* (1989) found a somewhat lower figure of 15 per cent, perhaps reflecting differences in practice between forces or in recording (or both).

Code B contains various safeguards in relation to consensual searches. For example, record keeping requirements apply equally to such searches. Bottomley *et al* (ibid.) found considerable variation in their research force in recorded use of consensual searches, even though most officers claimed they made such searches and in broadly similar circumstances. The variation in recorded use appeared to stem from a misunderstanding of the requirements of Code B.

Both Lidstone and Bevan (nd) and Bottomley *et al* (1989) found that officers generally preferred to act with consent, with legal powers available only as a back-up. In the former study, it was found that consent was often obtained in preference to an available legal power. Typically, the search power that could have been used was that available under s.18, since the great majority of with consent searches involved the arrest of a person for an arrestable offence. That it was not employed may have been in order to reduce the risk of repercussions if it was subsequently found that the search was not legally justified. Depending on consent had the advantage that neither the officers carrying out the search nor their supervisors had to consider whether there were the reasonable grounds for suspicion required to support a PACE search. The authors conclude that for some officers it was a matter of routine to proceed by way of consent rather than doing so only after they had concluded that a power to search was not available. In the same study it is also suggested that consent was sometimes obtained in order to minimise friction with householders. Officers might make occupiers aware that they had the power to search, but only as a way of obtaining consent. In other cases, the lack of formality was attributed to the reluctance of the police to make occupiers aware that they have the option of refusing consent: "to seek consent is inviting a negative answer".

Lidstone and Bevan (nd) argue that it is doubtful whether consent is genuinely given in many cases, characterising it as "submission to authority" in some of the cases they examined. If consent is not truly voluntary and if authorisation for a s.18 search has not been sought, this would render the search unlawful. They draw attention in particular to instances in which 'consent' was obtained from persons in custody – a situation which is in itself inherently coercive – without the detainee being made fully aware of his or her right to refuse. This is far removed from the concept of consent outlined in *Bowater v Rowley Regis Corp*[3] and quoted by Lidstone and Bevan:

---

3   (1944) K.B. 476

"A person cannot be said to be truly willing unless he is in a position to choose freely, and freedom of choices predicates, not only full knowledge of the circumstances on which the exercise of choice is conditional, so that he may be able to choose wisely, but the absence of any feeling of constraint so that nothing shall interfere with the freedom of his will".

Lidstone (1989) also points to the confusion which may arise where persons arrested sign to say they consent to the search of premises at which they live. Some householders, confronted by the signed document, wrongly took it to be a search warrant. Dixon *et al* (1990a) suggest that where a written record is made and consent obtained in writing, this is sometimes done in a way that robs it of all meaning, with a signature only being obtained immediately before officers depart from premises.

Lidstone and Bevan (nd) found that police officers themselves were not always happy with the practice of obtaining consent. To some it seemed a nonsense that they should have to obtain consent, even though they had already obtained an inspector's authority to carry out a search. They argued that properly trained officers and their supervisors, confident in the exercise of their statutory powers, should not have to resort to this expedient in order to 'cover their backs'. Searches dependent on consent alone were also subject to the weakness that detainees could change their mind or limit the extent of the search at any time. The officers then had no legal grounds for continuing the search without going to an inspector to obtain his or her authority.

Bottomley *et al* (1989) draw attention to shortcomings of Code B in relation to consensual searches and some of the dangers of this practice. They suggest that the Code does not take account of the complexity of the situations in which searches are carried out. Frequently, the police find themselves in people's homes for legitimate reasons but suspicions are then aroused. The point at which police presence might be defined as an entry and search becomes blurred. In these circumstances, the police prefer to work with consent, only recording searches where events do not go according to plan and officers need to guard against future comebacks.

They also note that the formal requirements of the Code – which require that before conducting a search the police state its purpose and that the person concerned is not obliged to consent sit uneasily with police preferences for working in an informal manner. They suggest (although they have little direct evidence) that consent tends to be assumed and is not genuinely informed as Code B (original version) envisages. Testing the householder to see whether he or she consents may also be used as a barometer of police suspicions and may itself be used to raise the level of suspicion.

As yet, there is no evidence available about the impact of revised Code B on police search practices. Changes to the Code aim to ensure that consent is genuinely given and informed. A new Notice of Powers and Rights must be given to the occupier, setting out on what basis the search is made, and summarising the powers of search and the occupier's rights. Further, if practicable, consent must be given *in writing* before the search takes place. Consent as thus envisaged, argue Lidstone and Bevan (nd) should be distinguished from the rather different situation in which the police are simply exercising a power with the suspect's or householder's *co-operation*.

Success rate of searches

Whether searches lead to the discovery and seizure of the property sought is a useful indication of the effectiveness of the important safeguard that there must be reasonable grounds for suspecting that stolen property or other evidence are to be found on the premises searched. Unfortunately, as Lidstone and Bevan (nd) found in their study, it is not a straightforward matter to assess the 'success rate' of searches in these terms because search records do not always specify clearly what was sought in the search. It is common for reference to be made simply to 'evidence of the offence' or 'stolen goods', for example. Lidstone and Bevan therefore relied on the rather basic criterion of 'success' of whether or not any property was seized. In fact, property seized because it is believed to be stolen may later turn out not to be. However, the authors were unable to follow cases through to establish this information. Judged by the above yardstick, they found that half of non-warrant searches were 'successful'. In virtually half of the cases in which property was seized this was believed to be stolen goods. In 40 per cent, the items seized were referred to simply as 'evidence' (most frequently this was correspondence), but there was no indication of its significance for the case.

Lidstone and Bevan (ibid.) also judge the 'success rate' of searches by putting them in the context of the total amount of crime recorded and detected by the police. By this criterion, they suggest that searches appear to play a relatively small part in the investigation and solution of offences. They found that one search was conducted for every 17 offences detected. Looking at 'successful' searches (see above) in relation to total recorded theft and related offences, they found that a search was conducted in less than one case per hundred.[4] However, as an index of the contribution of searches to the solution of crime it may be argued that the latter criterion is misleading. First, the use of search powers only comes into play once a

---

4   This figure is probably on the low side because, as Lidstone and Bevan found, there is a certain amount of under-recording of searches, particularly those made on the arrest of the occupier of premises - see above.

possible suspect has been identified. In very many cases there are no clear leads and no possible suspect whose premises may be searched. Secondly, some offenders commit numerous crimes and one search may therefore contribute to the solution of many offences. And, thirdly, it would be unreasonable to expect the police to carry out searches in all cases in which a possible suspect has been identified. There may be no grounds for suspecting that stolen property is to be found, or lack of police resources may limit the scope of enquiries. It is probable that searches are conducted with discrimination: for example, in higher value offences or ones where there are good grounds for believing that stolen property will be found. To regard all cases as having equal search potential and those in which no search is conducted as contributing to some kind of 'failure rate' is to ignore the circumstances of each case and the differential rewards that might be reaped from carrying out a search.

Nevertheless, Lidstone and Bevan's criticisms of the search rate as being low may have some force if they are correct in their view that the police are sometimes failing to search premises in circumstances in which they should do so. In some cases they found that this was due to lack of manpower. But there was also evidence that officers sometimes could not be bothered, despite the view promoted by many supervisory officers that a search should be routine practice in property offences. Officers may have been unwilling to take the time to go through the necessary bureaucratic procedures and to obtain assistance with the search from colleagues unless the offence was serious.

Supervision and monitoring of searches

Bottomley et al (1989) cast some doubt on the adequacy of the PACE provisions to ensure that searches are adequately monitored by supervisory officers or reviewable by outsiders. First, an unknown – but probably significant – proportion of searches do not appear on the search register, particularly those with consent, and details of some that do are incomplete. Second, there is a danger that the requirement for inspectors' authorisations of searches after arrest may amount to little more than a 'rubber stamp' – the basis on which the RCCP formerly criticised magistrates' granting of search warrants (see above). They point to the growing frequency of such searches and the rarity of refusals as evidence for this point of view. Lastly, they point to numerous potential loopholes in the specific responsibilities of officers for recording details of different types of search, the occupier's consent and authorisation which, they suggest, make proper monitoring and supervision impossible.

Lidstone and Bevan (nd) point to issues raised by searches with the suspect's consent. As has been noted earlier, there are doubts about whether the 'consent' obtained is always genuinely voluntary. However, proceeding with consent allows the police to evade the supervision intended by PACE and, in particular, the requirement for an inspector's authority to search premises occupied or controlled by a person under arrest for an arrestable offence. It would appear that this device is not unwelcome to supervisory officers themselves, since they avoid having to go into the case in any detail and they abrogate responsibility for anything that occurs at the premises during the course of the search. It would also appear to be quite common practice: the same study found that around 40 per cent of searches after arrest were carried out without the prior authorisation of an inspector.

Lidstone and Bevan (ibid.) found that the actual conduct of searches was generally left to junior officers. In only five per cent of cases was an officer of the rank of inspector or above in immediate charge of the search. The officers taking charge were constables in two-thirds of cases and sergeants in a quarter.[5] Consequently, the officer in charge may well be relatively inexperienced and the authors of the Sheffield report suggest that this may explain why up to 40 per cent of householders whose premises had been searched were dissatisfied with the way the search was conducted. However, the study does draw attention to the fact that it was rare for entry to premises to be effected forcibly. This occurred in only seven per cent of cases, and in half of these it was because the premises were unoccupied. In only a few cases was force needed because the occupier denied the police access or because the police feared that evidence might be destroyed.

Lidstone and Bevan (ibid.) point out that the scope for householders to oversee a search of their premises is limited. In theory, PACE searches are retricted to the extent that is reasonably required (ss.17, 18 and 32). However, even if the householder were aware of this limitation, it would be difficult to enforce where several officers search several rooms simultaneously.[6] Nearly three-quarters of house searches were found to be of the whole house. It is also difficult for the householder to guard against 'fishing expeditions' if he or she does not know what it is that the police are searching for. In their survey of householders, the Sheffield researchers found that in well over a third of searches this information was apparently not provided and, where it was, the description given was sometimes too vague to be of much use.

---

5   Maguire and Norris (1992) and Baldwin and Moloney (1992) provide further evidence of the relatively low involvement of middle ranking officers in the supervision of enquiries. See Chapter 10.

6   It was the norm for searches to be carried out by two or more officers; in nearly a third of cases, three or more police were involved.

The occupier's perspective

Consistent with the aims of ensuring that police powers are exercised fairly and openly, PACE and Code B make several stipulations about the way in which searches are to be conducted. In the case of searches under warrant, the constable carrying out a search must identify himself to the occupier, show his or her warrant card if not in uniform, produce the search warrant and supply a copy of it (PACE s.16(5)). The revised Codes of Practice make it clear that this should be done before a search begins (B, 5.5).[7] There are similar requirements in Code B, applying to all searches: again, the officer must identify himself and state the purpose of the search and the grounds for undertaking it before the search begins (B, 5.5).

The revised Code introduced a new requirement for all searches (whether under warrant, a PACE power or with consent) to provide the occupier with a notice specifying the basis for the search, explaining the PACE search powers and the occupier's rights (including that to compensation if damage is caused), and stating the availability of the Codes of Practice for consultation at any police station.

Lidstone and Bevan (nd) carried out an interview survey of over 130 occupiers of premises searched by the police, which casts some light on the level of satisfaction with the conduct of searches and on police practices in communicating information to occupiers.[8] Around half of those interviewed considered the manner in which searches were carried out was satisfactory or very satisfactory. The police were considered to be polite and fair and carried out the search without undue disruption. However, 40 per cent were dissatisfied to some extent, complaining, for example, of rudeness, lack of consideration and untidiness. The authors suggest that some of these shortcomings may be attributable to the inexperience of officers conducting searches and the lack of supervision by senior officers. They suggest that the conduct of searches needs to be given greater prominence in training programmes.

The survey also casts light on police practices in carrying out searches. In those searches conducted by plain clothes officers (just over half the interview sample), there was an apparent failure on the part of the officers conducting the search to identify themselves as police in over 40 per cent of cases.[9]

Turning specifically to searches on warrant (50 cases in the sample), 40 per cent of householders claimed that no copy of the warrant had been given to

---

7   Formerly, this was only implicit in PACE and the original Code B. An exception exists where there are reasonable grounds for believing that to alert the occupier 'would frustrate the object of the search or endanger the officers concerned or other persons'.

8   Their survey was carried out prior to the introduction of the revised Codes of Practice.

9   In 14 per cent of cases the householder was either not present or could not recall whether officers identified themselves. In the remaining cases, identification was correctly provided.

them (or left on the premises if they were absent). Where a copy was provided, there were some complaints that this was done only at the conclusion of the search or in circumstances which allowed no time to assimilate the contents before the search began.

In non-warranted searches, over 80 per cent of the 81 respondents interviewed reported that they had not been told what power authorised the search. While many of these (60 in all) said that they or a person in custody had 'consented' to the search, only 10 stated that they had given consent in writing. It would appear, therefore, that most had merely been acquiescing in the exercise of a PACE power and should have been told what power was being exercised.

The importance of the police providing the occupier with the information required by PACE and Code B is underlined by the finding that none of those interviewed were aware of the powers the police possessed to enter and search premises. Revised Code B introduced additional safeguards by requiring the police to provide a notice of rights to the occupier, including a statement of the authority under which the search is made. However, Lidstone and Bevan (nd) point out that this will be of limited value if the occupier does not have the opportunity to study it before the search begins. It is not unreasonable to argue that the more documentation that is provided the less chance the occupier will have to read it, since the occupier may feel under pressure to allow the police to proceed with the search. Furthermore, they point out that the effectiveness of the new provision is devalued by making the requirement to provide the notice prior to a search subject to a test of practicability (Code B, 5.8). They suggest that this may be called upon to justify delays in giving the notice until it is too late to be an effective protection to the occupier. Generally, they conclude that it is almost inevitable that, when reliance is placed upon the police conveying information which may operate as a constraint upon their actions, a minority of officers will either not pass that information on or do so only when it is too late to be effective.

Excluded and special procedure material

The PACE provisions

Prior to the enactment of PACE, police access to confidential information was strictly limited (Hewson, 1993). Certain statutes – many of which are still in force – allowed the police access to specific types of information (for example, under the Bankers' Books Evidence Act 1879 magistrates could order the inspection of certain banking records). Or, the police might obtain a witness summons to compel a third party to give such information in court. The limitation of these powers was that they generally applied once a charge had been laid or court proceedings begun, and were of little use during the investigative stage when the police needed them most. Other than this, the only other way of obtaining access was with the consent of the subject of the confidential information.

PACE divides material held in confidence into three groups.[10] *Legally privileged material* consists of communications between legal advisers and their clients in connection with the giving of legal advice or with legal proceedings. Such material cannot be searched for or seized. However, items held with the intention of furthering a criminal purpose are not included. Lidstone and Bevan (nd) point out that it may be difficult in practice to assess during the course of a search of a solicitor's offices whether material is held with this intention. It would appear that it is sufficient that a client or even a third party intends to use the material for a criminal purpose; the solicitor himself may be innocent of any criminal intent.

Excluded material includes medical records and samples and material acquired or created for the purposes of journalism, held in confidence. Generally, such material cannot be searched for or seized unless the police can satisfy a circuit judge that conditions laid down in Schedule 1 of PACE are satisfied.[11] If a judge is satisfied that the conditions are met, he or she may grant a production order requiring the holder of the material to give the police access to it, usually within seven days. In some situations the police may apply directly for a warrant to gain access: for example, where it is not possible to communicate with the person entitled to grant access or where going through the production order procedure may seriously prejudice the investigation. A search warrant may also be sought where a production order has been disobeyed.

Special procedure material consists of material acquired or created as part of a person's occupation and which is held in confidence, or journalistic material which is not excluded material (i.e. it is not in the form of documents or records nor held in confidence). As with excluded material, certain (but different) conditions have to be satisfied before a judge will grant a production order: an important one is that the police should first have sought to obtain access to the material with consent before pursuing a production order.[12] There are too some situations in which a warrant may be sought as an alternative. Both Levi (1993), in relation to the investigation of serious fraud, and Lidstone and Bevan (nd), more generally, draw attention to

10 Definitions of the three categories of confidential information are to found in PACE section 10 (legally privileged material), section 11 (excluded material) and section 14 (special procedure material). For a guide to the operation of the relevant PACE provisions see Hewson (1993).

11 The conditions are that: (a) there must be a reasonable belief that such material is to be found on the premises to be searched; (b) prior to PACE, the police must have been able to obtain a warrant under a previous statutory power to search for that material; and (c) the issue of such a warrant would have been appropriate.

12 The access conditions for special procedure material are: (a) there are reasonable grounds for believing that (i) a serious arrestable offence has been committed, (ii) that special procedure material is to be found on the premises to be searched, (iii) the material is likely to be of substantial benefit to the investigation, and (iv) the material is likely to be relevant evidence; (b) other methods of obtaining the material (i) have been tried unsuccessfully or (ii) have not been tried because it appeared likely that they were bound to fail; and (c) it is in the public interest that the material should be produced or that access should be given to it.

the importance of this category of material for police enquiries. It includes key targets in the investigation of offences of dishonesty such as bank and building society accounts and records held by profesional advisers such as accountants.

The procedures and safeguards relating to production orders or warrants for the above categories of material are similar to those relating to other PACE searches. For example, there is a requirement for a senior officer (of at least superintendent rank) to authorise police applications for production orders or warrants; and an officer of at least inspector rank must supervise searches under warrant.

Research on Schedule I

The Sheffield study (Lidstone and Bevan, nd) is the only research to date to have examined in any detail the operation of the PACE provisions allowing access to excluded and special procedure material, although Levi (1993) also touches on the use of these powers in serious fraud investigation in his study of this topic for the RCCJ.

Since the PACE Schedule 1 procedure is used most in the capital, the Sheffield researchers concentrated their attention there, carrying out interviews in the Metropolitan and City of London forces with officers involved in the investigation of fraud, robbery and drugs offences. They also sent a questionnaire to provincial forces which sought to establish the extent and nature of use of the Schedule 1 procedure and views about its value.

Extent and nature of use

The Sheffield study found that all provincial forces made use of the Schedule 1 procedure, but the extent of use varied considerably. Between 1 January 1986 (when the powers became available) and September 1989 the number of applications per force ranged from just two up to 150. In all, during this period there were 1,504 applications in provincial forces.[13] It was very rare for the judge to refuse applications in provincial forces – only seven refusals were recorded. In London, the refusals found were more akin to postponements, with judges asking applicants to redraft details of their applications. The authors note that the lack of refusals does not necessarily indicate 'rubber-stamping' of applications by the judiciary; in fact, judges asked pertinent questions about applications, particularly if there were deficiencies in the supporting documentation.

---

13   Precise figures about the number of applications made in London were not available. There is no requirement on the police to maintain records of production orders and warrants issued under Schedule 1 of PACE.

The vast majority of applications were for orders to secure access to special procedure material. The persons or institutions to whom the orders were directed (i.e. the respondents) included banks, building societies, solicitors, accountants, financial advisers and charities. Orders were sought to obtain access to a wide range of material including: documents relating to suspected mortgage frauds or illegal multiple share applications; television films that showed alleged offences; financial records to prove handling, forgery and murder; and records of telephone numbers dialled in order to catch drugs suppliers. Not surprisingly, those users of the Schedule 1 procedure who were interviewed placed a high value on it. Their comments were to the effect that it was an essential tool, particularly in the early stages of fraud investigations, and that effective investigation of such crimes would not be possible without it.

The existence of the Schedule 1 power was often enough to persuade respondents to reveal the relevant information without the police having to resort to a production order or a warrant. This was not always the case, however, for by refraining from producing material until obliged to do so by a court order members of professional groups protected themselves against accusations of breach of confidence to their client and sought to ensure that clients continued to trust them to maintain confidentiality in the future.

Lidstone and Bevan found that warrants to gain access to special procedure material were not often used (they do not provide figures). The warrant procedure carries the advantage of surprise and may, for example, prevent incriminating material being destroyed. However, the High Court has empha-sised that the procedure should not be abused and that it is essential that one of the conditions necessary to justify a warrant search has been made out (see above). That the police resort to warrants fairly infrequently suggests that this guidance has been taken on board.

Authorisation and execution of production orders

Code of Practice B (2.4) requires each application for a production order to be approved by an officer of at least superintendent rank. The Sheffield study found that in the Metropolitan area the senior officer's role was little more than to rubber-stamp applications. Since these often arose out of complex investigations undertaken by specialist officers, superintendents were often too divorced from the detail of the investigation to undertake any meaningful scrutiny. Instead, this task tended to be performed by investigat-ing officers' immediate supervisors. The authors of the Sheffield report suggest that the lack of scrutiny by superintendents does not result in any lack of thoroughness in the preparation of applications for production orders. The role of the circuit judge in examining such applications was sufficient to ensure due diligence on the part of investigating officers.

The police are required to send a copy of an application for a production order to the respondent (i.e. the holder of the material) but not to the suspect, specifying accurately all the information sought. Lidstone and Bevan draw attention to problems which sometimes arise with this procedure. One is that there is no obligation on the respondent not to inform the suspect that his or her affairs are under investigation. It is in order to prevent such tip-offs that the police sometimes apply directly for a warrant. Another problem is that, particularly in complex frauds, the respondent may have difficulty marshalling all the material required by the production order within the time allowed (normally seven days from the time it is made). The authors suggest that it should be good practice to inform respondents at the stage of applying for a production order about the extent of their obligations. Assuming they did not contest the making of the order, they would then be in a position to comply with the order at an early stage. However, they also note that, if the respondent does foresee difficulty in complying with an order within seven days, it is open to him or her to appear in court and argue for a longer period.

Lidstone and Bevan found some variation in the way applications for production orders are dealt with at court. Some forces use the CPS to present applications, while in others (the Metropolitan Police, for example) this is done by specialist police officers. The majority of applications are uncontested and, if there is full supporting documentation, the judge will often make his or her decision in chambers rather than in open court. Sometimes the applying officer will not be required to appear at all. Judges generally wish to ask some questions about applications, but these tend to be on points of clarification rather than about the substance of and grounds for the application.

Where applications are contested, objections tend to be of a procedural nature (that too little notice was given or that the material sought is inadequately specified, for example) rather than substantive. For, if the application has been well prepared, it is unlikely that the respondent will be able to find good grounds – other than that he or she does not have possession of the material – on which to object. It would appear that the courts are tending to decide in favour of the public interest requiring disclosure.

The execution of orders may present problems. Thus, where the material is held on computer an effective search of the data may be impossible without the co-operation of the respondent. And where the material sought is actually software, it may even be necessary to seize the computer hardware. Searches of lawyers officers present other problems. Legally privileged material, which the police may not seize, may be mixed with other material. It may be necessary in such situations to have a member of the law firm present at the search.

Conclusion

Lidstone and Bevan conclude that Schedule 1 has provided the police with an essential tool for investigating certain types of crime, and that it is operated fairly to respondents. Particularly in relation to fraud, much potential evidence, which formerly had been unavailable to the police because it was held in confidence by third parties, is now accessible. The Schedule 1 procedures have since been used as a model for other legislation aimed at obtaining evidence of serious crime (for example, the Prevention of Terrorism (Temporary Provisions) Act 1989). As a rule the problems identified as being associated with the Schedule 1 procedure are minor. However, one important drawback is raised by the Sheffield study, namely the lack of any requirement for respondents to provide any explanation of material produced in response to a court order. As they point out, it is often the explanation that accompanies the material that is crucial to the investigation. They compare the Schedule 1 procedure with the power possessed by the Serious Fraud Office under S.2 of the Criminal Justice Act 1987 to issue a notice requiring a person, who is believed to have relevant information, to answer questions and/or supply documents (see Levi, 1993, for a full discussion of this provision). In return, that person's answers (unless false) cannot be used against him or her in any subsequent prosecution. They argue that the extension of this power to the police is both desirable and logical.

Summary

- Searches on a magistrates' warrant have declined. Contrary to the requirements of PACE, applications for warrants are sometimes unspecific about the items sought. Applications are seldom turned down by supervisory officers or the magistrates.

- The police are frequently using their new statutory powers to enter and search premises on or after arrest. There may be some under-recording of searches made where the occupier of premises is arrested. Some searches occur where it is doubtful whether there is reasonable suspicion that stolen goods are likely to be found.

- Many searches are made with the consent of householders, either instead of invoking statutory search powers or in addition. This practice has both advantages (e.g. minimising friction) and disadvantages (e.g. consent may be withdrawn at any time; they are of low visibility to supervisors). It is doubtful in many cases whether consent is full and informed.

- Around three-quarters of searches on warrant and about half of non-warrant searches led to the seizure of property, usually goods believed to be stolen.

- About half of those whose premises are searched are satisfied with the conduct of the search, but there are frequent complaints that officers do not identify themselves, copies of warrants are not provided and officers do not state their search powers.

- The new PACE powers to obtain access to various kinds of confidential information were found to be valuable by the police. Applications for production order were usually thoroughly prepared. Compliance with orders sometimes presents problems where large volumes of papers are sought or where data are stored on computer. Another drawback is that there is no obligation on the holders of such material to provide any explanation of it.

4 Arrest and detention

The criteria for arrest and for detention differ under PACE: arrest requires reasonable grounds for suspicion, while detention is subject to the principle of necessity (see Chapter 1). The RCCP, in considering ways of limiting arrest to cases in which it was strictly necessary, had considered whether the necessity principle could be applied also to arrest. Given the circumstances of arrests, in which decisions often have to be taken urgently in the midst of disturbances or confused situations, they concluded that this would be impracticable (RCCP, 1981).

Arrests

It is difficult to draw firm conclusions about the impact of PACE on arrests because of the lack of published research in this area. The impact of the PACE provisions may well be complex because there are competing influences at work. On the one hand, police powers of arrest in arrestable (generally more serious) offences were broadened; arrest in non-arrestable (less serious) cases was also facilitated by the general arrest powers in Section 25 of PACE. On the other hand, arrest in non-arrestable cases was restricted to cases in which it is strictly necessary. For all offences, arrest must be justified on the basis of reasonable grounds for suspicion, while the fact that the arresting officer must satisfy the custody officer that detention is necessary once the suspect arrives at the station may act as a constraining factor.

Arrest statistics

The Home Office collects, but does not publish, a figure for total numbers of arrests (notifiable and other offences), but this is of little value in interpreting the effects of PACE because it is not broken down by offence. It is not therefore possible to distinguish trends in non-arrestable and arrestable offences nor to take account of the impact of new legislation other than PACE. The Public Order Act 1986, for example, recast public order law and introduced a new low-level offence of disorderly conduct which has resulted in considerable numbers of arrests (Newburn *et al*, 1990; Brown and Ellis, 1994). More detailed examination of the figures in individual forces has not proved to be helpful. Bottomley *et al* (1989), looking at arrest figures in their research force, were unable to draw general conclusions about the effects of PACE: variations over time may have reflected various changes in force policy as much as the effect of legislation.

Figures are published for those proceeded against in the magistrates' courts and whether they had been arrested and charged or summonsed (Criminal Statistics England and Wales, various years). These show a marked increase in the proportion of persons proceeded against for non-indictable offences by way of summons; this might be expected if the police are restricting arrest in minor cases to situations where it is strictly necessary. At the same time, they show that the proportion of persons proceeded against for indictable offences by way of arrest and charge has increased slightly. However, these figures are of no help in showing what proportion of persons are arrested but not proceeded against – a better, but still crude, indication of the standard of evidence on which arrest is based. Nor do they take account of the fact that a high proportion of those summonsed are first arrested and then released (pre-PACE research shows that this may be up to three-quarters in some forces: Gemmill and Morgan-Giles, 1980).

The basis for arrests

McConville *et al* (1991) suggest that the police are using arrest as much as ever, regardless of necessity. In a study of over 1,000 non-Road Traffic Act arrests and summonses in three forces, they found that reliance on arrest was almost total. Over 98 per cent of adults and 90 per cent of juveniles were arrested rather than summonsed. They draw upon this fact and anecdotal evidence from interviews they conducted with officers to argue that the police continue to rely on arrest because of the advantages of interviewing suspects on police territory. While this assertion may have some truth to it, they publish no details of the circumstances of arrests in their study or of the evidence against the suspect to support the contention that arrest was not always necessary. Nor is there any indication of the extent to which police officers hold the kinds of views of which isolated extracts from interviews are taken to be typical. Furthermore, as research for the RCCP indicated (Gemmill and Morgan-Giles, 1980), the extent to which forces use summons without arrest varies considerably and there is no contemporary data to assess whether practice in the research forces was typical.

McConville *et al* (1991) also argue that PACE and the requirement of reasonable grounds for suspicion has had negligible impact on the evidential basis for arrest. They cite evidence from previous studies to support the view that arrests are largely based on non-legal criteria (see, for example, Bittner, 1967; McBarnet, 1981; Holdaway, 1983; Smith and Gray, 1985). According to this argument, legal powers are fitted around the decision to arrest rather than vice versa. The criteria employed, it is argued, have deep historical roots, and are determined by police objectives and organisational pressures. Among the factors which may influence arrest decisions are: the need for the police to assert control when their authority is challenged; suspiciousness of particular classes or groups of people, particularly those 'known' to the police; the need to demonstrate success by returning good arrest figures; and the status of the victim. Anecdotal evidence of the employment of these various criteria is given from cases in their sample, backed up by extracts from interviews with arresting officers.

While initially persuasive, their claims are open to some doubt on critical examination. First, as Dixon (1992) points out, they assume that police culture is relatively immutable over time and between cultures (US studies are relied upon). This fails to take account of evidence of cultural changes within the police service in this country, wrought by PACE and organisational and technological reforms (Williamson, 1990; Willis *et al* 1988; Brown, 1991; Moston *et al*, 1990).

Secondly, the authors provide no assessment of the strength of pre-arrest evidence in cases in their sample.[1] If this is often inadequate, their hypothesis that non-legal criteria continue to determine arrest decisions may be valid. If, however, the evidence is generally adequate it is possible that the PACE requirement of reasonable suspicion may have taken precedence over other criteria. Alternatively, it may have interacted with these criteria so that, while non-legal criteria are important in attracting police attention to the possibility of arrest, arrests are made mainly where reasonable grounds for suspicion also exist.

Thirdly, without quantitative data, it is impossible to say whether non-legal criteria are as important, or more or less important in guiding arrest decisions than before the introduction of PACE. The qualitative data presented may not necessarily be invalid, but they may support a finding of diminishing applicability.

Fourthly, in a study primarily concerned with corroboration carried out for the RCCJ, but based on the same data-set as his earlier study, McConville (1993) himself points out that, where practicable, the police are generally careful to collect any available independent evidence before making an arrest (although, often such evidence is not available). He found that there were few cases in which relevant evidence was deliberately ignored by the police prior to arrest.

---

1   Such an assessment is made in a later study by McConville (1993) of a subset of the data. This is also open to criticism; see below.

Lastly, there is evidence from other studies that PACE has had an impact on arrest which runs counter to McConville's argument. In relation to the police's preference for arrest over summons, neither Bottomley *et al* (1989) nor Irving and McKenzie (1989) found evidence to confirm fears (see, for example, McConville, 1985) that the police are using powers of arrest unduly, particularly those under s.25 of PACE (the general arrest conditions in non-arrestable offences). In Bottomley's study, police officers interviewed maintained that the new powers had made arrest easier where minor offenders refused to provide sufficient details for service of a summons; but, equally, the existence of the powers of arrest sometimes enabled them to secure co-operation from members of the public more readily in providing such details. It should be noted, however, that neither Bottomley nor Irving and McKenzie carried out observation of arrests. Irving and McKenzie concentrated on more serious cases in which suspects were interviewed, and it is therefore difficult to see on what data they based their conclusions.

Turning to the evidential basis for arrest, Irving and McKenzie (1989), Bottomley *et al* (1989) and Brown (1991) all suggest that there may have been an increase in the standard of evidence on which arrests are based. Thus, Irving and McKenzie categorised the strength of the initial evidence as good in under a third of a pre-PACE sample of cases compared with around half in 1986 and 1987. They suggest that these changes may be attributable to police fears of disciplinary sanctions and the need later on to satisfy the statutory criteria for detention at the police station. Bottomley *et al* point out that PACE allows considerable scope for individual officers to interpret what constitutes 'reasonable suspicion', but despite this, many of those they interviewed considered that they arrested less 'on a hunch' than they used to. They suggest that this is part of a trend towards greater professionalism in policing.

In contrast, McConville (1993) categorised the evidence at arrest as 'strong' in only a quarter of a sample of post-PACE cases in his RCCJ study on corroboration. However, he classed evidence as 'strong' or 'weak' solely on the basis of its source, without any assessment of its quality. It is debatable whether some categories of 'weak' evidence would have been considered as such by other studies: for example, the unsupported evidence of a victim or a police officer.

Irving and McKenzie (1989) argue that one effect of the provisions on arrest has been for police officers to be more apprehensive about taking action based on their own suspicions, in the absence of independent witnesses or evidence. They back this up by reference to a decline in the proportion of arrests where suspect and crime were simultaneously identified by the suspect being found in possession of incriminating items. Such arrests typically result from stop/searches. At the same time, they found a large rise in arrests resulting from information from members of the public and informants.

A study by Brown (1991), that specifically examined the investigation of household burglary, also provides some support for the view that PACE has affected the basis for arrest, although not entirely in the ways suggested by the Brighton study. One change found was a reduction in arrests stemming from information provided during the interviewing of other suspects. This is attributed to less frequent interviewing (the result of increased regulation of interviewing by custody officers and the disincentive provided at that time by contemporaneous note-taking) and increased presence of solicitors at interview. Lengthier enquiries became more significant, suggesting that the police are going to greater lengths to secure firmer pre-arrest evidence. However in contrast to Irving and McKenzie, there was a slight increase in arrests stemming from stop and search, suggesting that the police are making productive use of the new s.1 PACE power (see above). The reasons for this may stem from differences in the pre-PACE stop and search powers available to the police in Brighton (where Irving and McKenzie carried out their study) and the research sites used in the burglary study.

The same study found a reduction in the burglary arrest rate (the number of suspects proceeded against for burglary/recorded burglaries X 100) at two out of three stations studied. Brown argues that this may be further grounds for arguing that officers are more careful to ensure that they have firm evidence on arrest.

Ethnic minorities

As a non-legal factor, race should have no bearing on the decision to arrest. Nevertheless, there is evidence from both pre-PACE (Stevens and Willis, 1979; Smith and Gray, 1985) and post-PACE studies (Home Office, 1989c; Walker *et al*, 1990) that Afro-Caribbeans are more likely than white people to be arrested.[2] FitzGerald (1993) notes that demographic factors (and particularly the higher proportion of young men in the Afro-Caribbean population) appear to explain much of the difference but by no means all. Thus, it appears that young Afro-Caribbean males are still arrested at a higher rate than their white counterparts (Home Office, 1989c).

The reasons for this over-representation are likely to be complex[3] and it is impossible to gauge from the available research information to what extent it is due to discriminatory application of the PACE arrest provisions or to other factors. There is, for example, a heated debate about the extent to which black people are responsible for a higher rate of offending and how this is

---

2   Until recently no national monitoring of the ethnic origin of those arrested by the police has routinely been carried out. However, from April 1996 police forces are required by the Home Office to carry out ethnic monitoring of arrests and their outcome, using the four point classification of White, Black, Asian and Other.

3   For a fuller discussion of this and other issues concerning ethnic minorities in the criminal justice system see FitzGerald's (1993) review of the relevant research, carried out for the RCCJ.

related to socio-economic factors (Reiner, 1993). Some evidence exists that a certain amount of discrimination may occur prior to arrest through proactive police strategies that impinge disproportionately on black people. Evidence that black people are stopped more often than white people has already been presented in Chapter 2. In addition, it appears that: they are more likely to appear in court on charges, such as drugs offences, which result from police activity; that those known to the police are more often arrested on 'suspicion'; and that property offences for which they are convicted are more often 'discovered' by the police than is the case for white people (Hood, 1992). Furthermore, evidence from the BCS suggests that there may well be a higher police presence in areas with large ethnic minority populations (FitzGerald and Hale, forthcoming).

In contrast, there is relatively little evidence that the arrest decision itself is influenced by the race of the suspect, in the sense that the police accept a lower standard of evidence to justify the arrest of ethnic minority suspects. There is some indication that Afro-Caribbeans are more likely to be arrested following a stop (see Chapter 2: Painter *et al*, 1989), but the reasons for this are not clear. Without knowing details of the evidence available it could just as well imply that such stops more often turn out to be justified or that the police are more blasé about arresting on weaker evidence.

Another possible explanation concerns the dynamics of police encounters with black people and the supposedly greater potential for friction. However, the evidence on this score is conflicting. Norris *et al* (1993), who observed stops of over 300 people, including over 80 black people, found that there was no evidence that such encounters were any more conflictual or troublesome than those with whites. They suggest that officers are well aware of the potential for trouble in such situations and deliberately set out to be non-confrontational. On the other hand, Brown and Ellis (1994), in a study of section 5 of the Public Order Act (which deals with behaviour causing alarm or distress) found that incidents involving Afro-Caribbeans far more frequently involved confrontation with the police, ultimately leading to arrest. Possibly, both studies may be 'right'. In the Brown and Ellis study, the police had intervened because some form of public disorder was already underway. Tempers may already have been frayed and it may have taken little for the situation to develop into one of confrontation with the police. In the Norris study, however, the police may have had more control over the encounter from the start and the opportunity to maintain a low-key approach. It is also likely that the state of police relations with ethnic minorities varies from area to area. It is not known which areas of London and Surrey Norris *et al* used for their research but, if they were ones in which police relations with the black community were good, this may have enabled stops to be carried out relatively amicably. This is a complex area which could clearly repay the attention of further research.

The authorisation procedure

Morgan *et al* (1991), in a study of the work of custody officers, note that PACE provides for the first time a clear statutory basis for the status of those who are 'helping the police with their inquiries'. The decision about whether suspects should be detained rests with custody officers, who are independent from the investigation (see Chapter 5 for further discussion of the custody officer's role). On the arrival of a suspect under arrest, custody officers must first ascertain whether there is sufficient evidence to charge (PACE s.37(1); if there is, they must decide whether to charge or release the suspect (s.37(7)). If there is insufficient evidence to charge, they must release the suspect, *unless* they have reasonable grounds for believing that his or her detention is necessary "to secure or preserve evidence relating to an offence for which he is under arrest or to obtain such evidence by questioning him" (s.37(2)).

Time of authorisation

If the outcome of the custody officer's assessment is that the suspect should be detained, detention is authorised from this time. The significance of this time is that reviews of custody (considered further below) are calculated in relation to it. However, the maximum length of detention is calculated from the time of arrival. Morgan *et al* (1991) note that there may in fact be a considerable gap between a suspect's arrival at the station and the time detention is authorised if the custody area is busy. In effect, periods of time that have not been officially authorised are spent in police custody. They found that the time of authorisation which custody officers entered on the custody record varied. Some recorded the time that suspects were given their rights. Others argued that authorisation was implied when the suspect arrived at the police station and they recorded a time close to or the same as this in order to reduce the time the suspect apparently spent waiting in limbo. Morgan argues that this practice runs counter to the underlying intention of the legislation, which makes authorisation dependent on an assessment of the evidence.

Deciding whether to authorise detention

The custody officer's assessment was intended to filter out unnecessary detentions. Several studies have noted that this objective is not being achieved. Morgan *et al* (1991) describe the authorisation procedure as a 'presentational fig-leaf'. They note that, although forces vary in the extent to which arresting officers are required to recount the evidence against the suspect, a failure to authorise detention was almost unheard of. Reporting on the same study, McKenzie *et al* (1990) found no evidence of any reduction in the numbers of people in police custody or reported for summons without arrest, which might be expected if the necessity principle was indeed having some impact.

Bottomley *et al* (1989) also report that the reception of suspects into custody is largely a routinised formality and arresting officers are not normally required to provide substantial details of the offence. Irving and McKenzie (1989) note that at Brighton a local instruction by the station superintendent specifically forbade discussion of the evidence resulting in arrest before the suspect, and custody officers therefore did not always know much of the circumstances of arrest. Similarly, McConville *et al* (1991), in their study of police and prosecution decision making, maintain that custody officers readily go along with the wishes of case officers in detaining suspects. Detention, they argue, is a routine response, displaced only in exceptional circumstances: for example, where the suspect is suffering from senile dementia. They found a failure to authorise detention in only five out of 1,080 cases in their sample. In the great majority of cases where detention was authorised, it was on grounds specified in PACE. But in just over 10 per cent of cases, the reasons did not fall into any legal category.

Evans (1993), in a study of the interviewing of juveniles, queries the justification for detention in some cases in his sample; officers interviewed felt it was sometimes needed as a 'frightener' or to raise the level of seriousness for the suspect. His analysis of interviews with juveniles showed that some were akin to 'fishing expeditions', raising doubts about whether there could really have been reasonable suspicion to justify detention.

Despite the criticism of the authorisation process which the above studies imply, Bottomley *et al* (1989) are of the view that, by and large, arrests appear now to be made on a firmer basis. However, this would appear to be despite, rather than because of, the institution of the authorisation process as a filter (see above).

There is a substantial difference of view between McConville *et al* (1991) and other studies in their assessment of the reasons for the nullity of the authorisation procedure. Morgan *et al* (1991) take the view that legal rules in this area do have the potential for achieving their object if adequately framed. In effect, the concept of regulation of police activity by the police themselves, through the agency of an officer independent from the investigation, is not necessarily doomed to failure. They argue that the reason it is currently failing is that the procedures are inadequate and other imperatives are over-riding. One is the belief that failure to authorise detention would amount to public criticism of another officer. Another, more important still, is fear of disciplinary consequences (on this issue see too McKenzie *et al*,

1990). They draw attention also to the lack of any clear procedure for not authorising detention, noting that Code C implies that a custody record should be opened for each person brought to the police station under arrest (C 2.1). If detention were not authorised, much of the form would remain blank and this might attract criticism from supervisors, as might the period suspects spend at the station without detention having been authorised. Furthermore, custody officers are concerned to protect investigating officers, who might also attract criticism for making unjustified arrests. In effect, custody officers prefer to take a discretionary decision, which may be wrong but of low visibility to supervisors, rather than complete forms 'incorrectly', something which is highly visible. Morgan *et al* (1991) suggest that alternative procedures and introduction of forms that allow for non-authorisation of detention might inject more substance into the authorisation procedure.

Bottomley *et al* (1989) identify two other reasons why the authorisation procedure is generally a formality. They note that pressure of work on custody officers can make it impracticable to carry out substantial enquiries. Thus, they encountered no case in which suspects were charged on arrival at the station, even though the custody officer is required to assess whether there is sufficient evidence to do so. They also suggest (although their evidence for the assertion is not strong) that the decision about the necessity of detention may, to some extent, have been brought forward to the time of arrest.

McConville *et al* (1991), on the other hand, argue that powerful structural factors are behind the ineffectiveness of the authorisation process. They maintain that the concept of internal regulation, with custody officers taking an 'independent' view of the case, cannot succeed because their shared interest with other police officers is too overwhelming. They argue that custody officers are unable to divorce themselves from the needs of policing – primarily, the goals of crime clearance which generally underpin police work – or from collegial ties with other officers, which cause them to be emotionally committed to believing their colleagues' versions of events. Therefore, they maintain, suspects are detained as a matter of routine rather than on the basis of individualised decisions. For presentational purposes, the grounds for authorising detention contained in the Act are cited as the justification for detention.

McConville's interpretation is at odds with the conclusions of other studies which have observed custody office practice at first hand (McConville relied on documentary analysis and interviews with police officers). The middle ground is perhaps taken by Morgan *et al* (1991). They do not dispute that custody officers back up arresting officers' actions but that they do so for different reasons (see above). They have a variety of tactics for dealing with arrest decisions with which they disagree: for example, communicating this to the officers concerned in private or ensuring that those wrongly detailed are rapidly released. They argue that there is a certain amount of communality of interest between custody officers and case officers, but the extent to which this exists may depend on the way in which custody officers are deployed. Their independence from the police culture is greatest where they are allocated to the post on a long-term basis. However, whether this communality of interest exists or not, they maintain that its effect is not to lead to subversion of the suspect's rights; rather, the suspect's rights are protected in order to ensure that the gathering of evidence fits the correct procedures and that cases stick.

Dixon *et al* (1990b), drawing on the Hull study, which included numerous hours of observation in custody areas and interviews with custody officers, argue that custody officers are marked out by a difference of outlook from investigating officers, which may be characterised (depending on one's point of view) as 'bloodymindedness' or 'commendable independence'. Maguire (1988) and Irving and McKenzie (1989) have also drawn attention to this independent trait among custody officers. Dixon (1992) and Bottomley *et al* (1989), like Morgan *et al*, also point to custody officers' unwillingness to lay themselves open to the risk of discipline as a motivating factor in ensuring PACE rules are adhered to. They are unwilling to risk their jobs in order to allow investigating officers to obtain admissions. Dixon agrees with Morgan that, by insisting on adherence to PACE, they may assist investigating officers by ensuring that evidence is accepted in court. He argues that McConville's view that "the prospect of an admission is much more important to [custody officers] than the 'rights' of any suspect" excludes the possibility that the best admission is one secured while the suspect's rights are maintained. He also draws attention to personal qualities of many custody officers and the pride they take in their work which makes their approach to the job distinctive. Although a dominant concern in observing PACE remains the avoidance of comebacks, their commitment to the job may also play a large part in ensuring that suspects are treated fairly.

Dixon (1992) has also levelled other important criticisms at McConville's analysis. Since his arguments apply not only to the authorisation of detention but to a variety of other aspects of PACE considered elsewhere in this review, no apology is made for referring to these at length here. He notes that McConville's interpretation of the impact of PACE stems from what he terms 'new left pessimism' about criminal justice reform, characterised by extreme scepticism about the possibilities of success in the face of dominant police culture. An underlying belief of those belonging to this school is that the police consistently seek to evade or stretch legal controls in the name of crime control, and that legal rules are turned to the service of this strategy by providing surface legitimacy for police actions. Dixon argues that because of McConville's preconceptions, the two of them arrive at radically different interpretations of broadly similar sets of data.

He argues that McConville oversimplifies the attitudes of the police towards controls by suggesting that their response is to mitigate the effects of restrictions and constantly try to extend the boundaries of legal behaviour. He argues that this exaggerates police commitment to crime control. There are other responses: one is the routinisation of tasks in the face of bureaucratic realities which make refusal to accept a suspect's detention or the conduct of any searching enquiry into the evidence problematic. Custody officers' approach to the authorisation of detention may be taken to exemplify this attitude rather than an over-riding commitment to crime control values. Examples which McConville himself gives from interviews with custody officers suggest the former approach rather than the latter.

Dixon (ibid.) argues too that McConville is guilty of over-generalising in several respects. First, he assumes to a considerable extent that a similar ethos, revolving around crime control, underlies most policing functions. Dixon argues strongly that this is not so and that there are substantial differences between police work at the station and that outside. The former is subject to much greater scrutiny by supervisors and there is little opportunity for custody officers to evade the very specific requirements placed on them by PACE.

Secondly, McConville makes geographical generalisations, whereas PACE research has in fact pointed to considerable inconsistencies between forces and stations in the way the Act is applied. Custody officers may, as has been noted, be deployed on a long-term basis in some areas, and this may help them maintain distance between themselves and investigating officers. This may not be the case in areas where sergeants may be expected to perform other duties besides that of custody officer (see, for example, Morgan *et al*, 1991).

The third generalisation is about the homogeneity of police culture and attitudes to crime. Dixon argues that this trivialises the differences between officers as well as providing no basis for assuming that their actions will be similar. He also makes the fundamental point that PACE exploits an important cultural difference in the police force, that between CID and uniformed officers. However, McConville would maintain that both are in league against the constraints of formal rules in pursuit of crime control values. He also points out that McConville himself draws attention to differences between custody officers: some are "all PACE, PACE, PACE" while others "will bend just a little bit". In order to maintain his argument, McConville must, on no firm basis, regard the former as atypical and the latter as predominant. McConville, he argues, also fails to take into account changes in police culture over time. Williamson (1990), for example, has referred to increasing professionalism in the police service; others (for example, Young, 1991) have pointed to a decrease in violence against suspects. Relatedly, police work at the station is increasingly subject to scrutiny by outsiders.

One further criticism made by Dixon (ibid.) relates to McConville's view that law reform in general – and PACE in particular – is concerned with 'empowering the police in relation to the suspect'. In effect, McConville's argument is that the broad scope of legal provisions makes it possible for the police to perpetuate their own working rules, of which those relating to authorisation of detention are just one example. Dixon argues that this is a mistaken conception. It understates the limits on police powers and the safeguards for the suspect contained in PACE. If these are unsatisfactory, they nevertheless compare favourably with the pre-existing situation, during which there was a far greater element of arbitrariness in the rules governing the detention of suspects. He also argues that a powerful determinant of reform was not the need to expand police discretion but simply to produce more efficient legislation through clarifying and codifying existing rules.

Reviews of detention

After detention has initially been authorised, PACE provides for the continuing review of the need to keep suspects in custody. Officers of at least inspector rank must enquire into the circumstances of cases at specified intervals, with the first review being not later than six hours after detention was first authorised, and subsequent reviews at not more than nine-hourly intervals after the first (PACE Section 40). Suspects may not be held without charge for more than 24 hours, except on the authority of an officer of at least superintendent rank in serious arrestable offences. If reviews are postponed, the reasons must be recorded in the custody record. Decisions about whether further detention is necessary must also be recorded on the custody record. The grounds for authorising further detention are the same as those relating to the initial authorisation of detention.

Bottomley et al (1989) raise serious doubts about the substance of the review procedure. Their observations suggest that 6-hour and 15-hour reviews are largely routinised procedures, with little heed being paid to representations made by, or on behalf of, the suspect. They found that inspectors depended to a considerable extent on custody officers for information about cases and effectively rubber-stamped their decisions. However, custody officers were not always as aware as they should have been about the circumstances of cases. Information may not have been passed on at changes of shift, for example, or investigating officers may not readily have been available.

Morgan et al (1991), basing their conclusions on observation in custody areas and analysis of custody records, found that around one-quarter of first reviews were delayed, without any reason being recorded. They also found that, in one-fifth of observed cases and 10 per cent of those taken from custody records, no review was recorded at all. Bottomley *et al* (1989) point to difficulties for custody officers in keeping trace of the times reviews are due when the station is busy. There may also be problems locating duty inspectors. In some cases, this leads to reviews being conducted over the telephone – a permissible procedure under Code C (15C), but less than satisfactory, since the review officer is unable to discuss directly with suspects any representations they may wish to make. It is quite permissible under PACE for reviews to be brought forward; this may be done where inspectors are unlikely to be available at the due time or where suspects are likely to be asleep. Brown *et al* (1992) found that, since the introduction of the revised Codes of Practice, there had been a greater tendency to advance review times. They suggest that this may be due to the new requirement to remind suspects of their right to legal advice at this point.

Length of pre-charge detention

PACE introduced clear limits to the length of time suspects can be held without charge. Other than in serious arrestable offences, the upper limit is 24 hours (PACE s.41). In serious arrestable offences, 36 hours is the limit on police authority alone (s. 42), and 96 hours the absolute maximum on the authority of warrants of further detention issued by a magistrates' court (ss.43 and 44). There is some evidence that the average length of detention without charge has decreased – this is consistent with the intentions underlying PACE – and that the pattern of time spent in custody has altered according to the seriousness of the offence.

The following studies have found decreases in detention lengths. Morgan *et al* (1991), drawing on samples of 1,800 pre-PACE and 1,800 post-PACE custody records, found the average length of detention fell from six hours and 20 minutes to five hours and 20 minutes. Mackay (1988), in a study in Bedfordshire, found that over 80 per cent of suspects in a post-PACE sample drawn from 1986 had been released by the six-hour mark, compared with three-quarters in 1982. Irving and McKenzie (1989) found a significant reduction: in their 1986 sample, the average figure fell by over two hours to eight hours and 35 minutes. One factor which they suggest contributed to shorter detention times was a significant reduction in the time that elapsed prior to first interviews with suspects. This may stem from tighter constraints on detention, which mean that investigating officers are less able to delay working on a case until they return to work on their next shift.

There is some evidence of differing trends in detention lengths according to the nature of the offence. Irving and McKenzie (1989) found some evidence that, at the lower end of the scale, those detained for less serious offences, who are typically held for short periods, were actually held for longer under

PACE. Morgan *et al* (1991) also found a clustering of detention times around the five- to six-hour mark. They suggest that officers may let detention drift up to the six-hour mark because they work on the principle that they are allowed up to six hours before they need to provide justification for holding suspects longer. It seems unlikely, however, given the superficiality of the review procedure (see above), whether the first review really does mark an important watershed for investigating officers.

At the more serious end of the scale, Irving and McKenzie (1989) found that detention lengths were shorter; this may be due to investigating officers' reluctance to approach superintendents for authorisation for detention beyond 24 hours. Such extensions are, in any event, limited to the relatively infrequent serious arrestable offences. Bottomley *et al* (1989) report a similar change in the pattern of detention lengths according to the seriousness of the offence.

There is agreement that the length of detention is related to a number of variables. Thus, it varies according to the outcome of detention. Those cautioned, summonsed or released without charge are held the shortest time and those charged the longest (Irving and McKenzie, 1989; Bottomley *et al*, 1989; Brown, 1989; Morgan *et al*, 1991). Those released, for example, are generally held for around four hours; those charged are held for six hours or more. Irving and McKenzie (1989) suggest that this pattern accords with the principles underlying PACE. If the Act is working correctly to safeguard the innocent, then it is to be expected that detention will be brief for this group. This interpretation is perhaps over simplistic. It should, it is submitted, also be the case that those against whom there is good evidence should be charged without delay if PACE is being strictly complied with (see Section 37 of PACE; also Code C, 16.1).

Detention lengths also vary according to the suspect's age. Bottomley *et al* (1989) suggest that the requirement to secure the attendance of appropriate adults for juveniles may have increased detention times for this age-group. Juveniles were held for more than an hour longer on average in their post-PACE samples of cases. Both they and Brown (1989) draw attention to longer detention times for those who receive legal advice. This is, of course, a factor, related to seriousness of offence. When this is controlled for, those legally advised are still held for longer than others, because of the time taken to secure the services of a solicitor.

It would appear that PACE time limits have generally not created difficulties for investigating officers. This is not surprising in view of pre-PACE findings, quoted by the RCCP (1981), that the vast majority of suspects were dealt with inside the 24-hour limit now applicable to most cases. Bottomley *et al* (1989) found that 40 per cent of officers interviewed felt the time limits had affected their work very little. Over 40 per cent felt there had been an effect, but half of these thought that this had been beneficial, in terms, for example, of introducing a more professional approach to investigation which entailed collation of firmer evidence prior to arrest. The remainder of those who thought there had been effect claimed this had been detrimental, referring to rushed investigations.

There is some evidence, particularly in more serious cases, of adverse effects. In a study of burglary investigation, Brown (1991) found that most detectives interviewed felt that the PACE time limits did not recognise the realities of police work and factors which pushed detention times up. These included: waits for solicitors and appropriate adults; the arrest of other suspects; recovery of stolen property; the requirement to allow suspects eight hours rest overnight; difficulties in co-ordinating interviewing where several suspects were arrested; pressure on interview rooms; and the constraints of the police shift system. Furthermore, while a case could sometimes be made that crimes should be classed as serious arrestable offences and that detention over 24 hours was justified, senior officers were reluctant to authorise this as they might have to justify their decisions in court later. These factors combined meant that, in more serious cases, enquiries were often carried out against a background of tension once an arrest had been made.

Outcome of detention

The decision to charge

After a person has been arrested, PACE requires the custody officer to determine whether he or she has sufficient evidence to charge (s.37(1)) and, if so, either to proceed to do so or release the suspect (s.37(7)). There is little indication that this clarification has led to any significant change in the pattern of outcomes to detention. Morgan *et al* (1991), for example, found little change in the proportions charged or against whom no further action was taken.

Irving and McKenzie (1989) suggest that the police may more frequently be using the facility in s.47(3) of PACE to bail suspects pending further enquiries. Around a quarter of suspects in 1987 were bailed – a fourfold increase over 1986. This may be a response to increased pressure of time brought about by PACE limits on length of detention. Bailing the suspect has the advantage that the custody clock is stopped; it also leaves the threat of re-arrest hanging over the suspect's head. Irving and McKenzie's study was restricted to just one station; other research has shown that the use of police bail varies considerably around the country (Brown, 1989). A recent study of burglary investigation, comparing practice in 1983 and 1987, revealed no increase in its use in burglary cases (Brown, 1991).

In attempting to regulate charging by objective criteria it is implicit that irrelevant factors, notably the race of the suspect, should have no part to play in the decision. Nevertheless, a study by Walker *et al* (1990) in Leeds and work on the monitoring of juvenile cautioning in seven forces (CRE, 1992) shows that young Afro-Caribbeans are far more likely to be prosecuted than white suspects. This mirrors the findings of pre-PACE research carried out in London (Landau, 1981; Landau and Nathan, 1983). However, as FitzGerald (1993) has pointed out, a major shortcoming of these studies is that they have not taken sufficient account of the extent to which Afro-Caribbeans were ineligible for a caution because of a failure to admit the offence against them. In the one area in the CRE study where data were obtained on admissions, it was found that Afro-Caribbeans were twice as likely as other suspects to deny the offence and that this largely explained the differences in cautioning rates. Other evidence that Afro-Caribbeans are less likely to admit the offence against them comes from Walker *et al*'s study in Leeds. The likelihood is, therefore, that the higher charge rate of Afro-Caribbeans is strongly related to this factor and that discrimination on other grounds at the point of charge is not proven.

Bail

Under s.38(1) of PACE there is a presumption that those charged with an offence should be released, with or without bail, unless specific conditions apply. These relate to the likelihood that the suspect will abscond, reoffend or interfere with witnesses. A recent study of police bail decisions in five forces by Burrows *et al* (1995) found that the most frequently used grounds for refusal of bail were the risk of the suspect failing to appear and to prevent the suspect from causing physical injury or causing loss or damage to property.

Brown (1989) found considerable variation between areas (32 stations were examined) in the rate at which suspects were remanded in police custody. Figures ranged from 13 to 32 per cent of those charged. He suggests that some of this variation is explained by differences between areas in the seriousness of offences. However, even for comparable offences, there was considerable variation: the proportion of burglary offenders kept in custody ranged from 21 per cent to 72 per cent, for example. Morgan and Pearce (1988), who compared police decisions in just two areas, Brighton and Bournemouth, also found different bail rates for similar offences. Thus, 47 per cent of violent offenders were remanded in custody at one station, compared with just 27 per cent at the other, and 41 per cent of fraud suspects compared with 22 per cent. Those of no fixed abode were most likely to be remanded in custody at both stations, presumably because of the perceived risk of absconding. Other factors that were relevant to the refusal of bail were: offence type and seriousness; the sex of the suspect; and whether he or she was employed. However, the stations appeared to give different weight to these factors and this may explain some of the variation in custody rates.

Brown (1991) suggests that differences in the proportion of juveniles in the arrest population at different stations may also help explain variations in their bail rates because juveniles are more likely to be bailed than adults. However, there remains considerable variation between stations in the granting of bail for offences in which juveniles are not heavily implicated. The range of variation suggests that the PACE criteria are being applied differently from place to place.

Recent work by Phillips and Brown (forthcoming) also examined the relationship between race and police bail decisions. When other variables were controlled for, the ethnic group of the suspect did not appear to have a bearing on whether bail was granted. This finding is in contrast to the situation once the suspect has reached court. The study of sentencing in the Crown Court by Hood (1992) found that black defendants were significantly more likely to be remanded in custody between court appearances than white or Asian defendants.

Burrows *et al*'s (1995) recent study of the bail process suggests that custody officers may find some difficulty in interpreting the PACE criteria relating to the bail decision, notwithstanding the publication of a Home Office circular aimed at providing clarification (Home Office, 1992). Many custody officers interviewed[4] felt that one of the criteria, 'to prevent interference with the administration of justice or investigation of offences', was insufficiently precise and were critical that there was no guidance as to the strength and nature of evidence that needed to be adduced to justify its use. One particular difficulty arose where custody officers believed that the suspect would reoffend if released on bail. Under s.38(1) of PACE, risk of reoffending was not in itself a ground for refusal of bail. The Criminal Justice and Public Order Act 1994 now makes the likelihood of reoffending on bail an explicit basis for refusal of bail. Burrows *et al* (1995) suggest that, under PACE, custody officers generally took the criterion of the 'prevention of injury, loss or damage' as relating to the risk of reoffending in general. Strictly, however, it was not appropriate where the potential offences were not likely to have one of these effects. Burrows *et al* (ibid.) suggest that there may have been a considerable amount of variability in the way custody officers interpreted this particular provision. They point out that this and other inconsistencies in the application of the bail provisions may be attributable in part to the lack of specific training for custody officers in the making of bail decisions.

---

4   Sixty-four custody officers from five forces were interviewed.

'Three day lie-downs'

Section 48 of PACE modifies a power formerly available to magistrates under Section 128(7) of the Magistrates' Courts Act 1980 to remand a person charged with offences to police custody for up to three days (commonly referred to by the police as 'three day lie-downs'). Section 48 now specifies that such detention shall be at a police station, where there is a need to detain someone for the purpose of inquiries into other offences. It also applies the necessity principle in determining how long such detention should be. Irving and McKenzie (1989) found that Section 48 was used more frequently than the previous provision. Brown (1991) found a particularly large increase in its use in burglary investigations. He attributes this to increased constraints on questioning before charge for offences to be taken into consideration (TICs). (Code C, in its original form, required a person to be brought before the custody officer for consideration for charging when there is sufficient evidence to prosecute: C 17.1.)

Bottomley et al (1989) found that remands to police custody sometimes caused conflict between investigating officers and custody officers. These were over the necessity for such detention. Custody officers sometimes suspected that remand to a police station was purely a matter of CID convenience to save them having to travel to prisons to talk to offenders. Also, they believed that in some cases, little was actively done in the way of pursuing inquiries and that detention was therefore not justified. However, Brown (1991) found that detention does not often reach the maximum three days allowable under the Section 48 provision, suggesting that the necessity principle is limiting the time suspects are held. It is possible that police practice in using Section 48 remands may have altered further in response to a revision to Code C which provides more latitude to delay charging suspects until questioning has been completed about other offences for which they have been detained (C 16.1 – revised Code).

Voluntary attendance

It was noted earlier in this chapter that detention appears to be authorised by custody officers largely as a matter of routine, partly because there is no established procedure for refusing to accept someone into custody. McKenzie et al (1990), in their study of custody officers, suggest that some forces are overcoming this difficulty through the practice of asking some suspects to attend the police station voluntarily to answer questions. They suggest that voluntary attendance might be used where a person was on the borderline between being a witness and suspect, or where the case was suitable for summons. This practice does not necessarily contravene PACE: Section 29 contemplates that some persons will attend voluntarily to assist investigations, but states that they are entitled to leave at will unless placed under arrest and should be told at once if the decision to arrest is taken. Code C also states that those attending voluntarily should be treated with no less consideration that those in custody, and enjoy an absolute right to obtain legal advice or communicate with those outside (C 1A).

McKenzie *et al* found voluntary attendance particularly prevalent in one of their research forces, with around a third of all suspects being dealt with in this way. On average, volunteers attended the station for just short of 80 minutes. The bulk of cases were dealt with by uniformed officers and were primarily less serious ones such as shoplifting, although some serious assault cases were included. In a survey of 23 forces, they found half used voluntary attendance, although in five it was minimal and in the others way below the level found in the force which they studied in detail. Bottomley *et al* (1989) also found the practice existed in their research force, but documentation was patchily completed and it was therefore difficult to assess its extent.

There are various dangers associated with voluntary attendance. McKenzie *et al* (1990) note that the dividing line between arrest and being a volunteer is dangerously thin. Both they and Zander (1990) point out that some 'volunteers' will really be at the police station under a degree of compulsion, wrongly assuming they are under arrest. For there is no obligation on the police to inform them that they are free to go although the police must say at what point they are under arrest. There is also the issue of proper accountability for those attending voluntarily (Zander, ibid.). For example, no obligation exists for the police to open a custody record (although McKenzie *et al* (1990) found that one of their research forces had a similar record for volunteers): thus, custody officers might be unaware of the presence at the station of volunteers until the point at which they left. McKenzie *et al* point out that this makes it impossible for them to fulfil the requirements of the Code of Practice (that volunteers be treated with no less consideration than those detained). There is also no requirement for volunteers to be told of their right to legal advice. Another danger is that voluntary attendance could be used to circumvent constraints on the length of detention: if the suspect is arrested later, time spent voluntarily at the station does not count towards total time in custody.

It should be noted that these findings on voluntary attendance are drawn from research carried out quite early in the life of PACE. At that time, some confusion may have existed about the scope of police powers to detain for questioning. It is not clear whether the practice of using voluntary attendance persists, either in the research force used in the study by McKenzie *et al* or elsewhere. There is some evidence, albeit by implication or anecdote, that voluntary attendance is not now used to any great extent. Thus, recent studies of the detention process by Brown *et al* (1992) and Phillips and Brown (forthcoming) contain no mention of the use of voluntary attendance at the wide range of stations and forces visited during the course of the research. Observers participating in these studies indicated that there were occasions on which persons attended for interview voluntarily, but these were rare and there was usually something unusual about the circumstances of the cases which justified this procedure.

Summary

- PACE has had little impact on police practices in arresting and detaining, rather than summonsing, those suspected of indictable offences. There is some evidence that the standard of pre-arrest evidence has improved, although not all studies agree.

- Black people are arrested at a higher rate than white people, but this does not appear to be because weaker evidence is used to justify their arrest.

- Although custody officers must examine the necessity for the suspect's detention, this rarely amounts to a searching scrutiny and almost all those arrested are detained. One line of research suggests that this is because custody officers share common aims with investigators, but others have convincingly argued that they exhibit strong independence and that other reasons explain why detentions are rarely refused.

- Reviews of detention at the six- and fifteen-hour mark are largely routinised procedures which simply confirm the suspect's continued detention.

- Since the introduction of PACE those arrested for serious offences are generally held for shorter periods than before but in less serious cases a number of factors (such as waiting for legal advice or the arrival of appropriate adults) have pushed the length of detention up.

- In the majority of cases, limits on detention lengths have not created problems for investigating officers. In some areas, suspects are commonly bailed for further enquiries as a way of stopping the detention clock running.

- There is considerable regional variation in the granting of bail to suspects after charge, probably reflecting different interpretations of the PACE bail criteria, particularly in relation to the risks of reoffending.

- In some areas, significant numbers of suspects are asked to attend the police station voluntarily for questioning.

5 Treatment of suspects

This chapter considers several aspects of the treatment of persons detained at police stations.[1] In particular, it examines the operation of the various rights and safeguards provided by PACE and the key role in their implementation played by custody officers. The latter are the holders of a new post, established by PACE in response to the RCCP's concerns that someone independent from the investigation should have responsibility for the suspect while in police custody (RCCP, 1981: 59). The custody officer fulfils this function; his or her specific tasks are to look after all aspects of the welfare of suspects, ensure that they are aware of their rights, and take decisions about their detention. Morgan *et al* (1991) describe the custody officer as "the linchpin of the whole system of safeguards".

One of his or her most important duties is to open a custody record for each person detained and record full details about the suspect's detention, as required by various PACE and Code of Practice provisions. A document of this kind was regarded by the RCCP as essential to the reviewability of events during periods of detention.

There are two other elements to ensuring the rules on the treatment of suspects are enforced. One is that breaches of the Codes of Practice render officers liable to police discipline (PACE s.67(8)). The other is that evidence obtained in breach of PACE or the Codes is liable to be excluded by the courts (PACE ss.76 and 78).

The post of custody officer

A number of studies suggest that several features of custody office work may have an important bearing on the custody officer's ability to act as an independent arbiter. Morgan *et al* (1991) make the point that, at most times, custody officers will have several prisoners in their charge, all at different stages in their progression through the system. There is therefore a considerable overlapping of tasks and unpredictability in the work. Brown (1989) has also drawn attention to the way in which the custody officer's job is made up of a mosaic of tasks. He notes that what appear to be fairly low workloads

---

1   Access to legal advice, at risk groups of suspects and interviewing are dealt with in later chapters.

(an average of four or five prisoners in custody at any one time) may entail a considerable amount of work in view of the differing demands engendered by juvenile, sick, drunk[2] or mentally disordered prisoners, requests for solicitors or outside contact, initial processing, review and charge procedures, and the demands of investigation officers for access to their prisoners. Bottomley *et al* (1989) have also noted that pressures on custody officers conflict and have to be resolved. In particular, the requirement to follow PACE procedures and avoid disciplinary consequences for failure to do so may compete with the demands of investigating officers.

Another relevant feature of the job is that the incoming flow of prisoners is beyond the custody officer's control. Brown (1989) draws attention to variation in the rate at which prisoners arrive according to the station, the time of day and day of the week. At a busy city centre station, for example, up to 20 per cent of the week's prisoners may arrive on a Saturday and most of these during the afternoon and evening. In general, the patterning is not unpredictable but, as both he and Maguire (1988) point out, unforeseen circumstances sometimes lead to 'log-jams' of prisoners which may place the custody officer under considerable pressure. A 'comfortable' rate at which a custody officer may cope with incoming prisoners is around three to four arrivals per hour (Maguire, ibid.; Barclay, 1986); however, Brown (1989) found several occasions during the course of a month on which seven or more prisoners arrived within an hour at busier stations. Morgan *et al* (1991) note how, when several prisoners arrive together, the charge-room becomes a hubbub of noise and confusion.

Morgan *et al* (ibid.) found that usual practice at police stations is to complete the formalities required by PACE and the Codes of Practice for each prisoner in turn in order of arrival before placing them in a cell. They note, however, that there is no requirement for this procedure to be followed, and it can lead to queues of prisoners building up. There may be undesirable consequences: for example, it may be difficult to maintain control; and juvenile suspects may find themselves alongside vagrants and prostitutes.

Bottomley *et al* (1989) point to situations in which the custody officer's independence may be compromised. At quieter stations, the officer filling the post may have to perform other duties, such as taking crime details from victims and even making arrests. In such situations, it may be hard to describe him or her as independent from the investigation. They also draw attention to the practice sometimes found of investigating officers making entries on the custody record where the custody officer is busy (although

---

2   Drunk prisoners may require considerable monitoring. Code C 8.10 requires visits every half hour. At some stations, up to 22 per cent of those arrested may be under the influence of alcohol, and up to a fifth of these may be suffering from significant impairment (Robertson, Gibb and Pearson, 1995).

custody officers would usually check entries later).

The custody officer has responsibility for the prisoner, while in his or her charge. However, Bottomley *et al* (1989) found that it was fairly common practice for gaolers (usually constables) to complete custody records and take key decisions on the custody officer's behalf. Inevitably, there are times at which custody must pass to officers carrying out interviews or searches of premises. Responsibility for ensuring compliance with the provisions of PACE passes to such officers (PACE s.39(2)), who must account to the custody officer when the prisoner is returned (s.39(3)). Bottomley *et al* (ibid.) and McConville and Hodgson (1993) both identify this as a weak point in PACE's provisions, because the distinction between the requirements of the investigation and the prisoner's welfare are blurred. The former study found that investigating officers' assurances to the custody officer were ritualistic; realistically, it is highly unlikely that an officer would report that PACE had not been complied with.

More serious doubts about the ability of custody officers to act as independent guardians of the suspect's welfare have been cast by McConville *et al* (1991). Their view (which has already been discussed more fully in Chapter 4 in relation to the authorisation of detention) is that custody officers are too closely allied with policing values to be able to divorce themselves from the needs of the investigation. This outlook may be to the prejudice of the rights and treatment of suspects. Others, notably Dixon (1992) have argued that these conclusions are unsound. He contends that custody officers are motivated strongly by fear of disciplinary consequences for breaches of PACE; they also recognise the value of achieving the ends of investigations within PACE rules so that cases do not fail later if irregularities come to light. He also suggests that custody officers have developed a distinct working culture, which emphasises independence.

Bottomley *et al* (1989), on the basis of interviews with custody officers, maintain that their attitude is one of assisting the investigation, but within the bounds of PACE and the Codes of Practice. At times, this *does* lead to conflicts with investigating officers, with the custody officer's point of view generally prevailing. However, they note that the same approach by custody officers can lead to a differential approach to the rules, depending on their substance. They found, for example, a degree of leniency in their willingness to allow investigating officers informal access to suspects in the cells. Such visits were generally recorded on the custody record, but in order that they could bear later scrutiny, went down as 'welfare visits' (see also Chapter 7). On the other hand, in relation to giving suspects their rights, minimum requirements were almost always observed.

In the same study, over 300 police officers were interviewed about their views on the impact of the post of custody officer. Their replies also provide little support for McConville *et al*'s standpoint. Nearly two-thirds considered that the post had affected police work for better or worse in various ways. Among the most frequently held views were that the rules on the detention of suspects were clearer, that officers had to justify their actions and decisions to a greater extent, and that custody officers had greater control over the enforcement of the rules. Some felt that police work had been impeded or slowed down. A significant minority, particularly among the CID, reported conflicts with custody officers: for example, about authorising interviews with the suspect.

Rights and entitlements

One of the most important tasks of the custody officer is to ensure that suspects are aware of their rights at the police station. Information must be given both orally and in writing about the three main rights: to have someone informed of arrest; to consult a solicitor;[3] and to consult the PACE Codes of Practice (C 3.1, 3.2). Under the revised Codes of Practice, introduced on 1 April 1991, custody officers must now give suspects a copy of an additional notice setting out their main entitlements over and above their statutory rights while in custody. These include the entitlements to a reasonable standard of physical comfort and to medical attention (see C 3.2 and C 3A). The revised Codes also stipulate that information should be conveyed clearly. Delay in providing information is only permissible if the detainee is incapable of understanding what is said (typically, if he or she is drunk), is actually or potentially violent, or in urgent need of medical attention (C 1.8). The detainee must be asked to sign the custody record to acknowledge receipt of the written notices and to indicate whether he or she wants legal advice.

Studies suggest that custody officers generally comply with the requirement to provide suspects with information about their rights. However, it is important to distinguish the two means whereby such information must be given: in writing and orally. The significance of the latter is that many suspects do not bother to read notices which they are given or may be unable to, if illiterate. Moreover, the way in which spoken information is conveyed may strongly influence the take-up of rights (Brown, 1989; Sanders *et al*, 1989; Brown *et al*, 1992).

Written information

Custody record data consistently suggest that 90 per cent or more of those detained are given a written notice of their rights: most suspects sign to indi-

---

3   The right to legal advice is discussed more fully in Chapter 6.

cate this, a small proportion refuse (Brown *et al*, 1992; Morgan *et al*, 1991; Sanders *et al*, 1989; Bottomley *et al*, 1989). Brown *et al* (1992) found several situations in which custody officers did not seek signatures to indicate that notices of rights had been given. Most frequently this was where detainees were not being held for offences (for example, those detained on warrant and missing persons) and were not classed by the police as PACE prisoners who needed to receive their rights. A signature was also often not obtained from suspects who were drunk or violent on arrival. However, in about a third of cases in which there was no indication that a notice had been distributed suspects were being held for offences and were not drunk or violent. Frequently these were juveniles. Some custody officers delayed raising the issue of the suspect's rights until an adult arrived. They then sometimes overlooked the provision of the notice and obtaining a signature where investigating officers were anxious to proceed with an interview.

Since the introduction of the revised Codes of Practice, Brown *et al* (1992) note an increasing tendency for custody officers to obtain a signature to indicate that a written notice has been given, particularly for non-PACE prisoners. This may reflect an attitude of 'playing safe' – there can be no harm in providing rights to those who may not strictly require them – and concern to avoid criticism or possible discipline for leaving sections of the record blank.

It is clear from both the work of Sanders *et al* (1989) and Brown *et al* (1992) that the presence of the detainee's signature is not itself a guarantee that a written notice of rights was in fact given. Both were able to use observation of custody office practice as a double-check and found that around five per cent of those who signed had not in fact received their rights. The latter research indicates a slightly smaller gap of four per cent, decreasing to three per cent with the introduction of the revised Codes. The same study found that the new notice of entitlements, provided for in revised Code C, was invariably distributed along with the notice of rights.

Spoken information

Estimates differ of the extent to which suspects are given spoken information about their rights. Sanders *et al* (1989) found that 15 per cent of suspects were not given a verbal explanation. However, in Brown *et al*'s (1992) more recent study of the revised PACE Codes, as well as in Morgan *et al* 's (1991) study of the work of custody officers, 95 per cent of detainees were heard to be given some explanation of their rights. Brown *et al* found that custody officers almost always mentioned legal advice and the right to have someone informed and, in a large majority of cases, the right to see a copy of the Codes of Practice. Possibly, custody officers' practice may have become more rigorous since early 1988 when Sanders *et al* carried out their study (although Morgan's data is not much more recent) or practice may differ between the sets of stations included in the studies.

McConville *et al* (1991) have drawn upon Sanders' findings to support the view that custody records are used by the police as a presentational tool to show compliance with legal procedures when the reality is in fact somewhat different. Like Sanders, they found that the overwhelming majority of custody records state that suspects are advised of their rights. Their study contained no observation of custody office procedures, but they quote Sanders *et al*'s study to support the view that this conceals a proportion of cases in which notices of rights are not given and that, where they are, explanation may be deficient or non-existent. This study has been examined in more depth elsewhere in this review (see above, Chapter 4), particularly its conclusions that custody officers are too closely identified with investigating officers and crime control values to act as independent guarantors of the suspect's rights. Here, it will be argued that it is doubtful whether their contention that custody records routinely misrepresent the provision of rights can be maintained.

First, as has been noted, Sanders' findings, on which they rely, are not in agreement with those of more recent, observational, research which found higher levels of explanations of rights. Secondly, a closer examination of Sanders' findings reveals that the gap between what custody records claim and the actual provision of rights is by no means as large as might appear. The figures used by McConville do not take account of the fact that in some cases rights were given later (when drunken suspects sobered up, for example) and that, in others, explanations of rights were given, although no written notices were seen to be passed across. Thirdly, the implication of McConville's argument is that the police seek to deny the suspect's rights where this is most to their advantage in terms of achieving crime control objectives. In fact, other studies suggest less sinister motives for inadequacies in the presentation of rights (Brown *et al*, 1992; Morgan *et al*, 1991). Cases typically involve drunks or those not suspected of crime who, in the police view, may derive little utility from exercising their rights. In other cases, involving juveniles, some failures to provide rights may be inadvertent or stem from a misguided zeal to press ahead with the case without further delay and secure the juvenile's release. The message of these studies is that very few suspects fail to receive either notices or explanations of rights where no mitigating factors are present.

Quality of presentation

There is general agreement that, in most cases, rights are given clearly by custody officers (Code C now specifically stipulates that information should be given clearly – C 3.1). Nevertheless, Sanders *et al* (1989), Morgan *et al* (1991) and Brown *et al* (1992) have all found rights to be given unclearly, incompletely or too quickly in minorities of cases. It is difficult to compare these studies because researchers may have used different standards to judge what amounts to adequate presentation of rights. However, Brown *et al* (1992) were able to compare the giving of rights on broadly the same criteria before and after the introduction of the revised Codes of Practice. They found that in around a quarter of cases in their later sample there were inadequacies in the clarity of presentation, compared with 16 per cent of cases in their earlier sample. They suggest that the apparent decline in standards reflects the fact that custody officers were not coping well with the additional information that they were required to provide under the revised Codes.

Morgan *et al* (1991) stress the difficulties for the observer of appreciating the perspective of the suspect, arguing that while "rights were generally stated in a manner which would be adequate for comprehension by the 'reasonable' man ... few suspects are in a 'reasonable' frame of mind at the time". Dixon (1992) makes a similar point, arguing that the routine way in which rights are given may fail to make allowances for individual differences in levels of comprehension. Brown *et al* (1992) suggest that statements of rights may be coloured by custody officers' perceptions of their utility to the suspect. Both they and Bottomley *et al* (1989), for example, remark on the cynical way in which the suspect's right to consult the Codes of Practice is sometimes described.

Comprehension by suspects

Brown *et al*'s (1992) research on the revised PACE Codes suggests that there is a high level of basic awareness among suspects about their rights. In a sample of nearly 550 suspects interviewed during their study, well over 90 per cent were aware from information provided by the police that they had certain rights while in custody and that these included the right to have someone informed of their arrest and to consult a solicitor (see Chapter 6 for a fuller discussion of suspects' knowledge about the latter right). Suspects are also now given a separate notice of entitlements which summarises essential information from the Codes. The same study provides some evidence that the new notice of entitlements has proved a useful source of information to suspects. Comparing the situation before and after the revised Codes were introduced, they found that substantially more suspects were aware of entitlements, such as those to eight hours sleep and to regular meals, and slightly more knew of their entitlement to medical attention if unwell. About a third referred to the new notice as their main source of information.

However, there were some sources of confusion, particularly about the distinction between the right to have someone informed and the entitlement to a telephone call. Although the police rarely told suspects they were entitled to a telephone call (this was done in no more than three per cent of cases), well over a third claimed they had been offered this facility. In fact, they had only been told that the police would contact someone on their behalf. In the same study, only around 40 per cent of suspects were aware that they had the right to consult the PACE Codes of Practice. Many more had been told of this right but, either not understanding what it meant or not perceiving it to be useful, may not have taken it in.

More severe doubts about the comprehensibility of the written information given to suspects – particularly those intellectually disadvantaged – have been raised by Gudjunsson (1991). Using established psychological techniques, he and others have analysed the notice of rights and both the original and revised Codes of Practice for reading ease (Gudjunsson, 1990 and 1991; Gudjunsson, Clare and Cross, 1992). They rate the notice of rights as 'difficult' to understand and estimate that barely a quarter of the population would be able readily to understand it. The original Codes of Practice were rated as 'very difficult' to understand and as accessible to only around five per cent of the population. In a small-scale study to test out these findings, a group of offenders with an average IQ of 82 experienced considerable difficulties understanding the notice of rights (Gudjunsson, 1990 and 1991). Only just over half the sentences were understood by all suspects. In a further study, conducted after the introduction of a revised notice of rights and the new PACE Codes of Practice, this figure actually declined, with well under half of the notice being understood by all suspects (Gudjunsson, Clare and Cross, 1992).

Gudjunsson (1991) makes the point that difficulties with the notice and the Codes may be greater at the police station than in the conditions of the study, since suspects could be expected to be under considerable stress. It should be noted, however, that at the police station oral explanations of rights are also given by custody officers and there is scope for officers to adjust their explanations to the suspect's level of comprehension (although, as noted above, the giving of rights sometimes leaves much to be desired). Furthermore, there is evidence that basic information about rights is understood, even if the more detailed descriptions of those rights are not. Gudjunsson (ibid.) notes that most suspects understand the basic fact that they can communicate with a lawyer. This is consistent with the findings of Brown *et al* (1992).

In a more recent study, conducted for the RCCJ, Clare and Gudjunsson (1992) have assessed the accessibility of information about the suspect's

---

4   The study also aimed to establish whether those in need of an 'appropriate adult' (for example, those suffering from mental handicap or reading difficulties) could be identified more satisfactorily through direct questioning by the custody officer. The relevant findings are summarised in Chapter 8 dealing with 'at risk' groups.

rights when presented in a simplified, experimental format.[4] One hundred experimental subjects took part in the study, and they were provided orally with information in everyday language about their rights, given a laminated card containing key points of the verbal exposition, and given a further information leaflet for reference. The latter was also assessed for reading ease, using the techniques employed in the earlier studies of the original and current notices to detained persons.

The study found that the experimental notice was considerably less complex to understand than the existing version. Nearly three-quarters of it was understood by all subjects; over 80 per cent understood their right to silence. There was particular success in communicating the information about rights orally and via the summary card to those with limited intellectual ability. In contrast, it was found that the information in the fuller leaflet added relatively little to basic understandings of rights. Clare and Gudjunsson (ibid.) suggest that the added detail it contained may have confused rather than assisted. They recommend that, for clarity and effective communication, suspects should be given information about their rights by just two of the means evaluated: oral explanation and the summary card.

It should be noted that, although the study provides a useful step towards better methods of communicating information to suspects about their rights, the conclusions are based on experimental research. There remains the question of whether Clare and Gudjunsson's findings would be replicated under 'live' conditions. These are likely to differ in important respects. As already noted, suspects may be under considerable stress and may have matters on their minds other than the information they are being given by the police. Furthermore, it is possible that the sample used for the study may differ from the arrest population at police stations, although little information is provided in the research report on which to draw firm conclusions. It would appear that the average intelligence level of members of the sample was similar to that of convicted offenders. However, convicted offenders may not be representative of those who pass through police stations, a significant minority of whom are juveniles or petty offenders typically dealt with by means of a caution (Brown, 1989). It would also appear that the sample contained a surprisingly high proportion of people who were identified as having past or present mental health problems, or learning or reading difficulties.

Right to have someone informed of arrest

The RCCP (1981) considered the right not to be held incommunicado an important element in minimising the effects of arrest and detention on the suspect. That right is contained in s.56 of PACE. The person to be informed may be a friend or relative, some other person known to the detainee or someone who is likely to take an interest in their welfare. The right is a restatement of a pre-existing one contained in s.62 of the Criminal Law Act 1977, but with tighter definition of the circumstances in which it is permissible to delay implementation and other procedural safeguards.

Take-up rate

No national data were collected on requests generally under s.62 of the Criminal Law Act, but only on cases in which intimation was refused for more than four hours after a request was made. However, several studies provide some indication of the level of pre-PACE requests for outside contact at specific sets of stations. The highest figure is provide by Mackay (1988): looking at six stations in Bedfordshire, he found a request rate of 28 per cent. Two other studies provide lower estimates. Softley et al (1980), looking at four stations in different forces, found that requests were made in just over a quarter of cases, while Bottomley et al (1989), in a study set at three stations in one force, provide a figure of 14 per cent. However, both Softley and Bottomley found that sizeable minorities of suspects – 30 per cent in the former study and 20 per cent in the latter – were not apparently offered the opportunity in the first place to have someone informed.

In contrast, Bottomley et al (1989) found that after the introduction of PACE suspects were invariably told of the right to have someone informed. However, it was not always possible to deduce this from custody records, which appeared to show that this had only been done in just over half of the cases. The reason for inadequate recording may be that Code C only requires requests for intimation to be recorded; there is no need for suspects to sign to say that they have been told of this right, whether they wish to exercise it or not.

It is doubtful whether the introduction of the s.56 right has substantially increased the rate at which suspects request that someone be informed. Mackay (1988) found a rise of just two percentage points to 30 per cent in the rate of requests in Bedfordshire. Bottomley et al (1989) found an apparently more substantial rise, from 14 per cent to around 25 per cent. However, they note that much of the increase is accounted for by under-recording of requests for intimation in pre-PACE records. Taking this into account, they found little substantial difference in pre-PACE and post-PACE request rates.

More broadly based figures on take-up are provided by Brown (1989) and Brown et al (1992) in studies set at 32 and 12 police stations respectively. The average request rate for intimation was found to be around 18 per cent.

The former study found considerable variation between stations, with take-up ranging from eight per cent to 29 per cent. Brown (1989) attributes some of the variation to factors which also explain differences in request rates for legal advice (see Chapter 6). Thus, those detained for serious offences are more likely to request intimation, probably because they are more likely to be held for longer. On the other hand, juveniles are less likely to make such a request. This is because the police must notify an appropriate adult. While this does not count as s.56 intimation, it may effectively suppress the need for anyone else to be contacted. Much of the variation is unexplained. Brown (ibid.) suggests that differences in suspects' foreknowledge of their rights and in the way custody officers convey those rights may be important, a point also made by Sanders *et al* (1989) and Brown *et al* (1992).

Brown *et al* (1992) note that, for several reasons, there is probably a given limit to the rate at which this right is exercised. Firstly, many suspects have good reasons why they do not wish anyone to know of their arrest; secondly, relatives often know of the arrest already; and, thirdly, others either see no practical benefit in contacting anyone or have no-one they feel would be interested in their arrest.

Delay of intimation

Under s.62 of the Criminal Law Act 1977 intimation could only be delayed where this was in the interests of the investigation or prevention of crime or the apprehension of offenders. Under PACE, the circumstances under which delay is permissible are more tightly defined. The crime must be a serious arrestable offence and the authorisation of an officer of at least superintendent rank is required. He or she must have reasonable grounds for believing that exercise of the right will lead to one or more of several injurious consequences, such as the alerting of other suspects. The maximum permissible length of delay is 36 hours.

Irrespective of these different criteria, it appears that delay in carrying out intimation was almost as unusual before PACE was introduced as it is now. Softley *et al* (1981) found that this occurred in just over one per cent of cases involving adult suspects, while information compiled separately for the RCCP also suggests that delay was an uncommon occurrence (RCCP, 1981a). Since PACE was introduced, Brown (1989) found that delay of intimation was authorised in just one per cent of a sample of 5,000 cases drawn from 32 stations. He notes that this relatively low figure is not surprising since few cases are serious enough to fall into the serious arrestable offence category. He also points out that, in some cases where a delay was authorised, suspects had not necessarily asked for someone to be informed; a ban on outside contact was instituted as a precautionary measure. More recent research by Brown *et al* (1992) found that delays are now imposed in barely a tenth of the proportion of cases found by the 1989 study. They suggest that this trend may ride on the back of a severe cut-back in use of the equivalent power to delay access to legal advice (see Chapter 6) since the two powers often tend to be exercised in tandem (Brown, 1989).

Bottomley *et al* (1989) found that the police may resort to informal means to delay carrying out intimation. This was typically found to occur where officers wished to search the suspect's home and feared that prior intimation of arrest would lead to stolen property being disposed of. In such cases, they would undertake to carry out intimation at the time they searched the premises. Strictly, if the person to be notified is on the telephone, this practice contravenes the requirement that intimation shall be carried out 'as soon as is practicable' (PACE s.56(1)).

Meeting requests for intimation

It appears that up to two-thirds of requests for intimation are known to be carried out (Brown, 1989; Brown *et al*, 1992). The main reason for failure is that the person requested is unavailable; in a few cases, suspects retract their requests before they can be put into effect. However, due to recording deficiencies in custody records it is not always clear whether intimation is made. Brown *et al* (1992) found that in around a quarter of requests for intimation, custody records provided no information as to whether contact was made, despite a requirement in Code C that a record be made of the action taken upon requests (C 5.8). They note that the outcome of requests is often lost where the task of carrying them out falls to beat officers or those conducting searches of premises. Bottomley *et al* (1989) also draw attention to the low priority accorded by custody officers to requests for intimation compared with requests for solicitors, particularly when stations are busy. Brown *et al* (1992) also note that requests may become 'lost' where initial attempts to make contact fail and further attempts are left to the next shift on duty.

The length of time taken to carry out intimation may reflect the priority accorded to this task as well as problems encountered in some cases. Brown (1989) found that a quarter of requests took over one hour to fulfil, and a large proportion of these took over two hours.

Terrorist cases

Terrorist cases present rather a different picture and are therefore considered separately. Brown (1992) found that 43 per cent of those detained under the Prevention of Terrorism (Temporary Provisions) Act 1989 (PTA) during the course of an 18-month period requested that someone be informed of their detention. In such cases, there is clearly a concern that detainees may wish to tip off other suspects or conceal evidence. However, Brown (ibid.) notes that many such persons are arrested at ports or airports and may genuinely need to contact those who are expecting them at the end of their journey.

The grounds available for delaying exercise of the right are the same as in PACE cases, with the addition of some applicable to PTA cases only. Delay is also permissible for up to 48 hours rather than 36. The power to delay intimation was found to be used extensively, with authorisation to do so being given in over 70 per cent of cases in which a request was made. Additionally, as a precautionary measure authorisation was given in a significant minority of cases where no request had been made. In total, a delay was authorised in 44 per cent of all PTA cases. The grounds most commonly applied were those specifically available for PTA cases. In a third of cases, however, the custody record mentioned no basis for delay despite Code C's requirement that such an entry should be made (C, Annex B). The delay imposed lasted for more than 24 hours in a quarter of cases and, in a few, for more than 36 hours.

The rate at which intimation was actually made was low, with contact known to have been successful in less than 40 per cent of requests. In a small proportion of cases in which intimation had been requested, no delay had been authorised but there was no reference in the custody record to any attempts to make contact.

Telephone calls

Telephone calls by the detainee pose more problems than intimation made by the police since there is the risk that the suspect may tip off others or ensure that stolen property is disposed of. The former Judges' Rules provided that those in custody should be able to speak to their friends on the telephone "[p]rovided that no hindrance is reasonably likely to be caused to the processes of investigation or the administration of justice" (Home Office, 1978). This allowed substantial scope for calls to be denied or delayed. There is now less scope for this to occur. In the original version of Code C, calls could be delayed (but not denied) in the same circumstances that intimation of arrest or access to legal advice could be delayed (i.e. in serious arrestable offences, in certain urgent situations on a superintendent's authority). The revised Codes ease this requirement somewhat, allowing calls to be delayed *or* denied, in *arrestable* offences, on an *inspector's* authority; the circumstances justifying denial or delay are as before.

There is no obligation on the police to inform suspects that they may make telephone calls. Brown *et al* (1992) found this was done in no more than three per cent of cases. However, the notice of entitlements now given to the great majority of suspects contains this information.

Estimates of the number of suspects who request telephone calls vary, depending on whether custody records or direct observation are relied upon for information. The former suggest that between six and eight per cent of suspects ask for a telephone call (Brown, 1989; Brown *et al*, 1992). Custody records show calls are rarely delayed or denied: this occurred in just four per cent of requests in the first of the above studies and two per cent in the second.

Brown *et al* (1992) suggest, however, that there may be some under-recording on the custody record both of requests for telephone calls and their outcome. Some requests, for example, may be entered as requests for intimation. Based on observational work in custody offices, they suggest that as many as 12 per cent of suspects actually request telephone calls. On the same basis, as well as from interviews with suspects, they also suggest that up to a quarter of requests are delayed or refused. Furthermore, this is sometimes done on an informal basis without recourse to a supervisory officer, a practice not in accordance with Code C.

Brown (1993) found a higher recorded level of requests for telephone calls among those detained under the PTA. This may reflect either more scrupulous recording of requests in sensitive cases or a genuinely higher level of requests. The latter explanation may have some validity, given that PTA detainees are held for longer than PACE suspects and may have various personal reasons for needing to contact those outside. Two-fifths of calls were officially delayed in PTA cases, a higher rate than in PACE cases, reflecting police concerns about alerting other suspects. Calls were eventually made in nearly 90 per cent of cases in which they were requested.

Visitors

Suspects have no absolute right to receive visitors while in custody but are entitled to visits at the custody officer's discretion (C 5.4), depending on the availability of manpower to supervise the visit and possible hindrance to the investigation (C 5B). This entitlement is listed in the new notice to detainees (C 3A). Brown (1989) notes that few visits are allowed (custody records tend not to record those not allowed): he found that only five per cent of suspects received visitors while in custody, and that a third of these visits were to those who had been charged. Brown (1993) records a higher level of visits – in eight per cent of cases – to those detained under the PTA. This, he suggests, is related to the greater length of detention in such cases, which makes the detainee's need for outside contact that much more important.

Physical conditions of detention

The PACE Codes of Practice make a number of stipulations about the conditions of detention. These relate, for example, to standards of physical comfort, provision of refreshments, detention of juveniles, use of reasonable force and the frequency of visits to check on welfare. Putting these standards into effect can entail considerable resource demands (both in terms of manpower and the costs of rebuilding work). Perhaps for these reasons, changes in the physical setting of detention have not been marked. For example, Irving and McKenzie (1989) found little change in the cell area at Brighton between 1979 and 1986, commenting particularly that nothing had been done to facilitate the increased surveillance of prisoners required by the Code.

Dixon (1990) raises the issue of the conditions in which juveniles are kept, noting that Code C prohibits the placing of juveniles in cells unless no other secure accommodation is available or it is impracticable to maintain supervision. In the force in which he carried out his research this requirement was complied with by designating specific cells as 'juvenile detention rooms'. These did not differ from ordinary cells.

Medical attention

Code C requires the custody officer to call the police surgeon immediately if a detainee appears be physically or mentally ill, injured, unconscious or semi-conscious, behaving abnormally or otherwise in need of medical attention (Code C, 9.2). It is not necessary for the detained person actually to request attention, although, if he or she does, the police surgeon must be called as soon as practicable. Entries must be made in the custody record in respect of requests for medical attention and the action subsequently taken (Code C, 9.7 and 9.8).

The effect of these provisions appears to have been for custody officers to call in the police surgeon far more frequently and for a significant minority of detainees to receive some form of medical attention. A study by Greater Manchester Police (1986), shortly after the introduction of PACE, found that medical costs had risen to two or three times their pre-PACE level. In the first quarter of 1986, doctors attended five per cent of prisoners throughout the force. An even higher figure of seven per cent was found in a more broadly based study set at 32 police stations (Brown,1989). In over half of these cases the police summoned a doctor on their own initiative; in a third this was at the detainee's request.

A study of police surgeons by Roberton (1992), carried out for the RCCJ, found that their work was dominated by attending detainees who were drunk or who had been drinking. Many had sustained minor physical injuries while under the influence of drink. The very drunk raise particular difficulties for the police and may require constant supervision. Police surgeons and custody officers in Robertson's study agreed that police stations lack the facilities to care for such prisoners. Nevertheless, he found it was rare for police surgeons to certify that someone was unfit to be detained: this occurred in respect of only eight per cent of drunk and/or injured prisoners. Usually, this pronouncement was made where some physical injury required hospital treatment.

Robertson (ibid.) found that nearly 10 per cent of call-outs were to examine those suspected to be under the influence of drugs. A further 10 per cent concerned detainees who were believed to be mentally ill or handicapped.[5] Examining detainees who had been involved in road accidents, and particularly taking blood samples to test for alcohol, constituted another nine per cent of police surgeons' workload. Brown (1989) found that the two groups requiring medical attention most frequently – each in one-fifth of cases – were missing persons, generally because of concern over their mental condition, and motoring offenders, usually to take blood samples from suspected drink-drivers. The need for doctors in the latter cases has certainly declined considerably with the widespread introduction of 'Intoximeter' machines at police stations (Robertson, 1992). Violent, sexual, criminal damage and public order offences also generated above average demand.

Both Brown (1989) and Robertson (1992) found large variations between stations in the call-out rate for police surgeons. This partly reflected differences in the predominant offences. It also reflected differences in policy and practice, with custody officers at some stations playing safe by calling a doctor whenever there was the slightest doubt about the detainee's condition. At others, custody officers were more willing to use their discretion about whether to call a doctor to treat minor ailments and injuries (a discretion provided for in PACE Code C, NG 9A). Medical call-outs in the Metropolitan Police were among the highest: both Brown and Robertson found that doctors examined a quarter or more of all detainees at some stations. Outside London, call-out rates as low as three per cent were found by Brown and nine per cent by Robertson.

Robertson (1992) notes that the provision of medical attention at police stations raises several contentious issues. One is that doctors need undertake no specialised training to carry out the role of police surgeon. Some local training initiatives exist but only a small minority of police surgeons have participated.

---

5   See Chapter 8 for a discussion of police treatment of mentally disordered and mentally handicapped suspects.

The need for training is indicated by increases in the complexity of the work and in challenges to forensic evidence in court. The situation is complicated by the fact that some police surgeons undertake very little work at police stations and might not feel that the effort devoted to training would be repaid.

Another issue relates to the confidentiality of exchanges between suspect and doctor and the status of evidence obtained during the course of medical examinations at the police station. Robertson (ibid.) notes that examinations are sometimes carried out within the hearing of police officers. There are no rules under PACE governing information disclosed in this way, in contrast to the situation where the police themselves are asking the questions. Robertson argues that it is wrong that examinations undertaken for therapeutic purposes (as opposed to forensic purposes) should be capable of leading to the obtaining of evidence. He suggests that the relationship between doctor and detainee in these circumstances should be the same as that between NHS doctor and patient and subject to the same assurance of confidentiality.

Summary

- Custody officers play a key role in looking after the welfare of suspects. Their effectiveness in doing so is constrained by pressure of work and lack of direct oversight of some aspects of the detention process. Contentions that they are unable to maintain the required degree of independence from the investigation are not well supported by the bulk of research.

- The great majority of detainees are given written and spoken information about their rights and entitlements, although explanations are not always given clearly. The provision of rights is sometimes overlooked in cases involving juveniles or where the prisoner is violent or drunk on arrival, but there is little evidence that rights are systematically denied in order to assist the investigation.

- A large and increasing proportion of suspects are aware of their basic rights. However, there remains some confusion over the right to outside contact. Suspects also find the detailed written information they are given hard to understand and there may be scope to introduce a simplified version which has been sucessfully tested under experimental conditions.

- Nearly 20 per cent of detainees ask to have someone informed of their arrest. In two-thirds of these cases it is known that contact is made, but in other cases, due to deficient record-keeping, it is not always known what the outcome was. It is extremely rare for exercise of this right to be delayed, other than in terrorist cases.

• The police rarely inform detainees of their entitlement to make a telephone call and not more than 12 per cent ask for one. Only five per cent of detainees receive visitors.

• Doctors are called to examine prisoners in up to seven per cent of cases. This most frequently occurs where detainees are believed to be drunk, but also in cases where drugs are involved or where the detainee is suspected to be mentally disordered or mentally handicapped. There is considerable variation between stations in the proportion of cases involving medical call-outs, with the highest rates (up to 25%) being found in the Metropolitan Police. Concerns have been expressed about the lack of specialised training received by police surgeons and about the confidentiality of information imparted to doctors by suspects.

6 Legal advice

The RCCP considered that an effective right to legal advice was a vital safe-guard for the suspect and an important element in reducing the coercive effects of arrest and custody (RCCP, 1981). Under the former Judges' Rules (Home Office, 1978) suspects were entitled to consult a solicitor privately at any time, but there was no obligation upon the police to inform suspects of this right. Furthermore, the police had considerable scope to delay or deny access to solicitors and the legal profession was not adequately geared up to providing advice.

The key question examined in this chapter is whether the statutory right to legal advice now contained in PACE is indeed an effective right. The extent to which suspects are informed of the right and the way in which this is done are both relevant to this question. So too is the working of the arrange-ments for delivering legal advice, and particularly the duty solicitor scheme.[1] Also important are the extent to which those interviewed by the police are able to consult a legal adviser beforehand and whether the police seek to delay or deny access to advice.

Several studies have included some consideration of the PACE legal advice provisions. One group of studies followed closely upon the implementation of PACE. They include research by Sanders *et al* (1989) on the duty solicitor scheme, by Brown (1989) on police detention, by Bottomley *et al* (1989) on the impact of rules on police conduct and by Morgan *et al* (1991) on custody officers. A second, more recent, group of studies has been under-taken to assist the RCCJ. Brown *et al* (1992) focused on the revised PACE Codes of Practice, while McConville and Hodgson (1993) examined legal advice and its relationship with the right to silence. The latter research formed part of a wider study of the work of defence lawyers at all stages of the criminal process, in which the practices of 48 firms of solicitors and three independent agencies were observed (McConville *et al*, 1994).

Informing the suspect about legal advice

Custody officers are required to provide persons entering police detention with information about their right to legal advice, both orally and in writing.

---

1   The Legal Aid Act 1988 deals with the arrangements for the provision of duty solicitor schemes. These are adminis-tered by the Legal Aid Board. Formerly, the arrangements were covered by s.59 of PACE.

From 1986 and up to 1 April 1991, the oral information to be given was essentially that the suspect had the right to consult a solicitor and that this right need not be exercised immediately. Written information, in a notice of rights, expanded on this slightly, drawing attention to the privacy of any such consultation and that it might be in person or on the telephone. A notice produced by the Law Society was also available, explaining the duty solicitor scheme and that advice was free; however, the requirement to provide this notice was contained only in a guidance note to the original Code C (3E).

The information to be given has been augmented in revised PACE Code C. In their oral presentation of rights custody officers must mention that any consultation is free and in private, with an independent solicitor and that the right to legal advice is a continuing right that may be exercised at any stage (C 3.1). The information must be given clearly (C 3.1) and no attempt made to dissuade the suspect (C 6.4). The written notice of rights now includes information formerly contained on the Law Society leaflet. A new poster is also to be prominently displayed drawing attention to the right to legal advice.

Compliance with PACE requirements

The best information about the extent to which custody officers comply with these requirements comes from studies by Sanders *et al* (1989) and Brown *et al* (1992). These studies have combined observation in custody offices and the analysis of custody records. Both examined the situation under the original Code C; the latter also examined the impact of the revised Code.

These studies point to a generally high level of compliance by custody officers with the requirements to provide information about legal advice. Sanders found that 88 per cent of those detained were given some form of spoken information about their right to legal advice. Brown provides a figure of 94 per cent; this rose marginally to 96 per cent after the revised Code was introduced. The written notice of rights was seen to be given out in 88 per cent of cases in Sanders' study; Brown found a similar figure of 89 per cent, rising to 95 per cent in the second phase of the study.

Custody officers are required to ask those detained to sign the custody record to acknowledge whether or not they want legal advice. Both studies found that the frequency with which the custody record was signed over-represented the number of cases in which detainees were actually informed of this right. Sanders found that more than five per cent of suspects signed in cases in which no notice about the right to legal advice was actually given.

Brown found a slightly smaller figure. People's willingness to sign forms that are put before them without enquiring into what they are signing for may account for these discrepancies.

There are several reasons why a minority of suspects are given no information about their rights. One is that around 12 per cent of those detained are categorised as 'non-PACE' prisoners by the police and there is some debate about whether they need to be given their rights. They include those detained on warrant or at a police station as a place of safety, and those detained for common law breach of the peace. Brown found that around a quarter of such prisoners were not told about their right to legal advice. However, the revised Code appears to have increased police scrupulousness in dealing with these detainees and in the second phase of this research there was an increase in the proportion told of their right to legal advice.

The studies by Brown *et al* (1992) and Sanders *et al* (1989), as well as a study by Mackay (1988), set in Bedfordshire, suggest that appreciable proportions of drunks are, for obvious reasons, not told of their right to legal advice on arrival, but nor are they told before release when they have sobered up. Code C permits information not to be given where someone is incapable at the time of understanding it (C 1.8), but does not excuse its complete omission. Brown also found that a higher proportion of juveniles than adults were not given information about their right to legal advice, although more were given information after the revised Codes came in. Failures to provide information could occur where rights were not given on the juvenile's arrival (although this is required by Code C, 3.11). Once an appropriate adult arrived, the giving of rights was sometimes overlooked where there had already been a long delay or where officers were anxious to proceed with an interview.

Information provided

Brown *et al* (1992) compared the information given to suspects about legal advice before and after the introduction of the revised PACE Codes. In the first stage of the research, the only information generally given (in about two-thirds of cases) was that suspects could exercise this right later if they did not want to do so at once. Hardly any were told legal advice was free. While this information was formerly contained on the Law Society leaflet,[2] the studies by Sanders *et al* (1989), Brown *et al* (1992) and Bottomley *et al* (1989) all agree that this was patchily distributed by custody officers at different stations, with anything from 80 per cent of suspects down to none at all being given a copy.

---

2   The revised notice of rights now contains the information formerly contained in this leaflet.

In stage two of Brown *et al*'s study, after the introduction of the revised Codes, considerably more information was given: nearly three-quarters of suspects were told legal advice was free and that it was a continuing right, and over half were told that advice was from an independent solicitor. However, hardly any were told that advice would be in private. The authors make the important point that few stations possess facilities for suspects to carry out private telephone conversations with solicitors. While there is the option of having a solicitor attend the station for a private consultation, suspects were not generally given to believe that this was a possibility.

Brown *et al* found considerable variation between stations in the information given to suspects about legal advice. Only just over half were told advice was free at one station, compared with over 80 per cent at another. The proportions told advice would come from an independent source ranged from one quarter to 84 per cent. They note that the poster required by the revised Codes (C 6.3) was found displayed at all stations in phase two of their study. However, the police very rarely drew the suspect's attention to it, other than where a foreign language translation was required.

Reminders

Under the revised Codes, suspects must be reminded at reviews of custody and prior to the beginning of interviews that they have the right to legal advice. Previously this was only best practice and not mandatory. There is a requirement that reminders at reviews should be recorded in the custody record, and that those given at interviews should appear in the interview record. Brown *et al* (1992) found that, in a sample of over 5,000 custody records examined after the new Codes were introduced, reminders of the right to legal advice were noted for only 16 per cent of reviews. Observation of reviews indicated that reminders were in fact given in over two-thirds of cases. The deficiency it would appear is mainly a recording one, with inspectors failing to make the appropriate entry in the custody record. The same study indicated that interviewing officers complied with the new requirement to remind those about to be interviewed of their right to legal advice.

Awareness among suspects

The right to legal advice can only be effective if suspects are aware of it and what it amounts to. The study by Brown *et al* (1992) of the revised PACE Codes of Practice provided the opportunity to interview a large sample of suspects (nearly 550) about their understanding of this and other rights. Both before and after the introduction of the revised Codes very high proportions of suspects recalled being told they had the right to a solicitor.

A significant minority in stage two (20 per cent) had also noticed the new poster advertising free legal advice. However, the study notes that a very high proportion of suspects (85 per cent in stage two) knew before they arrived at the police station that they had a right to a solicitor. The potential of the revised Code may therefore be more for enhancing awareness of the substance of the right than its bare existence.

This indeed appears to have occurred. There was a threefold increase in the proportion of suspects who were aware that legal advice was free, with over half being aware of this in stage two. The fact that the right was a continuing right that could be exercised at any time was remembered slightly less often. Some facts about legal advice do not appear to have registered: not many recalled being told that it would come from an independent source although over half were actually told this. And very few were aware of being informed that consultation would be in private. Few in fact were told this orally, although it is given in written information. Among those who went on to request advice, the proportion who said they were given information about the duty solicitor scheme doubled to two-thirds.

The demand for legal advice

Take-up rate

Pre-PACE data suggest that relatively few suspects requested legal advice. There is a need for caution in interpreting the figures, however, because most studies have covered relatively few stations or have been confined to particular sub-groups of suspects. The figures given vary widely, from three per cent up to 20 per cent. One of the more broadly based studies, by Morgan et al (1991), drawing on custody record data from nine stations in three forces (including the MPS) provides a request rate of 11 per cent. In Cleveland Constabulary, Young (1987) found a request rate of seven per cent in 1985, but in another force in the north of England Bottomley et al (1989) found a rate as high as 16 per cent in 1984. Softley et al (1980), in a study based at four police stations, found that 10 per cent of suspects requested a solicitor, although, where detainees were specifically asked if they wanted one, the figure rose to 20 per cent. Brown (1991), in a study confined to those detained for burglary, found an average request rate of six per cent although that at individual stations ranged from three per cent to 14 per cent.[3]

Initially, doubts were raised as to whether PACE would lead to any increase in the take-up of legal advice. Zander (1986) cited experience in the United

---

3   Markedly higher figures have been given by Zander (1972) for going to the Court of Appeal and by Baldwin and McConville (1979) for cases resulting in a contested trial at Crown Court.

States to the effect that suspects often could not be brought to understand the utility of legal advice. Informing suspects both in writing and orally of their right to advice and even telling them that it is free might not, he thought, lead to major rises in demand for legal services. In fact, there has been a significant increase in requests for legal advice among suspects since PACE was introduced. The most reliable indications of this come from studies by Brown (1989), Sanders *et al* (1989), Morgan *et al* (1991) and Brown *et al* (1992). All have sampled a wide range of stations in different forces and have found an average request rate for legal advice of around 24 or 25 per cent in the first few years after PACE was introduced.[4] The level of take-up varies according to the seriousness of the crime, with those detained for the most serious offences being the most likely to ask for a legal adviser. Brown (1989) found that 42 per cent of those detained for crimes such as robbery and serious sexual offences requested advice, compared with just 11 per cent of those held for minor public order and motoring offences.

Those studies which have been able to make direct comparisons between pre-PACE and post-PACE data collected at the same sites confirm a sharp increase in take-up. Thus, Morgan *et al* (1991) found a rise from 11 per cent to 24 per cent, while Young (1987), in his Cleveland study, found a more than threefold increase to 22 per cent. Bottomley *et al* (1989) found that requests increased by roughly half to 23 per cent in their research force. More dramatic was a sixfold increase found by Brown (1991) in burglary cases: in 1987 he found that 36 per cent of all burglary suspects sought legal advice.

A study by Brown *et al* (1992) of the impact of the revised PACE Codes of Practice indicates that there has been a further recent rise in requests to consult a legal adviser. Comparing the situation at a sample of twelve stations in 1990 and in 1991, when the revised Codes came into effect, they found that a third as many suspects again requested solicitors, with a request rate in 1991 of 32 per cent. This increase was statistically significant. They attribute it largely to the extra emphasis on explaining the suspect's rights demanded by the revised Code. Many more suspects than before, for example, became aware that legal advice was free. The report's authors also point out that whether or not to ask for legal advice is a finely balanced decision for many suspects, particularly those detained for offences of intermediate seriousness (a point also made by Maguire, 1988). The extra emphasis now given to the details of the right to legal advice may have swayed suspects increasingly towards requesting a solicitor. It is also suggested that there may have been some increase in suspects' awareness of their rights, independently of the information provided by the police. Evidence for this comes from the fact that, among those interviewed by the researchers, there

---

4   Brown *et al* (1992) found that the request rate increased after the introduction of the revised Codes of Practice in 1991; this is discussed further below.

was a slight growth in the proportion who were aware before they arrived at the police station that they had the right to consult a solicitor there.

Even more recent data, from a study set at ten police stations, suggests that there has been a yet further increase in demand for legal advice. Based on the observation of the processing of over 4,000 prisoners, it was found that no less than 38 per cent of suspects requested a lawyer (Phillips and Brown, forthcoming). This study was carried out during late 1993 and early 1994.

Variation in demand

An issue that has exercised several commentators is the great variation between stations in levels of demand for legal advice. A study by Brown (1989), based on data collected from 32 police stations in 1987, found request rates ranging from 14 per cent to 41 per cent among detainees generally, while a study of the duty solicitor scheme, conducted at 10 stations in 1988 by Sanders *et al* (1989), found a range from 17 per cent to 34 per cent. Morgan *et al* (1991), looking at six stations, discovered an even broader ranger, from 11 per cent to 37 per cent. In their recent study set at ten stations, Phillips and Brown (forthcoming) found request rates ranging from 22 per cent to 50 per cent.

Brown (1989) found that several factors were associated with these variations. The most important was the level of seriousness of offences; even so, differences between stations in this respect only accounted for one-tenth of the variation in demand. Other factors explained lesser amounts of variation: for example, whether some requests for court duty solicitors were included in the figures of requests for police station duty solicitors. This could occur where police station and court were adjacent and the suspect requested a solicitor for court. The proportion of juveniles held at stations was also relevant: they were significantly less likely than adults to request legal advice, and their representation in the prisoner population ranged from five per cent to 38 per cent. The type of duty solicitor scheme in operation (i.e. panel or rota) and police station workloads were only marginally relevant.

Nearly two-thirds of the variation between stations remains unaccounted for. Several explanations have been advanced for this lacuna. Brown (1989) has suggested that the extent to which legal advice services were already well-developed in an area before PACE was introduced and awareness among suspects of this situation may be an important influence.

One factor which has not been considered to any great extent is the influence of race. However, Phillips and Brown's (forthcoming) recent study was able to take this into account and found there to be important differences between the take-up of legal advice by white suspects and members of ethnic minority groups. While white suspects sought advice in 35 per cent of cases, as many as 50 per cent of Afro-Caribbeans and 47 per cent of Asians did so. The authors suggest that differences in the seriousness of the offences for which members of each ethnic group are arrested are partly responsible for these variations. In particular, white suspects are far more likely to be detained for public order offences, for which the request rate for legal advice is typically low, while Afro-Caribbeans are more likely to be arrested for offences of violence against the person and robbery, where legal advice is seen to be essential in many cases. Similarly, Asian suspects are more likely than whites to be arrested for fraud and forgery offences, again a group of offences generating above average demand for legal services. Phillips and Brown (ibid.) also suggest that distrust of the police, especially among Afro-Caribbeans, may also have a strong bearing on the propensity to request legal advice. Given these variations between ethnic groups in demand for legal advice, the ethnic composition of the arrest population at particular stations will clearly have some influence on the overall take-up rate for legal advice.

Morgan et al (1991) suggest that some of the variance is probably a function of less tangible factors which are hard to discern either from observation or records: for example, cultural differences between areas; suspects' attitudes to the potential usefulness of legal advice, resulting from folklore and experience; and general conceptions of the police. One important factor may be the way in which the right to legal advice is conveyed to the suspect. This is discussed further below.

The influence of the police

Several commentators have suggested that the police may exert considerable influence on the suspect's decision about whether to ask for legal advice (Maguire, 1988; Sanders et al, 1989). Studies have drawn attention to active discouragement by them of requests for legal advice (Morgan et al, 1991; Sanders et al, 1989). Equally, others have noted that custody officers may encourage suspects to have a solicitor in some circumstances (Bottomley et al, 1989). Attempts at dissuasion are now forbidden by the revised Code (C 6.4).

Views differ as to the degree of intent behind practices which tend to discourage suspects from taking legal advice. Perhaps the most extreme viewpoint is adopted by McConville et al (1991), who argue that custody officers share police cultural values to such an extent that they will connive with investigating officers to break the rules. Sharing the concern of investigating officers to place the suspect in an environment hostile to the suspect and favourable to the police, they will attempt to discourage suspects from requesting solicitors or secure the cancellation of requests so that the suspect may be interviewed in the absence of a solicitor. It has been argued elsewhere in this review that it is doubtful whether this view of custody officers can be sustained (see Chapters 4 and 5). In particular, it should be noted that the McConville study included no observation of custody office practice and relied principally on a reinterpretation of the findings of Sanders *et al*'s (1989) study for its conclusions in this respect. The authors of the latter study themselves appear to adopt a less extreme view, and express reservations about the extent to which the police have a coherent strategy to prevent suspects requesting solicitors, although they suggest that discouragement may be read into the way rights are presented.

More moderate opinions are expressed by Morgan *et al* (1991), Brown *et al* (1992), Bottomley *et al* (1989) and Dixon (1992). The first of these studies, based on extensive observation of custody officers' work, argues that it is a matter for subjective interpretation by the observer whether custody officers' intent is to discourage the suspect from obtaining advice (Morgan *et al*, 1991). Brown *et al* (1992), while not disputing that there are cases in which there is the intent to discourage requests for legal advice, argue that in many cases no such intent can be inferred. Dixon (1992) suggests that over-speedy and unclear renditions of rights may signify only that custody officers are all too familiar with what they are saying and fail to appreciate that those suspects to whom the information is new cannot take it in. Similarly, Bottomley *et al* (1989) note that advice that suspects can change their minds in favour of having a solicitor later could be sincerely offered, but could discourage take-up of the right until it is too late to be of any use.

Dixon (1992) argues that custody officers may often act according to what they think is in the suspect's best interests. There are clearly dangers in their doing so, but this does not mean that they are necessarily badly motivated or wrong. For example, information given about the time that it will take to obtain a solicitor may almost certainly be true. In trivial cases, warning suspects that a legal adviser is unlikely to be of much service may also generally be accurate. Bottomley *et al* (1989) also note that a common police view, which may be conveyed to the suspect, is that legal advice is of little value where the suspect is to be cautioned or intends to plead guilty. Both Dixon (1992) and Brown *et al* (1992) note too that there may be many reasons other than police influence why suspects do not request solicitors or cancel requests. They may not want to delay their stay, feel that the matter is trivial or that they can cope unaided, or may dislike lawyers.

Several studies, including those by Sanders *et al* (1989), Morgan *et al* (1991) and Brown *et al* (1992), have attempted to quantify and categorise the ways in which the police may influence the suspect's decision on legal advice. Sanders *et al* (1989), who refer to these as 'ploys', found that one or more was used in over 40 per cent of the 850 cases in their study. The most common, used in around 17 per cent of all cases, was the provision of rights too quickly, incomprehensibly or incompletely. Relatively frequently too, custody officers stressed that suspects were only going to be at the police station a short time or could change their minds later.

Brown *et al* (1992) reject the term 'ploy' in their analysis, which refers simply to 'influences on decisions regarding legal advice'. They too found that in a large minority of cases (28% in stage one of their study prior to the introduction of the revised Codes of Practice and 35% in stage two afterwards) suspects may have been influenced in a variety of ways against asking for legal advice. Lack of clarity or incompleteness in the explanation of rights was again the most significant and became more so after the Codes were introduced. The authors explain this change by reference to the new duty on custody officers to convey more information; custody officers did not always match up to these demands and omitted key items (see above).

Morgan *et al* (1991) also recorded details of cases in which they identified some form of discouragement against seeking legal advice. This they found to occur in 14 per cent of cases, far lower than the two studies so far discussed. However, they may have adopted a more stringent categorisation of what amounted to discouragement, principally including *active* discouragement, leading questions and incomplete statements of rights. They emphasise that in the great majority of cases, rights were stated in a manner adequate for comprehension by the reasonable person. But they also point out that many suspects are not in such a state of mind at the time they arrive at the police station; despite this, no attempt is usually made to ensure that suspects have understood their rights. They suggest that the way the right to legal advice is presented may vary according to the method of deploying custody officers. Those in post for long periods may provide more adequate information than those pressed into service for short periods. In contrast, Brown *et al* (1992) found that custody officers experience of the job was not necessarily linked with the provision of satisfactory explanations of rights.

Both Sanders *et al* (1989) and Brown *et al* (1992) have attempted to correlate the practices described above with the actual take-up of legal advice. They found that take-up was lower than average where two or more of what Sanders terms 'ploys' were used, although relatively few cases fell into this category. Where only one 'ploy' was used, the studies' findings differ. Sanders found a weak correlation between requests for legal advice and the use of 'ploys' (i.e. where one or more 'ploys' were used, the suspect was slightly less likely to request a solicitor). Brown, on the other hand, found that where one 'ploy' was used, requests for legal advice were *higher* than average.

Brown *et al* (1992) suggest, however, that attempting to correlate 'ploys' with take-up may produce highly misleading results because of the difficulty of disentangling cause and effect. They point out that the *non-use* of 'ploys' may be linked with both high and low take-up of legal advice. Thus, in some cases, the lack of any dissuasion may lead the suspect to request a solicitor. In others, no 'ploys' may be used because it is clear to the custody officer that the suspect does not intend to ask for a solicitor. Equally, they argue that the *use* of 'ploys' may also be linked with both high and low take-up. Thus, rights will sometimes be given very cursorily to experienced offenders because custody officers are aware that they are probably familiar with their rights. This would be recorded as a 'ploy' (unclear or incomplete statement of rights). But experienced offenders are also more likely to ask for a solicitor, and a spurious correlation between use of 'ploys' and high take-up of legal advice results. This obscures the effect of 'ploys' in cases in which the suspect is inexperienced and where the way rights are given may well lead to a failure to request a solicitor. Support for this argument is provided by Sanders *et al* (1989), who found that 'ploys' did have a more influential effect on those with no criminal record.

The conclusion that may be drawn from the above discussion is that there are some grounds for arguing that the police are able to influence suspects' decisions about legal advice by means of various cues, although the link is not necessarily as strong as might be assumed. For several reasons, it certainly seems doubtful whether there is sufficient scope for the use of 'ploys' to account for significant amounts of variance between stations in demand for legal advice. First, 'ploys' are found only in a minority of cases (albeit a substantial minority); secondly, suspects with no criminal record, for whom 'ploys' are most likely to be influential, form only around 30 per cent of the prisoner population; and, thirdly, the use of two or more 'ploys', which is most likely to influence the suspect, occurs in only a small minority of cases (around 10% in Sander's study, 5% in Brown's).

The provision of legal advice

The attrition rate

For a range of reasons, not every request for legal advice leads to its provision, although it is clear that the problem is now less significant than it used to be. Estimates of the proportion of pre-PACE requests for legal advice which failed to lead to any advice being given vary from around one-third (Softley *et al,* 1980; Brown, 1991) to half (Baldwin and McConville, 1979; Bottomley *et al*, 1989). Taken together, the low pre-PACE request rate for legal advice and the attrition of such requests meant that few of those interviewed by the police had received legal advice beforehand. Softley *et al* (1980) and Brown (1991) give a figure of just one per cent, although research on field trials of taped interviews gives a slightly higher estimate of three per cent (Willis *et al*, 1988).

PACE Code C now places considerable emphasis on suspects being able to receive legal advice before being interviewed and having a solicitor present at the police interview if desired (see Code C, 6.6 and 6.8). Only in certain urgent situations may an interview start if legal advice has been requested but not received. And, only exceptionally may a solicitor or representative be excluded from an interview. Advising a client not to answer questions is not sufficient grounds for exclusion (Code C, 6D).

Most requests for legal advice are now successfully met, in the sense that the suspect has some form of consultation with a legal adviser. The precise figures provided by studies vary due to differences in the range of stations sampled and in the basis for calculations. The estimates available include ones of 77 per cent (Sanders et al, 1989), 79 per cent (Brown et al, 1992), 86 per cent (Brown, 1991), 87 per cent (Phillips and Brown, forthcoming) and 95 per cent (Bottomley et al, 1989). The study by Brown et al (1992) suggests that the proportion of successful contacts with legal advisers has risen by about a tenth since the introduction of the revised Codes of Practice.

The combined effect of a higher request rate for legal advice and a higher proportion of successful contacts with legal advisers is that far more suspects than in pre-PACE days are receiving legal advice before being interviewed by the police. Compared with the pre-PACE estimates given above of one to three per cent, Brown (1989) found that around a quarter of suspects were legally advised before going into their first police interview. The proportion may have risen further, following a surge in demand for legal advice after the revised Codes of Practice were introduced. The study by Brown et al (1992) found that 29 per cent of suspects questioned by the police now receive pre-interview advice, compared with 21 per cent before the Codes were changed.

There are various reasons why not all requests for advice are met. A small number are not recorded by the police. Sanders et al (1989) found that six per cent of requests which they observed did not appear on the custody record. Ambiguous requests tended to be treated as non-requests; requests by those drunk on arrival were sometimes disregarded.

Sanders et al (ibid.) also found that 10 per cent of recorded requests, not subsequently cancelled by the suspect, were not taken forward by the police. Some of these cases involved juveniles who had requested legal advice on arrival but action on their request was delayed until a parent arrived. Brown et al (1992) also found evidence of a similar practice. In a few cases, Sanders suggests that the action of the police was apparently only explicable on the basis that they did not want the suspect to have legal advice.

Where requests are taken forward by the police, it does not necessarily follow that a solicitor will be contacted. Figures on non-contact vary. Brown (1989 and 1991) puts the proportion at around 10 per cent. This is a low failure rate compared with a figure of 26 per cent found by Sanders *et al* (1989) and 20 per cent in a more recent study by Brown *et al* (1992). However, the figures are based on different samples of stations. Some variation is also due to differences in the way the calculation is made: Brown (1989), for example, includes in the base figure cases in which suspects arrive with a solicitor, while Sanders *et al* (1989) do not.

Brown (1989) found that in nearly two-thirds of non-contact cases, suspects had cancelled their requests for legal advice. Around half of cancellations were prompted by the inability of the police to contact the solicitor of the suspect's choice. Sanders *et al* (1989) suggest that some cancellations are the product of police dissuasion, although providing no figures to support this contention. Where the suspect does not cancel a request, non-contact generally stems from the lack of a solicitor's availability (Brown, 1989; Sanders *et al*, 1989). Sanders et al (ibid.) found that the duty solicitor scheme was not significantly better at delivering advice than own solicitors. There was a failure to secure advice in 20 per cent of cases where duty solicitors were requested compared to 24 per cent where own solicitors were requested.

Recent research on the revised PACE Codes of Practice has found a decrease in failures to secure legal advice. Only around 13 per cent of requests taken forward by the police in this study failed to bear fruit, compared with 20 per cent before the revised Codes were introduced (Brown *et al*, 1992). The authors of the report suggest that a by-product of revised Code C's emphasis on the right to legal advice may be that custody officers are going to greater lengths to secure legal advice when it is requested.

McConville *et al* (1991) have drawn upon Sanders' figures for failures to record requests or take them forward as bolstering an argument, elaborated earlier in this review, that custody officers are in sympathy with investigating officers' aspirations to deny suspects access to solicitors. They argue, although without any supporting evidence, that requests not recorded are "presumably those in which the police most want to prevent the attendance of solicitors". The conclusions of this study about custody officers have been criticised earlier. While there may be an element of intent behind some of the practices Sanders identifies, the intentions may not be those hypothesised by McConville. There is evidence that cases in which requests for legal advice are 'lost' are often trivial ones in which custody officers feel that a solicitor would not benefit the suspect. In other cases, custody officers may feel that the suspect's youth or drunkenness makes them unable to make a valid decision about legal advice. Sanders *et al* (1989) and Brown *et al* (1992) both point to these as factors in cases where requests fall by the wayside. Dixon (1992) has argued that custody officers' decisions may be honestly made (although this does not necessarily justify them).

There are other possible explanations for the 'losing' of requests for legal advice which McConville and Sanders do not consider, including pressure of work on custody officers and lack of communication between officers at the changing of shifts. There may have been cancellations by the suspect which the researchers did not witness (although, in theory, these should have been recorded). Furthermore, it is by no means certain that Sanders' findings still hold good. The more recent research by Brown et al (1992) found little evidence either of under-recording of requests for solicitors or failures to take forward recorded requests (other than in some juvenile cases – see above). On balance, the evidence scarcely seems to support McConville's argument, the implication of which is that suspects are systematically denied legal advice in non-trivial cases in which the aim is to achieve interviews without the presence of a solicitor.

There is a further degree of attrition of requests for advice after a legal adviser has been contacted and has agreed to provide advice. This occurs in, at most, 10 per cent of cases (Brown, 1989 and 1991; Brown et al, 1992). In some less serious cases, legal advisers ask simply to be kept in touch with developments while, in others, the suspect is released before any consultation can occur. There are also some cases in which suspects cancel requests for legal advice after contact has been made, usually because they are unwilling to delay being interviewed until an adviser can reach the station. Provisions in the revised Codes of Practice are designed to ensure that this is a genuine change of heart and not the result of police pressure. Specifically, an officer of inspector rank or above must authorise the interview to proceed and the suspect must give his or her agreement in writing or on the interview tape (C, 6.6d). If the legal adviser requested is not available, the suspect must have been given the option of requesting the duty solicitor (C, 6.6c). Furthermore, if the suspect's legal adviser is already at the station, on the way to it or easily contactable by telephone, he or she cannot be treated as unavailable, and an interview cannot normally proceed without their presence (C, 6.8).

Mode of advice

Sanders et al (1989) note that when the duty solicitor scheme was first being formulated, the presumption was that solicitors would attend the police station to advise. There is a certain amount of guidance to solicitors on this question. The Law Society guidelines state that "[y]ou should attend personally ... when you consider that such an attendance is necessary for the protection of the suspect's interests. Each case depends on its own facts;

use your own judgement" (Law Society, 1991). More specific guidance is given in the current Duty Solicitor Arrangements (these are not binding on non-duty solicitors). These provide that solicitors shall attend in person in the following circumstances: the suspect requests their attendance; the offence is arrestable and the suspect is to be interviewed; an identification parade is to be held; or the suspect complains of serious maltreatment (Legal Aid Board, 1992). If the detainee is a juvenile or a person at risk, there should also be a presumption in favour of attendance. Guidance for solicitors generally, which reiterates and adds to these criteria is given by Cape (1993), in a manual for solicitors advising suspects at police stations. He notes that lack of confidentiality of advice given over the telephone should be further grounds for attending in person.

Sanders *et al* (1989) have suggested that suspects find telephone advice of less utility than personal attendance by a solicitor. Brown *et al* (1992) point to instances in which suspects did not proceed with requests for solicitors when they realised that advice would be over the telephone. They also note that telephone advice is rarely received in private, since police stations do not have suitable facilities or staff available to supervise calls. Conversations generally take place in the custody area in full hearing of those present, including investigating officers.

Nevertheless, the evidence suggests that a considerable minority of suspects are advised solely over the telephone. Estimates vary from 20 per cent (Phillips and Brown, forthcoming) up to 36 per cent (Brown *et al*, 1992), although the latter figure appears to be significantly higher than those quoted by other studies.[5] It is noteworthy that the 20 per cent figure is based on the most recent data and may suggest that advisers are increasingly attending in person.

There is agreement that the extent to which solicitors attend police stations to advise in person varies considerably around the country. Sanders *et al* (1989) found attendance rates ranging from 48 per cent to 96 per cent among the ten stations in their study; in Brown's (1989) study of 32 stations, the range was from 27 per cent to 96 per cent. Brown *et al* (1992), comparing the position prior to and after the introduction of the revised Codes of Practice found attendance rates ranging from 19 per cent to 94 per cent. Most recently, Phillips and Brown (forthcoming) found attendance ranging from 55 per cent to 92 per cent.

Sanders *et al* (1989), along with Brown *et al* (1992), believe that specific local and regional factors in the way the coverage of criminal legal advice work is arranged are most important in explaining the variations. Sanders *et al* (1989) also attribute a certain amount of the variation to different patterns of requests for duty and own solicitors. The former are generally less likely

---

5   Brown (1989), Sanders *et al* (1989) and Brown (1991) all found that between 22 per cent and 27 per cent of suspects were advised solely by telephone.

to attend the station, possibly because they are likely to receive more calls and ration their attendance to cases where they feel it is most required. Some of the variance depends on the mix of offences found at stations: solicitors will be more likely to attend for more serious crimes. The times at which requests are made is also relevant (although this does not vary greatly between stations): out of office hours requests are more likely to be directed to the duty solicitor.

Legal advice and police interviews

In line with the increase in demand for legal advice, many more suspects now have an adviser present during police interviews.[6] Some baseline figures are provided by Brown's (1989) study of 32 police stations. He found that legal advisers attended around 12 per cent of all police interviews. However, there are considerable regional differences. The same study found attendance rates at individual stations ranged from five per cent to 20 per cent. In a further study of burglary investigation, attendance at interviews at the three participating stations ranged from just three per cent up to 37 per cent (Brown, 1991).

Another – and probably more useful – way of looking at this issue is to consider the rate at which legal advisers attend interviews in legal advice cases only, since the overall attendance rate will vary according to the frequency with which suspects request legal advice. Sanders *et al* (1989) found that a legal adviser attended at least one interview in two-thirds of cases in which advice was provided. If telephone advice cases are excluded, legal advisers attended police interviews in 81 per cent of cases in which they consulted with their clients at the police station. More recent research by Brown *et al* (1992), looking at the impact of the revised Codes of Practice, provides somewhat lower figures, as well as pointing to a further decrease during the course of this two stage study. In the first half, carried out before the new Codes were introduced, advisers attended nearly 60 per cent of interviews in cases where they gave advice; in the second stage, this had fallen to 42 per cent. This may be because the rise in demand for legal advice has placed increased pressure on legal personnel, who may therefore be reluctant or unable to prolong attendance at the station by remaining for police interviews.

Sanders *et al* (1989) found that one important factor governing attendance at interviews was whether advice was given by own or duty solicitors, with the latter being far less likely to attend. The same study suggests that another reason why legal advisers did not attend interviews was because they felt

---

6   A study of the interviewing of juveniles by Evans (1993) found a slightly lower figure of 10 per cent for this group.

their attendance unnecessary where the suspect was going to admit the offence. In some cases the decision not to have a legal adviser present was made by suspects themselves in order to avoid delay. But in many cases, the study was unable to say for sure why many interviews were not attended. The authors do note, however, that they were witness to a number of successful attempts to manipulate suspects into proceeding without a solicitor where this would have involved undue delay.

There is considerable regional variation in the attendance of advisers at interviews. Looking first at all legal advice cases (i.e. whether advisers attended in person or gave telephone advice only), attendance rates ranging from 23 per cent up to 92 per cent and from 11 per cent to 90 per cent were found by Sanders *et al* (1989) and Brown *et al* (1992) respectively. As might be expected, this was partly a function of the proportion of advice given by telephone: thus, a high proportion of advice given in this form was linked to low attendance at interviews. But this rule is not invariable. Brown *et al* (ibid.), looking only at those cases where legal advisers consulted with clients at the police station, found that the attendance rate at interviews still ranged from 28 per cent to 86 per cent.

Attendance at interviews varies between offences as well as between stations. Notwithstanding the view expressed in a leading manual for those advising at police stations that "[t]here are relatively few occasions when a lawyer would be justified in not attending" (Cape, 1993), it appears that legal advisers are less likely to attend interviews relating to relatively minor offences. Brown (1989) found that advisers attended just eight per cent of interviews for shoplifting offences compared with 30 per cent of robbery interviews.

Use of non-qualified advisers

The present Duty Solicitor Arrangements provide that a clerk may only be sent to the police station if the duty solicitor has initially advised the suspect on the telephone, the clerk has been approved by the local duty solicitor committee, the police are prepared to allow the clerk the same rights of access as a solicitor, and the suspect is informed of the representative's status (Legal Aid Board, 1992). However, these criteria do not apply where suspects have nominated a particular firm as their 'own' solicitor. Some firms have established schemes whereby advice is given by employees who are not qualified solicitors or by outside agencies to whom some or all of such work has been contracted out (McConville and Hodgson, 1993; McConville *et al*, 1994).

Estimates of the extent to which advice is given by solicitors' representatives vary greatly. The highest figure is given by McConville *et al* (1994), who found that three-quarters of those giving advice at police stations were representatives[7] and only a quarter were admitted solicitors. Rather lower figures are provided by Sanders et al (1989), who found that around 30 per cent of those attending the police station to give advice were representatives, and, recently, by Phillips and Brown (forthcoming), who give a figure of 26 per cent. An even lower estimate is given in Brown et al's (1992) study of the revised PACE Codes of Practice, with 14 per cent of advice apparently being given by representatives.

It is likely that the wide differences between these figures may arise partly from changing trends in the way in which criminal legal advice is delivered and the movement towards using unqualified staff to attend police stations (McConville et al, 1994). However, they may also in part be an artefact of methodological and sampling differences. Sanders et al (1989), Brown et al (1992) and Phillips and Brown (forthcoming) all used the same method of obtaining their data: positioning observers at selected police stations for a sustained period of time. What they observed was the giving of legal advice across the board, whether by duty or own solicitors. The length of the study period in both studies was adequate to represent typical practice at the samples of stations included. McConville and Hodgson (1993) and McConville et al (1994) adopted a rather different method. Researchers accompanied staff from selected solicitors' practices and legal advice agencies on their visits to a range of police stations, as and when advice was requested from those firms. In total, these two studies examined the work of 39 firms of solicitors[8] and three independent agencies providing advice in London and eight other towns and cities throughout the Midlands, East Anglia and North and North West England.[9] It follows that the researchers are unable to say what proportion of advice given at any specific police station or at police stations generally was provided by solicitors or by representatives; they can only provide such estimates for advice given by the firms they were shadowing. More importantly, their studies were heavily biased towards firms where advice was given by legal advisers acting as 'own' solicitors rather than as duty solicitors. Thus, the incidence of advice by duty solicitors in the study was, at seven per cent, considerably lower than the actual incidence of duty solicitor advice, which has been put at anything from 25 per cent (Sanders et al, 1989) to 39 per cent (Phillips and Brown, forthcoming) or 40 per cent (Brown et al, 1992). Solicitors acting as 'own' solicitors have considerably more freedom than duty solicitors to use representatives to provide advice: both Sanders et al (1989) and Phillips and

---

7   Representatives were taken to include: articled clerks; staff and non-staff clerks; former police officers employed as legal advisers; and employees of outside agencies supplying legal advice services on contract to firms of solicitors.

8   A further nine firms were included but provided no police station advice during the course of the observation period.

9   McConville and Hodgson's (1993) RCCJ study reported on the work of 17 firms of solicitors and three independent agents. Confusingly, in a report written *after* the submission of their Royal Commission study (McConville et al 1994), they report the results of an earlier study, which covered the work of a further 22 firms. In the latter report, data from both phases of the research are generally aggregated. This report is therefore the one cited most frequently in this review.

Brown (forthcoming) suggest that only 10 per cent of advice provided by duty solicitors is given by representatives. It is highly likely, therefore, that the McConville study's under-sampling of duty solicitor cases has led to considerable overstatement of the amount of advice that is actually given by representatives at police stations. The study by Brown *et al* (1992), on the other hand, probably understates the position because the researchers did not have access to reliable information about the status of legal advisers. The source of information was frequently custody officers. It is more likely that unqualified advisers tended to be miscoded as solicitors than the other way round.

Even taking into account the oversampling of 'own' solicitor cases in McConville's work, the proportion of advice given by representatives appears unduly high. In contrast, Sanders *et al* (1989) and Phillips and Brown (forthcoming) found that own solicitors used representatives in just 50 per cent and 35 per cent of cases respectively. It is likely that, by sampling a number of specific firms, some of which were large practices employing non-legally qualified personnel solely to give advice at police stations, McConville obtained a rather different picture of the pattern of advice than would have been the case if they had taken a cross-section of the advice given at particular police stations.

Sanders *et al* (1989) draw attention to variation between areas in the extent to which representatives are used. In their study they advised in anything from 20 per cent to more than 80 per cent of cases in different areas of the country.

Both Sanders *et al* (1989) and McConville *et al* (1994) found that the key factor determining whether a solicitor or a representative advised was availability and, other than in a few firms, there was generally little attempt to match the status of the adviser to the gravity of the case. McConville and Hodgson (1993) argue that many solicitors' firms are more concerned with the expansion of their client base, by ensuring that someone, whether legally qualified or not, attends to advise at police stations, than with the quality of the advice given. There are economic advantages, too, to delegating such work, allowing solicitors to concentrate on more highly paid (and higher status) work, particularly advocacy.

McConville and Hodgson (ibid.) point to a number of difficulties arising from the use of non-qualified staff. They may lack legal expertise and confidence, both of which may be exploited by the police; or they may over-identify with the police, either because the viability of their job depends upon police co-operation or because they are themselves former police officers.[10] Problems may also arise where, as is typically the case, unqualified advisers do not reveal their status to their clients. Their influence with clients and the police may be undermined where the police later draw attention to this.

---

10   Over 20 per cent of advice in McConville and Hodgson's study was given by former police officers.

In theory, PACE Code C should act as a constraint on the use of unqualified staff. It provides for an officer of inspector rank or above to take certain steps where he or she considers that "a particular firm of solicitors is persistently sending as clerks or legal executives persons who are unsuited to provide legal advice ..." (Code C, Note for Guidance 6F). However, McConville and Hodgson (1993) argue that, perhaps not surprisingly, the police are happy with a situation in which solicitors send less than capable staff to advise and do not take any preventive action.

The time factor

Solicitors are normally contacted quite promptly and are obtained within half an hour in between 65 per cent and 80 per cent of cases (Brown, 1989; Sanders *et al*, 1989). The latter research found that own solicitors were slightly faster to respond, because requests for duty solicitors had to be filtered through a paging service. Both studies and the more recent one by Brown *et al* (1992) draw attention to very lengthy delays in a minority of cases. Requests for own solicitors outside office hours can cause particular problems: no home contact number may be available and the suspect may be unwilling to change to the duty solicitor. Some long delays occur with the suspect's consent, typically where an arrest is made at night, no interview is scheduled until next morning and there is little point in waking the suspect's solicitor.

Brown *et al* (1992) draw attention to a marked increase in the average time taken to contact advisers since the introduction of the revised Codes. They attribute this to increased strain placed on both duty and own solicitors by the large rise in requests for legal advice. They also note that an undue proportion of the burden is falling on duty solicitors, who are now requested by around 13 per cent of all suspects compared with nine per cent before the revised Codes were introduced. They found no evidence of any change in police practices which pointed to deliberate delay in securing a solicitor – a practice vetoed in the new version of Code C (C 6.2).

The studies by Sanders *et al* (1989), Brown (1989) and Brown *et al* (1992) tend to agree that the typical delay between a legal adviser being contacted and attending the station is around one hour. A longer delay of over two hours has been reported in Brown's (1991) study of burglary cases; however, this study was based on a much smaller sample of stations than the others and may reflect local difficulties rather than the general situation. All studies report lengthy delays in a minority of cases. In some instances, these occurred by agreement of all parties concerned, often where an arrest had been made during the night and no police interview was to take place until next morning. McConville and Hodgson (1993) also confirm that it is common practice for advisers to be notified to attend the station when investigating officers are ready to interview. However, Brown (1989) also reports that a significant proportion of requests for solicitors made during office hours led to delays of four or more hours before a solicitor could attend. Typically, delays were caused where solicitors were busy in court or attending meetings with clients.

The legal adviser's role

Familiarisation with the case

McConville and Hodgson (1993) point out that legal advisers' ability to provide effective advice to the suspect depends heavily on their prior knowledge of the facts of the case. Absence of this information may be a factor in their advising suspects to remain silent (Cape, 1993). The work by McConville *et al* (1994) and McConville and Hodgson (1993) is the only research to have examined in any detail how advisers acquire such knowledge. They point to some of the difficulties involved. Firstly, only sketchy information tends to be provided in the initial telephone contact from the police requesting their services. Secondly, where the adviser talks in person with a suspect on the telephone, it may be difficult to enter into any details because such conversations are often not private (see above; also Brown *et al*, 1992). Thirdly, only limited information may be available from the custody officer, who may be busy or lack close knowledge of the case; access to custody records is not uncommonly refused.

The best sources of information are investigating officers, although it appears that in nearly half of cases they are not approached by legal advisers. Where advisers do attempt to obtain information, they run up against the difficulty that police officers often have a vested interest in non-disclosure or selective disclosure in order to maintain the upper hand. Consequently, in nearly three-quarters of cases in which advisers sought information from the police prior to interview, McConville *et al* (1994) found that only bare details were provided.

Client consultations

The confidentiality of solicitor/client discussions has generally precluded researchers from carrying out direct observation of legal advisers' consultations with their clients. Sanders *et al* (1989) were largely unsuccessful in securing access to such consultations and depended on information from interviews with the parties involved. However, McConville *et al* (1994) were able to gain access to a large number of solicitor/client consultations and their study provides the most useful information about this important area (although reservations noted above about the representativeness of their sample need to be kept in mind).

The picture they present is one of variable quality in the adviser's dealings with his or her client. Consultations were often hurried, with nearly half taking less than ten minutes. In a minority of cases, advisers appeared to make little real effort to establish a rapport with their client and, in a few instances, requested no private consultation at all before a police interview began. They attribute this peremptory approach to three factors: pressure from the police to proceed with an interview quickly; lack of trust by advisers in their clients' veracity; and the cost inefficiency to solicitors' firms of having staff present at police stations for more than the minimum time. They argue that this cursory approach could be damaging to the client since advisers do not always establish important facts, particularly ones relevant to a possible line of defence. They categorised advisers' knowledge of the suspected offence prior to the police interview as 'superficial' in over 60 per cent of cases, while in 10 per cent they were ignorant of their client's version altogether.

There is a measure of agreement between studies that the bulk of advice given to suspects is either to co-operate with police questions or is relatively neutral in character. Advice to remain silent (considered further below) is less common and both Baldwin (1992a) and Dixon (1991b) note that lawyers do not generally view their role as being to help the guilty evade the consequences of their acts. McConville et al (1994) found that advice to co-operate with police questions was often given where the suspect admitted the offence and there were no grounds for doubting the police's ability to prove the offence. A co-operative attitude by the suspect could be of benefit later. Another important reason for advising co-operation was that this provided a means of establishing details of the police case. Advice to answer questions was also often given where the suspect wished to offer an explanation for his or her actions, to raise a defence or deny any involvement. Sometimes a co-operative stance was advised because advisers held the view that a refusal to answer questions would count against the suspect in court. McConville and Hodgson (1993) note that advisers were sometimes rather cavalier in advising that questions should be answered and did not always check that the police did possess enough evidence to make out their case.

Both McConville et al (1994) and Sanders et al (1989) observe that a common approach by advisers (in a third of cases in the McConville study) was to offer no real guidance, but broadly to go along with the suspect's own wishes. Generally, the tendency in such situations was for the suspect to answer police questions. McConville and Hodgson (1993) note that advisers often did not consider whether this was the best course, either because pre-interview consultations were rushed or, more importantly, because non-qualified staff lacked the competence to enquire into the factual and legal elements of the case.

Advice to remain silent

A contentious issue is that of the extent to which legal advisers counsel suspects to exercise their right of silence.[11] It is well established that suspects who are legally advised are much more likely than others to refuse to answer police questions (see Chapter 7). One study, by Moston *et al* (1990), concludes that: "... the use of silence shows a clear-cut pattern. Solicitors are routinely advising their clients not to speak to the police". One justification for the new provision in the CJPOA, which allow inferences to be drawn in some circumstances from the suspect's silence, was that the strengthened right under PACE for suspects to have a legal adviser present during interviews had increased the difficulties the police had in bringing the guilty to book (Home Office, 1989a).

The evidence from relevant studies is that there is indeed a link between legal advice and the exercise of silence, although it may not be as strong as has sometimes been assumed. On the basis of observing over 200 consultations between legal advisers and clients, McConville *et al* (1994) found that silence was advised in just over a fifth (22 per cent) of cases in which legal advice was given. They found little difference in the frequency with which solicitors and representatives of different kinds advised silence. A rather lower figure of 10 per cent is given by Sanders *et al* (1989). However, their estimate may be less reliable, given that relatively few consultations were witnessed.

Rather than routinely advising silence, legal advisers generally appear to do so for specific reasons. Baldwin (1992b), Dixon (1991b) and McConville and Hodgson (1993) suggest that these include: the lack of *prima facie* evidence or the police's unwillingness to reveal the evidence they have; the client's vulnerability to police questioning, particularly in the relatively uncommon situation where there is overt police hostility; and the suspicion of police malpractice. McConville and Hodgson add three further reasons: to protect the adviser, where he or she is inexperienced in police station work (in particular, it resolves the dilemma where the suspect admits the offence to the adviser but states his or her intention to lie to the police); to accord with the suspect's usual practice; and to emphasise that the police already have enough evidence to charge and should not interview further.

---

11   The Criminal Justice and Public Order Act 1994 now allows inferences to be drawn in certain circumstances from an accused person's failure during police questioning to mention any fact later relied on in his or her defence. However, the Act does not create an obligation on suspects to answer questions.

McConville and Hodgson (ibid.) found that the most significant of these factors was lack of information. They note that the controlled release of information is a central police interviewing strategy and a way of maintaining dominance. In response, a refusal to co-operate, in the hope of getting the police to reveal their hand in more detail, is one of the few resources that suspects and their advisers possess. The next most important reason for advising silence is the risk of unwitting self-incrimination by the suspect. This may be especially great in the case of suggestible or compliant suspects or those who do not appear to understand the meaning of the offence for which they have been arrested.

Several commentators have suggested reasons why silence is not advised more frequently. One consideration (which is discussed below) is the need of legal advisers to maintain harmonious working relationships with the police (Baldwin, 1992b; McConville and Hodgson, 1993). Another, drawn attention to by Dixon (1991b), is that, if it is clear that the suspect is likely to be charged, confession may have considerable advantages in terms of sentence when the case comes to court. Baldwin (1992b) also points out that many less serious cases are disposed of by way of caution, and this may stimulate co-operation at the interview stage. Both Baldwin and Dixon also argue that the right to silence is a relatively weak right. Silence may count against the suspect in court because skilled prosecuting counsel may find ways to introduce this fact into legal argument. This is particularly likely where the suspect has answered questions selectively, because the presence of a lawyer at the police interview may be taken to place the parties 'on even terms'. In these circumstances, the whole of the suspect's statement becomes admissible in evidence, not just those questions to which an answer was given (McConville and Hodgson, 1993).[12]

Advice to remain silent is not always followed by the suspect. McConville and Hodgson (1993) suggest several reasons for this: the advice may not be emphatic enough; some suspects are uneasy at not answering questions; and sometimes it is given in ignorance of the police and suspect's familiarity with each other and the usual pattern of their dealings. Hodgson (1994) also draws attention to the relative powerlessness of the suspect compared with the police and the pressures this creates to capitulate to their expectations. In the face of these pressures, legal advisers may face an uphill struggle to persuade the suspect to trust them and to behave in a way which openly conflicts with police demands. McConville et al (1994) draw attention to specific tactics sometimes used to persuade silent suspects to answer. These may include: attempts to marginalise the adviser, perhaps by placing him or her physically at a distance from the suspect out of easy eye contact, or by denigrating the advice given; and stressing to the suspect that silence could

---

12 These views were expressed before the recent changes made by the Criminal Justice and Public Order Act 1994 permitted the suspect's silence to be a matter of legitimate comment, irrespective of the presence of a lawyer or whether all or only some questions were refused.

be taken as indicative of guilt and that an innocent person would wish to speak in their defence.

Some suspects who are *not* advised to remain silent nevertheless refuse to answer questions. McConville and Hodgson (1993) suggest that in some cases this is due to the suspect's distrust of the advice received or an obstinate belief that silence will provide protection against self-incrimination, despite the weight of evidence. In others, it may simply stem from dislike of the police. Dixon (1991b) goes further, arguing that silence often constitutes an antagonistic refusal to co-operate with the police or an attempt to protect accomplices. This analysis does not necessarily conflict with that of McConville and Hodgson, since they looked only at cases in which suspects were legally advised. Those not advised, who exercise their right of silence, may well do so for the reasons Dixon suggests.

The adviser's role during police interviews

Legal advisers appear to have relatively little impact on the course of interviews. Two studies which have sought police views on this issue, those by Sanders *et al* (1989) and Bottomley *et al* (1989), have found that the presence of a legal adviser apparently had little effect on the way questioning was carried out. Some officers in the latter study stated that the presence of an adviser meant that they did not conduct off-the-record questioning; however, this particular effect may be expected to have disappeared now that almost all interviews are tape-recorded.

Several studies have sought to quantify and categorise legal advisers' interventions. Five of these (Greater Manchester Police, 1988; Brown *et al*, 1992; Baldwin, 1992b; Evans, 1993; and McConville and Hodgson, 1993) have concluded that legal advisers interrupt questioning quite rarely – although the figures given vary quite considerably – and that interventions by advisers to push their clients' interests are quite unusual.

Three studies put interventions by legal advisers at a very low level indeed. In the Greater Manchester study, advisers were found to intervene in only six per cent of cases (GMP, 1988). They generally did so to seek clarification or slow down the pace of questions so that they could take adequate notes. In the study by Brown *et al* (1992), there were interruptions in just eight per cent of cases; only half of these were to give advice that may have impeded the flow of questioning, such as to remain silent. In a quarter, the advice may have assisted the interview: for example, advice to tell the truth or admit the offence. The third study, by Evans (1993), was concerned solely with juvenile suspects and confined to just one force. The sample of cases in which solicitors attended interviews was also small (just 18). This inevitably detracts from the strength of the conclusions, although it should be noted that they are in line with the studies already referred to. Evans draws attention to the particular risks that arise in cases involving juveniles: for example, their failure to appreciate the legal implications of police questions and of their own answers. He also identifies instances of oppressive police questioning of juveniles. Despite the special considerations applying to such cases, this study too found that solicitors very rarely intervened during interviews: in only one out of the 18 cases in which solicitors attended interviews did this happen, despite the fact that in half of these cases persuasive tactics were used and a confession obtained.

The studies by McConville and Hodgson (1993) and Baldwin (1992b) have found rather higher rates of participation by solicitors. However, there are reasons to doubt whether either study is representative.[13] While differing somewhat in the way in which they classify advisers' interventions, they agree that these rarely obstruct the course of the interview. McConville and Hodgson found that multiple interventions are very rare, although effective when they occur. In all, this study found that legal advisers intervened in 22 per cent of interviews. In three-quarters of these cases, interventions were on the adviser's own initiative. Where these occurred they were most frequently to object to improper questions (for example, their client could not reasonably be expected to know the answer) or to explain or reinforce their client's refusal to answer. Some interventions were to seek information from the police, to clarify the suspect's account, or to check that their client had understood police questions. In the remaining quarter of cases, the adviser's intervention was either requested by the client, usually seeking advice about whether to answer a police question, or sometimes by the police.

In Baldwin's (1992b) study legal advisers had something to say in around a third of cases. However, as already noted, his sample too may not have been representative of interviews involving legal advisers. It was originally drawn as part of a study of video-recorded interviews: two-thirds of cases involved such interviews while, for comparative purposes, one-third included taped interviews. The former particularly may have occurred in more serious cases, one indication being that 30 per cent of interviews were attended by legal advisers – a higher than average proportion. However, Baldwin too found that advisers were often attempting to facilitate questioning (in nine per cent of cases) and they could, in effect, play the role of a 'third interviewer'. Most frequently, they sought to clarify matters (in 12 per cent of cases). Only in eight per cent were they described as 'pushing their client's interests': for example, by curtailing repetitive police questioning, calming down angry suspects and clarifying legal points. In two per cent of cases solicitors were considered to be obstructive.

13   The methods of McConville and Hodgson's study are discussed earlier in this chapter under the sub-heading 'Use of non-qualified advisers'.

Both Baldwin (1992b) and McConville and Hodgson (1993) argue that intervention by solicitors to promote their client's interests was often called for but did not occur. They draw attention particularly to interviews in which interviewing officers appeared to assume guilt, failed to allow suspects an adequate chance to give their side of the story, questioned the suspect repetitively or oppressively, or were unnecessarily confrontational. Irving and McKenzie (1989) also found cases in which the police used various manipulative tactics during interviews, but no instances in which solicitors intervened to curtail them. Some extreme cases of this type are drawn attention to in a recent report by Justice (1994). These include the so-called 'Cardiff Three' case,[14] where the Court of Appeal described police questioning in the following terms: "[s]hort of physical violence, it is hard to conceive of a more hostile and intimidating approach…". No intervention was made by the solicitor present during a lengthy period of oppressive questioning. In another case of aggressive and repetitive questioning, during which a duty solicitor was present, another lawyer who took on the case after charge commented that the suspect 'might as well as have had a cleaning lady present through his interviews'.

There may be a number of reasons why solicitors generally play a passive role. Baldwin (1992b) points out that Code C emphasises that the solicitor's duty is to advise without obstructing the interview. Interviewing officers may remove solicitors who persistently obstruct questioning (although advice not to answer particular questions is not sufficient basis nor are challenges to improper questions or a request to give a client further legal advice – Code C,6D). Guidance from the Law Society also tended to stress mutual co-operation with the police, ensuring fairness was observed and looking after the suspect's physical welfare rather than an adversarial stance (Law Society, 1988), although more recent guidance (Law Society, 1991) is less conciliatory. Baldwin (1992b) notes that solicitors very much see their role as being to advise suspects about their position *prior* to interview and, to this end, to obtain as much advance information about the case as possible. *During* interviews they see their task as being to observe that questioning is conducted fairly. Their stance is by and large non-adversarial and they do not see their role as being to secure the acquittal of guilty clients.

Several studies have also drawn attention to legal advisers' need to maintain harmonious working relations with the police (Baldwin, 1992b; Sanders *et al*, 1989; Irving and McKenzie, 1989; Dixon, 1991a; McConville and Hodgson, 1993; McConville *et al*, 1994). The first two of these studies note that legal advisers are often young and relatively inexperienced, and may be too ready to accept interviewing officers' preferred role for them of passive observer. Should they wish to challenge the interviewer, they may be no

---

14   R v. Miller, Paris and Abdullahi, Court of Appeal, 16.12.92.

match for more experienced officers. Baldwin (1992b) notes the significant fact that interviews take place on police 'territory' and that lawyers are there on sufferance so long as they behave appropriately. Bottomley *et al* (1989) draw attention to conflicts between solicitors and interviewing officers in the early days of PACE when this convention was not observed. Cape (1993) notes that interviewing officers may make life difficult for lawyers they perceive as obstructive, for example by manipulating the seating arrangements in the interview room to the lawyer's disadvantage.

Sanders *et al* (1989), Dixon *et al* (1990b) and McConville and Hodgson (1993) note that legal representatives, particularly but not exclusively those who are former police officers, may identify more with the interests of the police than with those of their clients. Baldwin (1992b) points out that in the interests of maintaining good relationships with the police it is often easier for solicitors to take the line of least resistance. Thornton (1989) notes that, where legal advisers are co-opted to the police point of view, this is more important than any manipulative tactics by the police, because suspects no longer feel that they have an ally on their side in the interview room.

McConville and Hodgson (1993) maintain that in a few cases legal advisers do not intervene because they judge that their clients are coping well enough without their intervention.

Denial or delay of access to legal advice

Under PACE, no suspect who requests a solicitor may be prevented from seeing one. Compliance with a request for legal advice may only be delayed, at the most for 36 hours, in serious arrestable offences if certain conditions are met and a superintendent's authorisation is given. Formerly, the Judges' Rules, while stating the principle of private consultation between solicitor and client, in fact allowed considerable scope for access to a lawyer to be delayed or barred (Home Office, 1978). The evidence is that, particularly in more serious cases, it was rare for suspects to be allowed unimpeded access to a solicitor (Baldwin and McConville, 1979; Zander, 1972).

Studies since the introduction of PACE suggest that access to legal advice was seldom delayed formally under s.58 of PACE in the early days of the Act. Brown (1989) found that superintendents' authorities to do so were successfully invoked in only one per cent of all cases. There is now evidence that use of this power has all but fallen into disuse following Court of Appeal decisions which have clarified the circumstances in which delay is permissible.[15] Brown *et al* (1992), in their study of the revised PACE Codes of Practice, found only one case in over 10,000 in which this power was used.

---

15   R v. Samuel (1988) 2 W.L.R., 920-934; R v. Alladice (1988) 87 Cr. App. R. 380.

Cases of detention under the Prevention of Terrorism (Temporary Provisions) Act 1989 are something of an exception. Access to legal advice may be delayed on the same basis as non-terrorist cases, but there are two additional grounds. A study by Brown (1993) of all persons detained under the Act over an 18-month period, found that access to legal advice was delayed in just over a quarter of cases. It should be noted, however, that all detentions under the PTA rank as serious arrestable offences for the purpose of delaying access to legal advice. Also, the most frequently used grounds for delay were those specifically provided for terrorist cases. In almost all cases where delay was instituted, it was to solicitors generally. Brown (ibid.) suggests that the breadth of the ban may reflect police concerns in such serious cases that any outside contact may, albeit, unwittingly, lead to members of terrorist organisations evading capture or destroying valuable evidence.

Brown also draws attention to the absence of any statement of the reasons for delaying access to legal advice in nearly half of the PTA cases in which this occurred, despite the requirement in the PACE Codes of Practice to record this in the custody record (Code C, Annex B, para 11). He also points to the length of delays in contacting solicitors – more than a day in a quarter of cases. Less than 60 per cent of those who wanted legal advice went on to see a solicitor.

Apart from legally sanctioned delays of legal advice, there is some evidence that in a very few (non-PTA) cases suspects are still denied access to a lawyer without any legal justification. Evidence of such malpractice has emerged in a number of miscarriage of justice cases documented in a recent report by Justice (1994). In 33 out of a sample of 71 cases examined,[16] suspects complained of legal advice being refused, not offered or not being available at crucial times. In one case, for example, a suspect was allegedly refused a solicitor during the course of 12 hours of interviews.

Summary

* The great majority of suspects are given written and oral information about their right to legal advice. This information is most likely to be omitted in the case of those detained other than for an offence, drunk and violent suspects, and juveniles. Suspects are generally reminded about this right by review officers, although the fact that this has been done is often not entered on the custody record.

* The amount of information provided has increased since the revised PACE Codes of Practice were introduced. This has raised awareness among suspects that advice is available free.

---

16   These cases are not necessarily representative in any way. They are a subset of cases referred to Justice, in which alleged miscarriages of justice rested on disputed confessions.

- Requests for legal advice have, at the very least, doubled under PACE. Soon after the Act was introduced one-quarter of suspects requested advice but this has now risen to 38 per cent. There is considerable regional variation.

- Take-up of legal advice varies between ethnic groups: Afro-Caribbeans seek advice in half of all cases, while the demand among white suspects is much lower at 35 per cent.

- Custody officers may influence the suspect's decision whether to seek legal advice. However, some studies may have overstated their impact on take-up and have misinterpreted their motives in trying to dissuade some suspects.

- Eighty per cent or more of those who request legal advice eventually receive it. Where advice is not received, this is often because suspects cancel their request where the adviser of their choice is not available or where they wish to expedite matters. Some requests by juveniles are not taken forward once their parents arrive.

- In around 70 per cent of cases in which legal advice is given, the adviser attends the police station, but in the remainder advice is given solely over the telephone. Where advice is given in person, it is common for advisers not to stay on for police interviews with the suspect. There are large regional variations in these patterns.

- A significant proportion of legal advice is provided by non-qualified solicitors' representatives, although estimates vary considerably and there are, again, considerable regional differences.

- Legal advisers often obtain only sketchy information about cases from the police, either because they do not ask for it or because the police withhold it.

- Generally, consultations with clients prior to police interviews are brief. Advice given is usually either neutral in character or to co-operate with police questions. Estimates of the extent to which silence is advised vary but, at most, this occurs in around a fifth of legal advice cases, typically where the police are not forthcoming about the evidence they have or where the suspect runs the risk of self-incrimination.

- In the majority of police interviews legal advisers are silent throughout. At most, they intervene in one-third, sometimes to object to questions but also to facilitate the interview or obtain clarification.

- Legal advisers do not often intervene, even to curtail oppressive or repetitive questioning or to allow suspects to present their version of events. This may be because lawyers need to maintain good relationships with the police, or because some are inexperienced or identify with police interests.

- Access to legal advice was occasionally delayed when PACE was first introduced but this now occurs only exceptionally, other than in terrorist cases.

7 Interviews with suspects

The PACE provisions on the interviewing of suspects reflect the RCCP's concern with minimising the risk of false or unreliable confessions. At the same time, they are designed to make the police's task easier by providing clear rules about the conditions under which interviews are to be conducted. Detailed guidance on interviewing is to be found in Codes of Practice C (on the detention, treatment and questioning of suspects) and E (on tape-recorded interviews).

Neither PACE nor the Codes attempt to define tactics that are and are not permissible during interviews: the RCCP considered that, for various reasons, this would be neither practicable nor desirable (RCCP, 1981: 109). Code C does, however, abjure against oppressive questioning and the offering of inducements. Under the Act itself, confessions made in consequence of such questioning are liable to be excluded as evidence (s.76). Evidence is also liable to be inadmissible if it was obtained in circumstances which would mean that it would adversely affect the fairness of the trial (s.78).

Other PACE provisions seek to enhance the reliability of interview evidence in a number ways. First, there are procedures designed to prevent prolonged holding without charge for questioning. Detention may only be authorised where this is strictly necessary to secure or preserve evidence or obtain evidence by questioning; the same test is applied at reviews of custody, which are conducted at prescribed intervals by an officer not directly involved in the investigation (see Chapter 4). Secondly, there are safeguards relating to the presence of third parties at interviews. All suspects are entitled to have a legal adviser present at interview. In the case of juveniles and the mentally disordered or mentally handicapped, an adult (referred to as the appropriate adult) must be present unless there are exceptional circumstances. Thirdly, there are provisions designed to improve the accuracy of recording of interviews,[1] in order to avoid disputes about their content. Lastly, the Codes contain measures which are intended to reduce the stress of the interview situation. They provide for breaks for refreshments and overnight rest, and they lay down standards relating to the physical conditions of the interview setting.

---

1   When PACE was first introduced, this was achieved by interviewing officers taking contemporaneous notes of interviews. Almost all interviews are now tape-recorded or, in a minority of cases, video-recorded as well.

Research on interviewing

Several studies have dealt with the interviewing of suspects under PACE conditions. Only one, that conducted at Brighton by Irving and McKenzie (1989), has provided a direct comparison of interviewing before and after the introduction of PACE. Other studies include an examination by Moston *et al* (1990) of police interviewing styles and the exercise of the right of silence. Two studies, both conducted for the RCCJ, have focused on groups for whom there are special safeguards under PACE,[2] namely juveniles (Evans, 1993) and psychologically vulnerable suspects (Gudjunsson *et al*, 1993). In addition, there are studies of the tape and video recording of interviews by Willis *et al* (1988) and Baldwin (1992c) respectively. Williamson (1990) has also looked at the impact of PACE, new technology and organisational change on interview practice. In the context of a study of custody officers, Morgan *et al* (1991) have examined the decision to detain for questioning and voluntary attendance at the station. Also relevant are studies of the duty solicitor scheme (Sanders *et al* 1989), the impact of PACE rules on police decision-making (Bottomley *et al*, 1989), police detention (Brown, 1989), burglary investigation (Brown, 1991), police case building (McConville *et al*, 1991), the revised PACE Codes of Practice (Brown *et al*, 1992), custodial legal advice and the right of silence (McConville and Hodgson, 1993) and the organisation and practices of criminal defence lawyers (McConville *et al*, 1994). For the most part, these studies have drawn upon audio or video tapes of interviews for their data. The major exceptions are the studies by Irving and McKenzie (1989), McConville and Hodgson (1993) and McConville *et al* (1994), in which researchers carried out direct observation of significant numbers of interviews.

The Brighton research

Because of the unique position of this research in providing a direct pre- and post-PACE comparison, and because considerable reliance is often placed upon its findings, it is useful briefly to outline the aims and methods of the study and offer some critical comment. The research is a double replication of a study of police interrogation carried out during 1979 for the RCCP (reported in Irving, 1980). The aim was to test a number of hypotheses about the effects of PACE on interviewing: for example, that the use of tactics to elicit confessions would fall, as would the confession rate (Irving and McKenzie, 1989). Fieldwork was conducted in 1986, and again in 1987 to explore possible longer-term effects. Interviews were observed in 68 cases in both years at Brighton police station. Generally, the findings suggest PACE has had a substantial effect on interviewing, broadly in line with the aims of the legislation.

---

2   See too Chapter 9.

The study has been heavily criticised by Dixon (1992), firstly on the grounds that the findings may not be representative. Both the 1986 and 1987 samples comprised only 68 cases, some of which were selected on the basis of their complexity, and the research was confined to one station. His second criticism is that the researchers may greatly have underestimated the impact of their presence and of officers' awareness of the research on the behaviour studied. Irving and McKenzie (1989) argue that the issue of representativeness is academic because there are no other data against which the findings may be assessed. However, this is not an argument for accepting the findings as valid. Dixon (1992) suggests that it is unlikely that police officers, who are traditionally resistant to oversight by others, would not have modified their behaviour. One feature of the research that may particularly have affected practice was the copying by researchers of the contemporaneous notes of interviews which they observed.

Dixon (ibid.) also argues that the pre-PACE study may have led to organisational change at Brighton which made it unrepresentative of stations generally. He notes that the study was heavily backed by senior officers, that it had been critical of what it found and that it was politically significant. It was unlikely that senior officers would not have taken its messages to heart and ensured that changes in practice were effected. It is also significant that other studies that have examined various aspects of post-PACE interview practice – for example, work on interviewing outside the station (Brown *et al*, 1992) and on informal questioning (Bottomley *et al*, 1989; Sanders *et al*, 1989) – have not always agreed with Irving and McKenzie's findings. While the study may accurately portray what occurred at Brighton, its findings may not be generalisable. It should be noted, too, that it reflects a system of interviewing (using contemporaneous notes) which has now largely disappeared. Some significant findings of the study relate to the effect of interviewing under such conditions.

Condition of interviewees

An important aim of Code C is to ensure interviews are not conducted with suspects who are unfit to be questioned. Appropriate adults must be summoned for juveniles or those suspected to be mentally disordered or mentally handicapped (C 3.9). Medical attention must be provided for any person who appears to be physically or mentally ill, injured or acting abnormally (C 9.2). Those unfit through drink or drugs should not normally be questioned in that state (C 12.3).

These provisions appear to have succeeded in curtailing interviews with those who are clearly not suitable to be questioned, although a recent report from Justice (1994) suggests that they have not been eliminated entirely. Irving and McKenzie (1989) categorised the mental state of suspects interviewed as 'abnormal' in over 40 per cent of cases in 1979, but in only 13 per cent in 1987. However, they included as 'abnormal' those who appeared frightened. Unless fear is extreme (perhaps pointing to mental disorder) it is doubtful whether this alone would justify not interviewing. The most marked change was the virtual elimination of interviews with those rated as intoxicated: only two per cent of suspects were interviewed in this condition in 1987 compared with 18 per cent in 1979. More recent work for the RCCJ confirms this tendency not to interview those affected by alcohol (Gudjunsson *et al*, 1993). Brown (1989) and Robertson (1992) also point to the alacrity with which custody officers now summon medical assistance whenever there is any doubt about the suspect's condition. The advice given may result in the postponement or cancellation of interviews with the suspect.

Drug addicts present particular problems for the police. It appears that, notwithstanding the provisions of PACE Code C, interviews with those under the influence of illicit drugs do sometimes occur (Gudjunsson *et al*, 1993). This raises the possibility that such detainees may make false confessions.[3] Robertson (1992), for example, has noted that, motivated by the need to obtain more drugs, members of this group may comply with any procedure which hastens their release, including the provision of unreliable evidence during police interviews. Others have suggested that this is most probable where the suspect is withdrawing from opiate dependence (Davison and Forshaw, 1993; Sigurdsson and Gudjunsson, 1994). In other cases, the effect of drugs appears to be to make suspects confused and less able to think clearly. This might raise the chances of them providing misleading or erroneous accounts but would not necessarily generate a false confession (Sigurdsson and Gudjunsson, ibid.).

Another group, those suffering from psychological conditions, are not always easily identified. Gudjunsson *et al* (1993) are sceptical about whether PACE has made a significant difference to identifying those at risk. In a study of psychologically vulnerable suspects, carried out for the RCCJ,[4] they found that, while the police were good at identifying the most disabled and vulnerable, there were likely to be many more persons at risk who were not spotted because their condition was not readily apparent, even to trained psychologists. Whether it is appropriate to interview those identified as mentally disordered is a decision left to the police surgeon. Robertson (1992) found evidence of some difference in practice here between the MPS and elsewhere. In London, there was a tendency for doctors to certify that the suspect was fit to be interviewed with an appropriate adult present; elsewhere, it was usual practice to state that the suspect was not fit to be interviewed at all.

---

3   False confessions are discussed briefly later in this chapter.
4   This study is discussed more fully in Chapter 9.

Robertson (ibid.) draws attention to the lack of established criteria for deciding whether someone is fit to be interviewed. For example, in relation to suspects who had been drinking, he found large variations between stations in the extent to which they were certified as 'fit to be interviewed'. He suggests that one way of standardisation would be to lay down what constitutes a reasonable blood/alcohol level and require suspects who are affected by drink to pass a breathalyser test before being interviewed. Other than this, he argues that it is probably difficult to lay down hard and fast rules. Lack of comprehension and irrational responses may be reasonably reliable indications of unfitness, but other conditions, such as a high degree of anxiety, are more problematic. Sometimes it may only be possible after the event to conclude that evidence given was unreliable because of the suspect's condition. At the time the suspect is detained the best that medical examiners can hope to do is ensure that the suspect appears to be rational and free of physical discomfort.

The extent and timing of interviewing

Frequency

The introduction of PACE appears to have been linked with a reduction in the frequency of police interviews, although the situation varies between stations and according to the offence. For example, Irving and McKenzie (1989) found that in 1979 over 40 per cent of suspects at Brighton were interviewed more than once, but this declined to one-third in 1987, a statistically significant change. However, in a study of burglary investigation, Brown (1991) found only very marginal reductions in interviewing activity at two of three stations examined. He suggests that varying local resistance to changes in practice may be important in determining whether fewer interviews are conducted. He also notes that pre-PACE frequency of interviewing differed between stations and suggests that the likelihood of a decline in interviewing was greatest where interviewing previously had been most frequent.

When PACE was first introduced, the requirement to make contemporaneous notes of interviews, which detectives regard as cumbersome, may have deterred the police from interviewing as frequently (Brown, 1991). This reason is no longer applicable with the extension of tape-recorded interviews to the whole country. However, there is little evidence to suggest that taping has reversed the trend towards less frequent interviewing (Willis *et al*, 1988; Brown, 1991). The most wide-ranging studies to have examined the frequency of interviewing under taped conditions suggest that less than 20 per cent of suspects now receive more than one interview (Brown, 1989; Brown *et al*, 1992).

Other PACE-related factors may also have contributed to less frequent interviewing, including the regulation of access to prisoners by custody officers and limitations on the range of interview tactics that are permissible (Irving and McKenzie, 1989).

Length of interviews

Assessing the effect of PACE on the length of interviews is complicated by the fact that two different methods of recording have been used since 1986 – contemporaneous notes and taping.[5] The available research provides no clear picture, other than showing that interviews where contemporaneous notes were used took longer than those carried out using pre-PACE methods of recording (Irving and McKenzie, 1989; Bottomley et al, 1989).

Taping may well produce shorter interviews: in a study of burglary investigation set at three stations, Brown (1991) found taped interviews were significantly shorter than both pre-PACE untaped interviews and contemporaneously noted interviews. Home Office field trials of tape-recording also suggest that taping leads to slightly shorter interviews (Willis et al, 1988), although it should be noted that these trials were conducted prior to the introduction of PACE.

Looking at the overall time spent on interviews per case, the impact of PACE would appear to vary on a station by station basis, depending, for example, on the frequency of pre-PACE questioning. Irving and McKenzie (1989) found that, despite longer interviews (because contemporaneous notes were used at this time), less frequent interviewing meant that overall questioning time at Brighton decreased significantly. Bottomley et al (1989), however, found an increase in overall interviewing time in their Hull study. This was because the rise in individual interview lengths in their study outweighed the reduction in frequency. In his study of burglary investigation, Brown (1991) also found a mixed pattern, depending on changes in the frequency of interviewing, and whether taping or contemporaneous notes were used.

With tape-recording now in place in almost all designated police stations and with generally less frequent interviewing, it is submitted that the typical situation is probably for the overall time spent on interviewing per case to have declined.

---

5   Before the introduction of PACE, contemporaneous notes were not generally taken, except in some serious cases. Instead, a note was generally made after the interview of relevant factual material, with an attempt to reproduce exact words if admissions were made (Royal Commission, 1981: 71). Taping was only used in areas participating in the Home Office field trials of tape-recorded interviews.

Despite the PACE safeguards, it appears that instances of protracted interviewing still occur on occasion. A recent report by Justice (1994) draws attention to cases in which suspects were repeatedly interviewed for a total of 12 hours or more (and in one case 29 hours). In terrorist cases, Brown (1993) found that four per cent of a sample of 251 detainees were interviewed for more than 12 hours, extending up to 21 hours of questioning in one case.

Timing of interviews

One aspect of interviewing which troubled Irving in his pre-PACE study of interrogation for the RCCP was night-time interviewing. The suspect may be at a low ebb and questioning may thus be inherently more coercive (Irving, 1980). In his post-PACE study he found no reduction in interviewing between the hours of 2200 and 0600, with approximately one-quarter of first interviews being carried out between these times. Code C states the requirement for suspects to be allowed eight hours rest in any period of 24 hours, free from questioning, and that this period should normally be at night (C 12.2). However, certain exceptions are allowable, one of which is that allowing such a period of rest would 'delay unnecessarily the persons' release from custody'. It appears that this proviso may readily be invoked by investigating offices keen to press ahead with a case to justify night-time interviewing. Pressure on cell space at Brighton, caused by the lodging or remand prisoners, may have been a particular factor contributing to night-time interviewing.

Brown (1992) provides evidence that the requirement to avoid night-time interviews is more scrupulously observed in terrorist cases. He found that only eight per cent of interviews with those detained under the Prevention of Terrorism Act were begun between 2300 and 0700, the great majority being first interviews justified by urgent circumstances.

The interview setting

The physical environment in which interviews take place may have an important bearing on the way they are conducted. Code C of PACE lays down only the basic requirements that interview rooms should be adequately heated, lit and ventilated (C, 12.4) and that persons being interviewed should not be required to stand up (C, 12.5). Beyond this, the police have considerable control over the interview conditions. McConville *et al* (1994) suggest that these are manipulated to the police's advantage and may contribute to the pressure on the suspect to confess. They found, for example, that seating was sometimes arranged in such a way that suspects could have no eye contact with their legal advisers; and tables were some-times removed so that officers could close in on the suspect. Other features of the interview room set-up to which they draw attention are: the lack of aural and visual stimuli; the immobility of the suspect's chair; and the posi-tioning of the main interviewer directly opposite the suspect. It may be suggested, however, that the interpretation which they place on some of these features is over-sinister. Tables may sometimes be removed, for example, to allow the police to concentrate on the suspect's non-verbal behaviour – something stressed in the National Interviewing Package – while the absence of aural and visual stimuli is to ensure that there are no distrac-tions from the purpose of the interview. Chairs used by suspects are some-times fixed to the floor to prevent them being picked up and used as weapons.

The purpose of interviewing

Code C (original version) advises that the purpose of any interview is: "to obtain from the person concerned his explanation of the facts, and not necessarily to obtain an admission" (C 12A). Over-emphasis on securing admissions, which may have led the police into adopting tactics likely to produce unreliable statements, is a consistent feature of past miscarriages of justice (Williamson, 1990). Five studies (Irving and McKenzie, 1989; Williamson, 1990; Moston *et al* 1990; McConville and Hodgson, 1993; Stockdale, 1993) have considered why police officers undertake interviews. The first two claim to provide some evidence that, under PACE, the purpose is less often to obtain a confession. However, there are grounds for doubting whether these conclusions are dependable.

Irving and McKenzie (1989) found a significant decline between 1979 and 1987 in the proportion of cases in which the stated purpose of interviews was to obtain a confession as the *principal* evidence against the suspect. This was cited as a reason for interviewing in 15 per cent of cases in 1987 compared with 25 per cent in 1979. Far more frequently than before, the purpose was to secure a confession as *additional* evidence. That other evidence was available is, they maintain, a further reflection that arrests are more firmly based (see Chapter 4). Furthermore, both they and McConville (1993), in a study of corroboration, point to a concern with gathering more evidence to strengthen the case after arrest but before interview. McConville found this occurred in over half of cases. If so, the urgency of securing admissions during interviews may have reduced accordingly.

Irving and McKenzie (1989) note that a considerable proportion of inter-viewing is for what they term 'administrative' purposes. There may be *prima facie* evidence, but questioning is deemed necessary to establish *mens rea.* The amount of interviewing for this purpose has, according to them, changed little under PACE.[6]

It may be argued that Irving and McKenzie ignore aspects of their own findings and, specifically, do not draw attention to the statistic that obtaining a confession of some kind was in fact mentioned by *more* officers in the post-PACE phase of their research than the pre-PACE phase. Whether to obtain main or additional evidence or for administrative reasons, confession was an aim of interviewing in no less than 75 per cent of cases in 1987 and 74 per cent in 1986, compared with only 54 per cent in 1979. They also offer no explanation as to why obtaining a confession as main evidence was as important in 1986 as in 1979, only declining in their 1987 sample. This may be due to chance variation in small samples, in which case their conclusions generally may be flawed. Officers' responses to the researchers may also have been influenced by increasing awareness of the aims of PACE and reflected what detectives believed to be the correct answer rather than actual practice (see Dixon, 1992).

Williamson (1990) also claims that obtaining a confession has become a less important objective. In a questionnaire survey of 80 detectives in the MPD, he found that only 12 per cent rated the main purpose of interviewing suspects as being to obtain a confession. The majority considered that the aims of interviewing were to arrive at the truth, obtain an explanation of the facts or secure evidence. One difficulty with this conclusion is that the aims of interviewing listed by the majority are not exclusive of the desire to secure a confession. It might be argued, for example, that obtaining 'the truth' may be little different from securing a confession, particularly where the interviewer is sure of the suspect's guilt. It is likely, therefore, that the 12 per cent figure seriously understates the current significance of obtaining a confession. Furthermore, the survey asked detectives their views in the abstract and may have produced idealised responses. Where real cases are at issue, answers may be very different.

There are other criticisms of this study, and since it will be referred to again later, they may be mentioned here. An important one (which is also relevant to most studies in this area) is that Williamson is unable to provide baseline pre-PACE data against which to compare his study of current practice. Another point concerns Williamson's own standing as (at that time) a superintendent in the Metropolitan Police. As Dixon (1992) notes, it is not surprising that detectives should respond to a senior officer's survey in terms which showed that they were aware of and conformed to the Code of Practice's definition of an interview. Williamson indeed acknowledges elsewhere that

---

6   McConville and Hodgson (1993) note that interviews are also conducted in a minority of cases where there is no intention of securing a confession or charging: for example, this may be to establish that the matter is primarily a civil one or to confirm that a person arrested was not involved in an offence.

there may indeed by a gap between what detectives say and what they do (Moston *et al*, 1992).

Lastly, the study is restricted to the MPS and there is the distinct possibility that, even if the findings accurately reflect detectives' approach to interviewing there (which is in doubt), they may not apply to other forces. The MPS, perhaps more than any other, has been at the heart of criticisms for malpractice of various kinds: the Confait case, for example, raised the issue of interview malpractices (Fisher, 1977), while corruption has also been an important issue (Cox *et al*, 1977). One consequence is that recent Commissioners have taken various steps, independently of PACE, to improve professionalism. The first such drive was undertaken by Sir Kenneth Newman in the mid-1980s (Metropolitan Police, 1985). Some of this programme may have affected interviewing practice, as Williamson acknowledges. Some evidence for this is provided by Stockdale's (1993) study, which included the Metropolitan Police along with four other forces. Officers interviewed in the capital were the only ones not to state that trying to get a confession was the basic aim of an interview with a suspect.

Williamson's (and Stockdale's) findings in relation to the MPS conflict with the results of research by Moston *et al* (1990). In a study of police interviewing styles, they included a survey of detectives, who conducted interviews in over 1,000 cases at nine MPS stations. Interviewing officers were asked to complete questionnaires before and after each interview, recording (among other information) the purpose of the interview. This study, more than any other appears to point to the continued primacy of the confession, with fully 80 per cent of responses pointing to this as the objective of interviewing.[7] Confession was viewed as the main evidence in 30 per cent of cases and in 50 per cent as additional evidence. The figure of 80 per cent is not significantly higher than the overall proportion of cases in Irving and McKenzie's study in which confession was referred to in some guise as the object of interviewing. The proportion of cases in the Moston study in which confession was viewed as providing the *main* evidence was higher, however. This may be an artefact of the responses available to officers for, unlike the Brighton study, there was no category of confessions for administrative purposes. Where this was the aim of the interview, therefore, officers may variously have classed this as main or additional evidence. This study may be taken to support the view that, in concrete cases (cf. Williamson, 1990 and Stockdale, 1993) detectives still view confession as of crucial significance.

---

7   A very similar estimate is provided by McConville and Hodgson (1993). In their study of legal advice and the right to silence, they characterised 83 per cent of interviews as focusing primarily on a confession. However, there is a need to treat this estimate with caution since it is not clear how it was arrived at: the inference is that it is based on direct observation of police interviews. Also, there are reasons to doubt whether the sample of cases in this study was representative of interviews generally. See Chapter 6 for a discussion of this study's methods.

Interview tactics

Pre-PACE research pointed to the use of a variety of police tactics designed to elicit confessions, with those involving various forms of deception causing the most concern (Irving, 1980). PACE and Code C now specifically forbid the use of oppression or the offering of inducements, while s.76 deals with the exclusion of evidence obtained by such methods. The Act and Codes also aim in various ways to enhance the fairness of procedures surrounding interviewing and evidence obtained in breach of those procedures may, in some circumstances, be excluded under s.78 of PACE.

PACE and Code C stop short of specifying what tactics are and are not permissible in police interviews. The RCCP took the view that it was too difficult a task to lay down a precise dividing line between allowable and prohibited tactics (RCCP, 1981). They emphasised instead the need for police officers to receive interview training which would equip them to recognise the dangers of particular tactics producing false confessions. However, McConville and Hodgson (1993) point out that the fundamental weakness of this approach is that tactics liable to produce false confessions may equally produce true ones. They argue that the consequence of the failure to place hard and fast restrictions on particular tactics is that there remains considerable doubt about what constitutes acceptable questioning. Others have pointed to the difficulty of determining when a 'robust' interviewing style becomes 'oppressive' (Maguire and Norris, 1994). Baldwin (1992c) contends that "[p]olice interviewers continue to operate in a sea of uncertainty, and it is not possible for them to be sure what conduct (short of physical violence and intimidation) the courts will be prepared to tolerate". Some police manuals on interviewing themselves advocate tactics which are of debatable propriety (see, for example, Walkley, 1987). More recently, however, attempts have been made by the police service and Home Office jointly to inject a more ethical approach into interviewing (Central Planning and Training Unit, 1992a and 1992b).

Nevertheless, it is clear from relatively recent cases in which the courts have decided to exclude evidence that the police have continued to use various kinds of unacceptable interview tactics and to breach PACE procedures designed to inject greater fairness into interviewing (Justice, 1994). It is beyond the scope of this report to review these cases which are adequately dealt with elsewhere.[8] It would appear that, while the courts have been reluctant to interpret police actions as oppressive under s.76(2)(a) of PACE, they have shown some preparedness to exclude evidence under s.76(2)(b), on the basis that things said or done by the police are likely to have rendered

---

8   For details of the courts' interpretation of ss. 76 and 78 of PACE see, for example: Zander, 1990; Birch, 1989; Gelowitz, 1990; Allen, 1990; and Parker, 1992. A recent report by Justice (1994) provides some particularly flagrant examples of the use of oppressive or unfair tactics in police interviews.

confessions unreliable. A broader view still has been taken of s.78, which permits the exclusion of evidence that would have an adverse effect on the fairness of court proceedings. Decided cases have made it clear that confessions may be challenged under this section as well as under s.76 (Zander, 1990). It has been held in R v. *Samuel*,[9] for example, that evidence should be excluded where there has been wrongful denial of access to a solicitor and in R v. *Canale*[10] that a conviction should be quashed where there had been flagrant and deliberate breaches of the rules in Code C about the recording of interviews.

Decided cases provide no evidence of the frequency with which various interview tactics are used nor of the way in which the police generally approach questioning under PACE procedures. There is information on this score from several sources, including Irving and McKenzie's (1989) Brighton study and Moston *et al*'s (1990) research on police interrogation styles. McConville and Hodgson (1993) and McConville *et al* (1991) also provide qualitative evidence on the type of tactics used by the police.[11]

The Brighton study

Irving's (1980) pre-PACE study identified a number of tactics used at that time to influence suspects into providing information or making admissions. These have been drawn upon as a framework by some later studies and are as follows:

(i)   Police discretion: allusion to police power over decisions such as the nature of charges and granting of bail;

(ii)   Provision of expert knowledge: playing upon knowledge of the criminal justice system: for example, to suggest to the suspect how co-operation will affect the attitude of the court;

(iii)   Consequences of confession to suspects: making admission look attractive by playing upon the way others will view this positively; playing down undesirable consequences.

(iv)   No decision to be made: giving the suspect to understand that the police already have all necessary evidence for a conviction; and

---

9   [1988] Q.B. 615
10   [1990] 2 A.E.R.
11   These studies in themselves do not indicate whether police interview practices would lead to exclusion of evidence; this is a matter for interpretation by the courts.

(v)   Proactive use of custody conditions: manipulation of the physical conditions under which suspects are confined and of access to those outside.

Comparing their 1979 and 1986 data, Irving and McKenzie (1989) found a major change in use of these tactics. All were used far less frequently in 1986. The overall proportion of cases in which at least one form of tactic was employed fell from 73 per cent to 57 per cent. And whereas the norm in 1979 was to try other tactics if the first one used did not work, this practice had become almost non-existent in 1986. The number of times a tactic of some kind was used declined to one-quarter of the 1979 level. The only tactics still used to any extent were the exercise of police discretion and proactive use of custodial conditions, although – probably because of increased control by custody and review officers – the latter became restricted more to general displays of police authority. Irving and McKenzie (ibid.) suggest that the proscription in Code C (C 11.3) of unsolicited advice to suspects about the action the police propose to take in the case has largely been successful.

By 1987, however, they report some resurgence in tactical interviewing, although the frequency with which tactics were used still remained at half the 1979 level and the overall proportion of cases involving use of tactics only rose to 62 per cent. The tactic predominately used was to tell the suspect there was no decision to make (because the police had good witness or forensic evidence). The authors suggest that use of this tactic may be related to the availability of a higher standard of independent evidence (see above). Confronting suspects with such *real* evidence contrasts with the pre-PACE situation in which interviewing officers may have tried to persuade suspects with *imaginary* evidence.

Other research

Irving and McKenzie's conclusion that it has become rare for the police to exploit their power over bail and charge decisions is not entirely shared by other studies. McConville *et al* (1991) and Sanders *et al* (1989) both cite instances of such tactics. The McConville study gives examples of detectives holding out charge reduction, the possibility of bail or the taking of offences into consideration as inducements to confess, although the authors provide no evidence of the extent to which these tactics were used. Since those studies were conducted, tape-recording of interviews has become the universal rule. Clearly, this renders interviews open to the possibility of external scrutiny and this might be thought likely to have had a deterrent effect on the use of unacceptable tactics.

This does not appear to be the case. Looking at a sample of cases where interviews were taped or videoed, Baldwin (1992c) discovered instances of suspects being offered unfair inducements to confess. These primarily consisted of detectives providing misleading information about the likely sentence if suspects agreed to have offences taken into consideration. McConville and Hodgson's (1993) recent study for the RCCJ also examined the use of the tactics described by Irving and McKenzie. Since there are reservations about the extent to which the sample of interviews in this study was representative,[12] it is unsafe to draw conclusions about the overall frequency with which certain tactics are used although it is perhaps permissible to draw tentative conclusions about their relative frequency. The authors found that it was most common for the police to maintain that there was no decision for the suspect to make because they had other good evidence. Second to this was a tactic not identified by Irving and McKenzie, namely a resort to accusation and abuse, especially where the suspect denied the offence or refused to answer questions. Next in order, the police often sought to influence the suspect's assessment of the consequences of admission (for example, to hold this out as being a courageous act). This was followed by a further tactic, again not originally singled out by Irving and McKenzie, which was to persuade the suspect that this was one last chance to confess, usually if all other tactics had failed. There was relatively little use of the tactics of police discretion (cf. Sanders *et al*, 1989 and McConville *et al*, 1991), exploitation of expert knowledge or use of custodial condtions, although there was a tendency for the police to exert dominance during interviews in a generalised way if their authority was challenged by the suspect or legal advisers.

Another important study to have examined the way in which interviewing is conducted under taped conditions is that by Moston *et al* (1990). The study was confined to CID interviews, and is not therefore representative of cases generally. Data were collected from two sources. Detectives completed questionnaires both before interviews, recording details such as the aim of the interview and the strength of the evidence already available, and afterwards to obtain information about the outcome. The sample obtained was large, with details being gathered of over 1,000 cases. The researchers also analysed the tapes of interviews in nearly 450 cases.

The researchers note that the interviewer's belief in the suspect's guilt may be an important determinant of interviewing styles (a point also made by Baldwin, 1992c). They found that, in nearly three-quarters of cases, the interviewer entered the interview sure of the suspect's guilt. This led to accusatorial styles of questioning, aimed at securing confessions, sometimes backed up by presenting the evidence in the police's possession to the suspect.

---

12   See Chapter 6 for a discussion of this study's methods.

Questioning aimed at gathering information was less common and took two forms. It might be open-ended, with no reference to the allegation; but where the interviewer believed in the suspect's guilt, it might revolve around the allegation and could be a means of putting pressure on the suspect to confess.

Depending upon which style of interviewing was adopted, questioning could be regarded as coercive to varying degrees. In the researchers' assessment, the most coercive was that in which the suspect was directly accused of the crime, along with supporting evidence, implying that admission was the only acceptable course. However, the researchers found no evidence that Metropolitan Police detectives used manipulative tactics of the kind identified by Irving (1980) and Irving and McKenzie (1989), which stress the advantages and disadvantages of confessing. They attribute this to the fact that interviews are now taped – allowing detailed scrutiny of interviewing practices later.

A somewhat different view of questioning is provided by Williamson (1990), although this is based solely on questionnaires completed by detectives themselves. Detectives were asked a range of questions about their attitudes to interviewing suspects: for example, about their measure of a successful interview and about preferred questioning styles. His general conclusion is that there has been a 'sea-change' in the way detectives question suspects. Partly as a result of PACE, there has been a growth in professionalism, and interviewing is now less inherently coercive and more a process of enquiry than one of persuasion to confess.

Williamson (1990) justifies the view that interviewing standards have risen on several grounds. Some relate to the impact of PACE and the Codes and include: the provisions on exclusion of evidence (ss. 76 and 78); closer definition of what amounts to an interview; the advent of tape-recorded interviews; the increased presence of third parties (solicitors and appropriate adults) at interviews; oversight of the detention of suspects by custody officers, review officers and superintendents; the possibility of disciplinary consequences for breaches of the Codes of Practice; and an increase in the strength of evidence on arrest, meaning that police interviews are not conducted from a position of weakness. While his conclusions are plausible, they are open to criticism (see above for a more detailed critique of this study). In particular, his standing as a superintendent in the force may have produced answers that subjects felt he wanted to hear and which conformed with the legislation and Codes. Also, responses were not located within the context of practice in specific cases; nor do the findings correspond with those of some other studies that have examined the aims of interviewing.

Some further insight into police interviewing practices comes from a study of the right to silence by Leng (1993). His analysis is based on a sample of over 1,000 cases of all levels of seriousness. One issue he examined was the way in which interviewers respond when defences are raised by suspects (this occurred in just under 40 per cent of cases). In the overwhelming majority (94 per cent) of such cases the interviewing officer attempted to break the defence down. While this might tend to suggest that interviewing is a coercive process, Leng found that these attempts apparently failed in 95 per cent of the cases, implying that robust interviewing tactics were not generally persisted with. A very similar view of the relative lack of success of police interviewing techniques is provided by Baldwin (1992c) in his study of video-recorded interviews. He found that in only 20 out of 600 interviews (3 per cent) did suspects completely change their story in the course of the interview and admit the offence. Even then, this appeared to be attributable to police tactics in just nine cases.

According to Leng (1993), the reason that interviewing officers usually fail to break down suspects' defences is because it is difficult to controvert them: this is the situation where the suspect simply denies having the appropriate intent, for example. In other cases, officers were confident in obtaining a conviction without undermining the suspect's defence or did not regard the case as important enough to expend the requisite effort on further questioning. In a few cases the suspect's explanation was accepted and no further action followed. Baldwin (1992c) lays more emphasis on the generally low level of competence of the police as interviewers. His view is that they simply lack the high level psychological skills needed to 'turn' suspects. He rated over a third of interviews in his study as poorly or not very well conducted. He particularly notes various kinds of ineptitude (such as nerves and lack of confidence) and poor interview technique (for example, losing control of the interview, failure to allow suspects the chance to give their account and lack of grasp of the legal elements of the offence).

The content of police questions

Some studies have looked beyond the broad tactics used by the police in interviews and at the detailed content of the questions put and the dangers that particular forms of questioning may raise. Certain types of question are unproblematic: for example, questions unrelated to the offence, perhaps to put suspects at their ease and neutrally phrased questions, seeking information about the suspect's movements or an explanation for apparently incriminating behaviour (McConville and Hodgson, 1993). The structure and form of some other types of questions raise potential difficulties. Gudjunsson and Clark (1986), McConville et al (1991) and a report by Justice (1994) all note that questioning may play upon the suggestibility of the suspect in various ways and raise the possibility of a false confession.[13] McConville and Hodgson (1993) and others have identified several such lines of questioning. Leading questions, for example, seek to persuade the suspect to give a particular answer by foreclosing other possible answers. Baldwin (1992c) notes that such questioning comes close to putting words into the suspect's mouth and that the value of any resulting admissions may be equivocal. In similar vein, McConville and Hodgson (1993) also refer to 'statement questions', which aim to secure the suspect's assent to an incriminating version of events recounted by the police. Another variation is to accuse the suspect of the offence and, in doing so, disclose the evidence possessed by the police. This runs the danger that it will be impossible to prove that the information contained in any 'confession' was not simply fed to the suspect by the police.

McConville and Hodgson (ibid.), along with Sanders *et al* (1989), Evans and Ferguson (1991) and Evans (1993), also point to the practice of asking 'legal closure questions. These amount to an attempt to force the suspect's responses into appropriate legal categories (for example, inviting an admission that the suspect *stole* goods), as a short cut to proving the elements of the offence. Interviewing officers may, it is argued, play on the suspect's ignorance of legal definitions – recklessness is sometimes cited as an example – to secure admissions to the appropriate degree of intent. Another practice identified by McConville and Hodgson is that of seeking to persuade the suspect to adopt a police statement or opinion, which has the effect of incriminating the suspect.

There is some evidence that these problematic forms of question are used with some frequency, although the estimates available need to be treated with some caution. McConville and Hodgson (1993) found, for example, that legal closure and 'statement' questions were each used in around a third of interviews and leading questions in a fifth. Evans (1993) also found that leading questions were used in a fifth of cases but legal closure questions were only found in 12 per cent of cases. However, the former study contained only cases in which suspects received legal advice and may not even have been strictly representative of these (see Chapter 6), while the latter is also limited in its coverage, being restricted to a sample of juveniles who admitted or did not clearly admit or deny offences.

Non-verbal tactics

One aspect of police interview tactics is the use made of non-verbal cues. A standard interviewing manual for the police lays considerable emphasis on the interviewer's ability to tell from the suspect's behaviour or from physio-

---

13   False confessions are discussed further below.

logical signs (such as a rumbling stomach or sweating) whether the suspect is lying (Walkley, 1987). However, in a review of research on the detection of deception, Moston (1991) has shown that some types of physical manifestation which are often perceived as being linked with deception are not indicators of actual deception. In relation to some other perceived indicators of deception, there is no evidence whether they are or are not linked with actual deception. He concludes that the guidance given to police officers in the detection of deception is often, in consequence, misleading. Nonetheless, McConville and Hodgson (1993) claimed that interviewing officers took facets of the suspect's behaviour – for example, an averted gaze or nervous laughter – as indicating guilt and exploited these in the course of questioning to apply pressure to confess. They observe that tape-recording of interviews has enabled the police to concentrate more on the suspect's response. In contrast, Irving and McKenzie (1989) who carried out their research when contemporaneous note-taking was in use, had found that interviewers paid relatively little attention to the behaviour of the suspect during questioning.

Confessions

A range of studies have pointed to the centrality of confessions in the investigative process, for they are viewed by the police as a quick and useful way of clearing up crime (Mawby, 1979; Morris, 1980; McConville and Baldwin, 1981; McConville et al, 1991; Evans, 1993; Mortimer, 1994). There have been recent attempts to change this 'confession culture'. A joint Home Office and ACPO initiative has sought to inject a more open-minded approach into investigative interviewing, stressing the importance of allowing suspects to present their own version of events and of keeping the possibility of the suspect's innocence clearly in view (Mortimer, 1994; Central Planning and Training Unit, 1992a and 1992b).

Whether these moves will alter interviewing practice and the frequency with which confessions are secured remains to be seen. Most research on interviewing under PACE conditions has been undertaken prior to the relatively recent introduction of the 'investigative interviewing' package and it is with this body of work that this section is concerned. It considers the frequency with which confessions are obtained in PACE regulated interviews and some of the inherent dangers of such evidence.

Frequency of confessions

The pre-PACE evidence suggests that just over 60 per cent of interviews led to confessions (Softley et al, 1980; Irving, 1980). The study by Irving and

McKenzie (1989) provides the only opportunity to compare the confession rate at the same location before and after the introduction of PACE. They found no clear-cut effect. In 1986, despite a reduction in the use of tactics to a quarter of their 1979 level, there was actually a slight rise in the proportion of suspects admitting offences during interviews, from 62 per cent to 65 per cent. In 1987, when there was some return to the use of tactical interviewing, the admission rate fell to 46 per cent. However, the 1987 sample contained a higher proportion of serious offences than the earlier samples and is not strictly comparable with them.

In seeking to account for these developments, they suggest – rather unsatisfactorily – that the existence of better evidence prior to interview may have counteracted the reduction in the use of tactics, but it is unlikely to be the sole factor explaining the high 1986 confession rate. Their difficulty in providing an explanation increases with their 1987 sample. This had been boosted to include more serious cases. Their theory was that, in such cases, more pressure would be brought to bear through interview tactics and this would be related to suspects' decisions to confess. However, even when cases were taken out of the analysis in which the evidence was strong and interview tactics might not be expected play a significant role, the rate of admissions was still found to have fallen despite a doubling in the use of tactics. They suggest that some of the power of police tactics may have been destroyed by the unwieldy contemporaneous note-taking procedure or the loss of the investigating officer's control over the conditions of custody. Tape-recording may have now counteracted the effect of the former.

It is more likely that the small samples used in the Brighton study are responsible for much of the variation. In view of this and the fact that the study was limited to one station, it is doubtful whether it is sound to make generalisations about the effect of PACE on confessions from this one piece of research. It is also relevant to note that the study did not take account of any possible impact of legal advice on admissions. Irving and McKenzie have themselves noted that there was a very large increase in attendance of solicitors at Brighton police station in 1987.

More reliable data on confession rates are undoubtedly provided by more broadly based studies drawing on larger samples. One estimate is provided by McConville (1993). In a sample of 465 cases drawn from six stations confessions were obtained in 59 per cent, only marginally lower than pre-PACE estimates. The same figure is given by Moston and Stephenson (1993), drawing on a sample of 558 cases from three forces. Phillips and Brown (forthcoming) found a slightly lower admission rate of 55 per cent in a sample of nearly 3,000 suspects interviewed at ten police stations, while a similar figure of 54 per cent was found by Sanders *et al* (1989) in a sample of nearly 250 cases, also at ten police stations.

There is agreement that the confession rate is lower where suspects have received legal advice. Moston and Stephenson (1993) give a figure of 51 per cent in legal advice cases compared with 63 per cent in others. More strikingly, Phillips and Brown (forthcoming) provide figures of 37 per cent and 65 per cent respectively, and Sanders et al (1989) quote rates of 44 per cent and 60 per cent. The extent to which the advice given by solicitors is instrumental in determining whether suspects confess has been touched on earlier (see Chapter 6). In brief, the general conclusions of researchers in this area are that solicitors do not often intervene in interviews and that advice given prior to interview is largely in line with the suspect's own inclinations (Sanders et al, 1989; Baldwin, 1992b; McConville and Hodgson, 1993; McConville et al, 1994). This suggests that the increase in legal advice to suspects may not, in itself, have significantly affected the confession rate. In effect, suspects who now receive legal advice but who would not have done so in the past, have not generally changed the nature of their response to police questioning.

The studies show that the confession rate is related to a number of variables, one being seriousness of offence. In cases handled by the CID, for example, Moston et al (1990) found an admission rate of just 41 per cent in a sample of over one thousand cases in the Metropolitan Police. McConville (1993) found a confession rate of 39 per cent in personal violence cases, compared with 59 per cent in cases generally. Phillips and Brown (forthcoming) found that as many as 72 per cent of suspects confessed in cases they defined as 'minor' (for example, shoplifting and public order offences), compared with 46 per cent in very serious cases.

There is some evidence that juveniles are more likely to confess. Phillips and Brown (forthcoming) found a confession rate of 62 per cent among juveniles, compared with an average of 55 per cent for suspects generally. In a study of the interviewing of juveniles for the RCCJ, Evans (1993) suggests that the figure may be as high as 68 per cent (although this includes five per cent of cases in which police records were misleading and where there may not actually have been a confession). It must be kept in mind that juveniles who are interviewed by the police are the product of a different filtering process from adults. In particular, it is likely that more will be informally warned, cautioned or released without interview. This would tend to suggest that those who are interviewed may be those who are less likely to admit their offence and it raises concerns if the confession rate among this group is higher. There may be particular pressures on juveniles to confess. As Evans (ibid.) notes, parents who attend as appropriate adults may condemn their child's behaviour and assist in obtaining a confession. Furthermore, solicitors are less likely to attend interviews with juveniles. Neither they nor social workers intervene significantly during the interview.

The confession rate also appears to be related to the ethnic origin of the suspect. Phillips and Brown (forthcoming) found that 58 per cent of white suspects provided admissions, compared with 48 per cent of Asians and 44 per cent of Afro-Caribbeans. To some extent these differences are accounted for by the varying arrest profiles of the different ethnic groups. For example, white suspects are more likely to be arrested for public order offences (typically drunkenness), and admissions run at a higher rate for such offences, regardless of the ethnic origin of the suspect. However, this is by no means a complete explanation. For some categories of offence the admission rate for Afro-Caribbeans is lower than that for white suspects. The reasons why this should be so remain to be explored more fully. The practical consequence is that Afro-Caribbeans are less likely to be eligible for police cautions (which require suspects to admit their guilt) than white suspects and more likely to plead 'not guilty' at court.

Not surprisingly, the confession rate also varies in relation to the strength of the evidence: the stronger the evidence the more likely is the suspect to confess. It is difficult to make comparisons between studies on this point because they have drawn on different samples and used different measures of the strength of evidence. Moston et al (1992), in their study of CID cases in the Metropolitan Police, found that 67 per cent of suspects made admissions where the evidence was 'strong', 36 per cent where it was 'moderate' and only 10 per cent where it was 'weak'. McConville (1993), looking at suspects generally, found a similar but less marked pattern. Where the evidence was 'strong', 64 per cent confessed, compared with 46 per cent where it was 'weak'. Phillips and Brown (forthcoming) used a rather different measure of evidential strength, looking at whether there was sufficient evidence to charge at the point of arrest. They found that 67 per cent of suspects against whom there was sufficient evidence at this point confessed, compared with only 36 per cent where the evidence had not reached this standard.

Earlier in this review (see Chapter 4), it was noted that there was some indication that the standard of evidence on which arrests are based has risen since the introduction of PACE. It might be expected that the confession rate would, in consequence, have risen too. As the preceding discussion has suggested, there has in fact been little change – or possibly a small decline – in the confession rate. The research does not provide any clear indication of why this should be the case. Two explanations may be offered. One relates to deficiencies in the research. It is, for example, inadequate to gauge the extent and nature of the increase – if any – in the standard of evidence, nor is it sensitive enough accurately to indicate trends in the confession rate. In other words, it is by no means certain that there have not been changes in the expected direction. The other explanation is that the impact of a higher standard of evidence may have been counteracted by the influence of other factors. Among those that might be relevant are the increase in legal advice to suspects (see Chapter 6), greater use of the right to silence (see Chapter 8), and less use of manipulative tactics during interviews.

False confessions

The significance of false confessions[14] and the safeguards against them cannot be understated, given that the RCCP and, later, PACE had their genesis in the Confait case, which raised precisely these issues. The risks of false confessions are probably greatest in the case of two (overlapping) groups of suspects: juveniles (Evans, 1993) and psychologically vulnerable suspects, such as the mentally handicapped (Gudjunsson *et al*, 1993; Justice, 1994). The latter pose particular problems in terms of identifying those at risk. These are discussed in Chapter 9. Those withdrawing from opiate dependence may also be at risk of providing false confessions if they perceive this to be a way of securing their release and access to drugs (Davison and Forshaw, 1993; Sigurdsson and Gudjunsson, 1994).

Several studies have drawn attention to the scope for particular styles of interviewing to produce false confessions.[15] Moston et al (1990), Baldwin (1992c) and McConville and Hodgson (1993) all suggest that styles which involve confronting suspects with the evidence ranged against them raise particular dangers of false confessions (or accusations that confessions may be false). Moston *et al* (1990) note that, in order to validate a confession, suspects must provide information independent of that put before them by police interviewers, which must then be double-checked by the interviewer. Their sample contained cases in which suspects offered little information beyond that which was contained in interviewers' questions; in their view, such cases positively invited defences based on the suggestibility of the suspect. Evans' (1993) study of the interviewing of juveniles found that in nine per cent of cases in which juveniles confessed there was no other evidence against them or that other evidence was only weak. He notes that it is important in such cases to consider whether juveniles make ready confessions simply to ensure that they are released from uncomfortable and threatening situations.

McConville *et al* (1991) and Evans (1993) single out other lines of police questioning which, they argue, also heighten the risk of false confessions.[16] These forms of questioning exploit the suggestibility of suspects by leading them towards accepting forms of words which amount to a confession without their appreciating this. Thus, interviewers may be able to capitalise on suspects' ignorance about the requisite mental element for offences in order to obtain admissions of intent. Or, without realising the significance of

---

14   For a full review of the literature in this area see 'False Confessions' by Clive Hollin (1990), report to the Guildford and Woolwich Inquiry; also 'Confessions and the Mentally Vulnerable Suspect' by Camilla Parker (1992).

15   See also the earlier section of this chapter entitled 'The content of police questions'

16   See also McConville and Hodgson (1993) and McConville *et al* (1994).

what they are saying, suspects may provide the responses the police wish for in reply to leading questions or questions seeking agreement with the police view of what happened.

Moston *et al* (1990) and McConville (1993) note that officers are sometimes too ready to accept confessions without further validation. In his study of corroboration for the RCCJ McConville found that, in eight per cent of cases, police investigations came to an abrupt end once a confession was obtained, notwithstanding that other important evidence was available and could have been collected. To some extent, this practice may be attributable to the requirement in Code of Practice C (original version, C 11.2) that questioning should cease once there is sufficient evidence for a prosecution to succeed. Revised Code C now allows more latitude about continuing with questioning after this point (C 11.4). However, Moston *et al* (1990) maintain that the real reason detectives stop questioning once a confession is obtained is that this is all that they really want and they are unwilling to proceed to obtain further information that might help validate the confession. They point out that detectives do not generally question the confessions they receive. McConville *et al* (1991), along with other commentators (see, for example, Parker, 1992; Irving and Dunnighan, 1993; Mortimer, 1994) have noted that, where police officers are convinced of the guilt of the suspect, this may detract from exploring other avenues, including possible defences.

Evans (1993) suggests that the dangers of false confessions may be particularly acute in cases involving juveniles. He found, for example, that leading questions (i.e. ones supplying their own answer such as 'so you knew the goods were stolen, didn't you') were used in 20 per cent of juvenile cases in which confessions were made and 'legal closure' questions in 12 per cent. He argues that there is less chance of detecting unreliable confessions later in cases involving juveniles because the majority are diverted from court by means of police cautioning, and there is no public opportunity to examine or contest the evidence.

Corroboration

The risks attached to confession evidence are reduced – although not eliminated – where there is independent evidence to implicate the suspect (Justice, 1994). Although PACE did not alter the general rule in English law that there is no bar to the conviction of a defendant on the basis of a confession alone,[17] PACE may have had an indirect effect on the standard of evidence. The quality of pre-arrest evidence, for example, has been

---

17   Section 77(1) of PACE introduced one qualification to this rule by requiring a warning to be issued to juries in cases where the case depends on confession evidence from the accused, where that person is mentally handicapped and has confessed in the absence of an independent person.

mentioned earlier (see Chapter 4). The introduction of the CPS, and their independent review of the evidence, may also have encouraged the police to seek corroborating evidence where possible.

Establishing whether PACE has contributed to any such effect is made difficult, as so often, by the lack of directly comparable 'before' and 'after' data. One pre-PACE study by McConville and Baldwin (1981) related only to Crown Court cases. They found that, in view of the lack of corroborative evidence, about 13 per of cent cases would have been fatally weakened if confession evidence had not been taken into account and a further per four cent would probably have resulted in acquittal. Vennard (1980), looking at contested cases in magistrates' courts, found that around 12 per cent rested mainly on a confession or damaging admission. It is likely that this is a considerable under-estimate of confession-dependent cases generally, since defendants pleading not guilty are less likely to have confessed.

More recently, the question of corroboration has been examined by McConville (1993) in a study for the RCCJ. His conclusions are based on a sample of 524 suspects charged by the police, 305 (58%) of whom had made confessions. The study was not restricted to Crown Court cases, but included ones dealt with in the magistrates' courts, whether contested or not, as well as those discontinued by the CPS. He found that in only eight per cent of cases was a confession the only real evidence – a lower proportion than was obtained by the two pre-PACE studies (which, in turn, probably under-estimate the proportion in cases generally). In the bulk of cases there was other admissible evidence from an independent source. Even where a confession alone was depended upon, McConville estimates that other evidence may possibly have been available in two-thirds of such cases. Only in the remaining third (3% of all cases) was there no apparent possibility of providing corroboration. The study therefore may be taken to support the view that the police have become increasingly alive to the need to obtain independent evidence.

Recording of interviews

The method by which police officers record details of interviews with suspects clearly has an important relationship with confession evidence. Prior to the introduction of PACE, there were frequent disputes about whether suspects had actually made confessions in the terms alleged by the police. This problem was inherent in the method of recording frequently used at the time, whereby interviewing officers transcribed questions and answers from memory after the interview had been completed. This method of recording also carried the disadvantage that there was no independent means of checking whether the interview had been conducted in an oppressive manner or whether other irregularities had occured.

Contemporaneous notes

The PACE and Codes of Practice provisions on the recording of interviews were designed to introduce greater integrity into the process of recording interviews. The method initially adopted was for interviewing officers to make verbatim, written notes of questions and answers while interviews were in progress ('contemporaneous notes'). This practice was made desirable – although not essential – under the provisions of the original Code C (11.3). It is arguable whether this represented a substantial improvement on what had gone before. Several research studies have reported that this method of recording had severe effects on the flow of police interviews and styles of interviewing and often proved a severe frustration to the police (see, for example, Maguire, 1988; Bottomley *et al*, 1989; Irving and McKenzie, 1989; Brown, 1991). Bottomley *et al* (1989) found that a majority of officers sometimes or always avoided the worst constraints of contemporaneous note-taking by clarifying suspects' stories with them informally before interviews began. Irving and McKenzie (1989) found evidence too that some exchanges were omitted from the record, especially where they revealed police tactics that may not have been acceptable. The record therefore served as a validation of police practice, showing that officers appeared to have complied with the formal requirements of the Codes.

It is not intended to dwell on the findings of studies in this area since, with the advent of tape-recording, they are largely of historical interest. However, they illustrate how procedural changes may have a major impact on police working practices.

Audio-taping

The overwhelming majority of interviews with suspects at the police station are now tape-recorded, as provided for in s.60 of PACE. Code of Practice E covers procedures in taped interviews. Home Office field trials of tape-recording were conducted between 1983 and 1985 and provide a considerable amount of information about the impact of tape-recording on pre-PACE police practice. This literature is not reviewed here.[18] Little systematic information is available about the impact of taping under PACE procedures. However, various studies have referred to specific aspects of taping and these have been referenced at various points in this review. For example, it has been found that taping produces shorter interviews than those contemporaneously noted (Brown, 1991). Here, points not previously covered are dealt with.

---

18   Readers are referred to reports of the research by Willis (1984), Willis *et al* (1988) and Macleod (1991). The field trials found a number of benefits to be associated with taping, including fewer challenges to interview evidence in court, a greater tendency for defendants to plead guilty, and a greater likelihood that contested cases would result in conviction.

Police views of taping

Williamson (1990) notes that there was initial police scepticism about the value of tape-recording. However, surveys of detectives that both he and Brown (1991) conducted some while after its introduction found responses to be largely in its favour. They maintain that taping produced more naturally flowing and quicker interviews than contemporaneous notes. It also allegedly brought greater professionalism to interviewing because the ground had to be better prepared. The accuracy of the record was also cited as important in relation to possible later disputes about what was said. On the other hand, the requirement to produce written records of interviews[19] for use by the CPS was viewed as a time-consuming chore which detracted somewhat from the benefits.

Purpose and nature of taped interviews

Williamson (1990) argues that methods of recording interviews influence the purpose of questioning. He suggests that taping is equally well-attuned to the gathering of evidence as to eliciting a confession while, in contrast, pre-PACE methods of recording were in line more with the latter. He too argues that taping, along with the broader effects of PACE and organisational change in the police service, has led to a growth of professionalism in the questioning of suspects.

The issue of the purpose and nature of questioning have been discussed more fully above; so too have criticisms of Williamson's methodology. In sum, there is some doubt about whether his contentions stand up to scrutiny. Several studies have pointed to continuing deficiencies in the conduct of taped interviews. In particular, Moston et al (1990) maintain that interviewers often lack the necessary questioning skills required to conduct a professional interview, in part perhaps because these have been lost during the period of contemporaneous note-taking but also because the tactics employed by interviewers draw upon psychological techniques which lack any sound basis. Various deficiencies in the conduct of interviews have also been identified by Baldwin (1992c), Baldwin and Moloney (1992) and Stockdale (1993). These include: poor preparation; repetitive and laboured questioning; inflexibility; and responding to external and self-imposed pressures. As has been noted earlier in this chapter, a number of researchers, including Moston et al (1990) have also argued that confessions, rather than a more neutrally disposed enquiry for the truth, are still a prime concern of interviewers.

---

19   This topic is dealt with further below.

Records of taped interviews

Police officers are required to complete a record of taped interview (ROTI), which provides an account of relevant parts of the interview for use by the CPS. It should include details not only of points favouring the prosecution case, including verbatim details of admissions, but also points in mitigation which may be drawn upon by the defence. Research on ROTIs by Baldwin and Bedward (1991) and Baldwin (1992a) has pointed to the reliance placed upon them by both prosecution and defence to conduct the case. They found that it was rare for either Crown Prosecutors or defence solicitors to listen to tapes. The former study noted that defence solicitors requested tapes from the police in only 12 per cent of cases.

Given the significance of ROTIs for the prosecution process, it is important that they should be compiled accurately and without bias to either side. Several studies have, however, drawn attention to shortcomings. In a study of the interviewing of juveniles, Evans (1993) found that, in an important minority of cases, ROTIs stated that the suspect had admitted the offence for which he or she was being questioned. In fact, scrutiny of interview tapes by researchers showed that there was no clear admission or even a denial. He notes that injustice may result where suspects who have not admitted offences, nonetheless receive formal cautions, which are recorded by the police for future reference.[20]

Studies by Baldwin and Bedward (1991) and Baldwin (1992a) have also identified considerable shortcomings in ROTIs. The first of these studies, conducted in just one force, found that around a half of ROTIs were deficient. A third, for example, provided misleading or distorted accounts of the interview, with much irrelevant information included – sometimes at considerable length – but salient facts omitted. The authors note that police officers are often ill-equipped for the difficult task of producing competent précis but there is generally no-one else to undertake it. In a study of the management and supervision of interviews, Stockdale (1993) notes that police officers interviewed for her research were themselves well aware of their limitations in this area.

In the second study, which was conducted in four forces (Hampshire, Leicestershire, Northamptonshire and the MPS), Baldwin (1992a) sought to ascertain whether best practice found in some forces had resulted in discernible benefits in the preparation of interview records. One of the forces examined (Northamptonshire) used civilian summarisers, while another (Hampshire) used civilians to type out passages marked by officers

---

20   It should be noted that before a suspect accepts a formal caution he or she must sign a form to say that they admit the offence. However, this is not a guarantee that the form will be explained to the suspect, nor that they will read it before signing.

in the case. The methods of the study were simple and might be criticised on the basis that they reflect one person's subjective judgement. Baldwin listened to tapes of 200 interviews (50 per area) conducted in 1990 and 1991 and then assessed whether the ROTI provided a fair summary that could be relied upon by both prosecution and defence. No independent assessment was made to validate his judgements.

The results were as discouraging as the earlier study – more so, if it is considered that the study was examining examples of supposedly good practice. Furthermore, Baldwin notes that the great majority of interviews were short (85 per cent took less than half an hour) and should not have presented major difficulties. In his estimation, half of the ROTIs omitted too much relevant detail or were 'misleading, distorted or of poor quality'. Some were far too long, without necessarily including all essential information. Large amounts of verbatim material were sometimes provided without any linking narrative to enable the reader to keep track of the interview.

The other half represented reasonable outlines, but over a third of these were also far too long and sometimes, quite unnecessarily, amounted virtually to transcripts of the interview. Generally, the longer the interview the less satisfactory was the record of it. Where the record did not fairly represent the interview, it was far more common for the bias to favour the prosecution than the defence. The exception was Northamptonshire (which used civilian summarisers) where the balance was roughly equal. Elsewhere, the ratio was about three to one in favour of the prosecution. Baldwin suggests that this is probably not surprising but, on the basis of his analysis of the data and discussions with police officers and lawyers, discounts the possibility that this is through any intentional mischief on the part of the police but attributable more to incompetence and misunderstanding as to what is required. Schemes involving civilians were not markedly better than those involving the police alone. While fewer Northamptonshire records were classed as 'misleading, distorted or of poor quality', they were subject to the same problems of prolixity as those in other areas.

Baldwin's overall conclusion is that, despite several years of police experience in their production and Home Office guidance,[21] ROTIs remain "crude and risky" documents in a high percentage of cases, and fail to reflect accurately what was said in the interview room. He rates the prospects for improving the position greatly as poor. Police officers, because of their "temperament, aptitude, educational background, tradition and training", are unlikely to be predisposed to summarise complex material in a way that can

---

21   The preparation of records of taped interviews has been the subject of two Home Office circulars (39/1991 and 21/1992). They provide guidance on, for example, which material should be recorded verbatim (principally, admissions and questions leading up to them) and differences in 'straightforward' and 'complex' cases, with the latter requiring lengthier summaries.

safely be relied on by other parties, particularly the defence. Nor does Baldwin believe that the Home Office circulars that have been issued on the subject will help to improve practice greatly. His criticisms are that they require too much verbatim material, even in straightforward cases and, given the unstructured nature of many police interviews, this is liable to produce confusion rather than clarity in the interview record. Furthermore, too many cases fall into the 'complex' category, for which fuller records are required, even though many such cases are not serious offences. He also criticises as impractical the requirement for officers to note the tape counter times of key points of the interview (e.g. admissions, salient points and aggravating and mitigating factors). This is very difficult for an interviewing officer to do, if working alone, but, more importantly, it will often only become apparent when the interview is complete which are the key points. The view that Home Office circulars have had only a limited impact on practice is confirmed by Stockdale (1993), who found that the contents had often not percolated down clearly to officers: some, for example, were unaware of the distinction between simple and complex cases. The requirements of the Circulars also sometimes conflicted with those of Administrative Support Units or local CPS branches.

Baldwin (1992a) proposes that one way forward is to involve civilians increasingly in preparing ROTIs, arguing that they may be less inclined to view cases through a "prosecution prism". However, he suggests that they would need more adequate training in précis skills and legal knowledge than at present. In the last analysis, given the importance of interview evidence to both prosecution and defence cases and the dangers of taking ROTIs on trust, Baldwin argues that there is no substitute for the (inevitably costly) option of CPS and defence lawyers playing the tapes themselves in order to make their own judgements about the evidence.

A somewhat different emphasis is provided by Stockdale (1993), who advocates supervisors maintaining stricter quality control over ROTIs and providing appropriate feedback to those preparing them. Maguire and Norris (1992) also favour a system of quality control, although they have in mind some form of random audit by a dedicated quality control unit rather than by line managers. A difficulty with these solutions is that line managers may not have the appropriate expertise to assess the performance of their staff. Stockdale (1993) counters this objection by proposing that line management should undergo training to develop competency in assessing interview records. Evans (1993) and Baldwin (1992a) argue strongly that an essential feature of any such assessment must be a comparison of the contents of the interview tape and of the ROTI[22] in order to guard against the production of distorted or misleading interview records.

---

22   This practice is indeed recommended in the Home Office Circular 21/1992.

The quality of ROTIS, along with the resources devoted to their preparation, is the subject of a further recent report by consultants who carried out a Home Office sponsored review of administrative burdens on the police (Cresswell *et al*, 1993). They made a detailed examination of procedures in six police forces, reaching conclusions not dissimilar from those of Baldwin, but going further in their suggestions for change. They considered, but rejected on cost grounds, the radical option of dispensing with police summaries and having CPS and defence lawyers review taped interviews themselves. Accepting that ROTI preparation needed to stay with the police, they argue that greater use could be made of appropriately trained civilian summarisers and typists. They argue too that the summariser's task could be simplified in several ways, notably by upgrading the quality of interviews. Thus, in common offences, interviews might be conducted in a more structured manner, perhaps by working through a checklist of key points. Generally, interviewers should be better trained, and there should be regular feedback from supervisory officers about the quality of interviewing, a point echoed by Stockdale (1993) in her research.[23] In conjunction with these improvements, they argued for a 'graduated approach' to the provision of interview records. In straightforward cases, only brief summaries of the main points might need to be provided. In more complex and contested cases, they argue for a dual approach, depending on the length of the interview. In the case of short interviews, a transcript could be provided, avoiding the need for a summary and the associated risks of inaccuracy or bias. In cases involving longer interviews, summaries should be provided, but increasingly prepared by civilians. These proposals have as yet to be tested in practice.

They have been given recent impetus by further Home Office funded work, which was designed specifically to explore the relative quality and cost of civilian and police produced ROTIs in more depth than previous work in this field (Hooke and Knox, 1995). By the time this work was undertaken in late 1994, a number of forces had made advances in the use and training of civilian summarisers. Perhaps in consequence, Hooke and Knox found that civilian prepared ROTIs were consistently of higher quality those those prepared by police officers. This was true in terms of freedom from prosecution bias, coverage, accuracy, relevance, coherence and literacy. Furthermore, these conclusions held good for both straightforward and complex cases. These conclusions are based on a quality assessment exercise, in which CPS lawyers and police officers rated 300 ROTIs prepared according to different methods in six forces. On the basis of activity survey work, the same study also found that there were considerable cost advantages to using civilian summarisers.

---

23   This point is expanded in a later section on 'Supervision of interviews'.

Video-taping

Neither PACE nor the Codes of Practice make provision for the video-taping of interviews with suspects and this topic will only be touched on briefly here. While many, particularly in the police service, have seen video-taping as the next logical step forward from audio-taping, the RCCJ expressed some reservations and recommended further research (RCCJ, 1993). They were partly concerned about technical dificulties associated with videoing, but they were also anxious about whether viewers would be distracted from listening to what was said by the visual impact of the video-recording.

Their views on videoing were influenced by research conducted by Baldwin (1992c), which remains the only study in this country to date to have looked at this area. He examined the video tapes of 400 interviews. These were conducted at four stations in 1989 and 1990 in three forces which were then experimenting with video-recording (MPS, West Midlands and West Mercia). He compared them with 200 audio recordings from two stations in the West Midlands. One limitation of the study is that the cases included were not necessarily representative of offences generally. Not all officers, for example, availed themselves of the videoing facility. And, in the West Midlands, videoing was used mainly for more serious cases.

Technical problems

Baldwin found frequent technical problems of varying degrees of seriousness with video equipment.[24] In nearly half of cases problems arose, ranging from minor irritations like the interviewing officer being obscured to more serious ones such as the suspect being off-camera, equipment malfunctions and tapes being so poor as to be unusable. The most sophisticated systems appeared to be the least reliable. Up to one in seven interviews were vitiated by camera malfunctions. Picture quality was a problem where the system in use sought to capture both interviewing officers and interviewees; quality was far better where the camera focused on the suspect. The former option has value in terms of being able to follow the behaviour of the interviewing officers. On the other hand, more subtle details, such as facial expressions or small movements are lost. Baldwin suggests that the simpler (and cheaper) equipment may prove to be the most serviceable, given the lack of technical problems it presents.

---

24   The study may underestimate the technical problems because Baldwin looked only at cases where officers had proceeded with videoing interviews. There may be other cases in which videoing was not even begun because of equipment problems.

Added value of videoing

A key question is that of the extent to which videoing provides advantages over and above audio-taping. Baldwin sought to address this question in several ways: through subjective assessment; by interviewing officers who had used the videoing facility; and by looking at the extent to which prosecution or defence lawyers or the court played the tapes.

Baldwin notes that videoing gives a third party the opportunity to make a firm and confident assessment as to whether an interview has been conducted fairly. He adjudged that in 20 per cent of cases videoing provided clearer information on this score than audio-taping. Nevertheless, it was only in a third of these cases (6 per cent of all cases) that he considered that it was critical to be able to see the suspect in order to assess the propriety of the questioning. He notes, however, that some of these cases were very serious in nature and that: "it might well have been critical in court to be able to see, rather than hear, suspects' spontaneous outbursts or else to form judgements about their expressive demeanour or their attitude and reactions". He adds that: "[t]hese phenomena seemed well captured on the video recording and were very relevant in aiding an observer to form a view as to the propriety of interviewing procedures".

A possible advantage of video-recording is that it may help courts to arrive at a view of whether suspects are telling the truth. In the past, interviewing manuals for detectives have stressed the importance of being able to read from the suspect's body language whether he or she is telling the truth (see, for example, Walkley, 1987). However, there is probably a need for caution and probably further research before concluding that courts may use video-recorded interviews to help draw such conclusions. The RCCJ was particularly concerned that there might be the risk of prejudice to suspects arising from irrelevant and possibly unfair surrounding circumstances (RCCJ, 1993). It was noted that suspects will seldom be at their best at the police station, and may be nervous or in a state of shock. There is the consequent danger that even trained observers may "mistake small gestures and tricks of demeanour for symptoms of guilt when they may be symptoms only of nervousness or anxiety". Moston (1991), in a manual on investigative interviewing, has also drawn attention to the difficulties of detecting deception from behavioural clues. The RCCJ (1993) also point out that the visual impact of the interview may distract the court from what was actually said.

One clear advantage of videoing is that it provides a valuable management tool that enables supervisors to monitor standards of interviewing and take any necessary remedial steps. However, set against this, as both Baldwin (1992c) and Stockdale (1993) have noted, is the apparent reluctance of supervisors to carry out any such scrutiny (see below under 'Supervision of interviews'; also Chapter 11).

Baldwin (1992c) suggests that the possibility of interviews being seen later by others may deter interviewing officers from any impropriety. It is submitted, however, that videoing may have limited added value in this respect. Much of the headway here has probably already been made through the introduction of audio-taping, which has reduced challenges to interview evidence in court (Willis *et al*, 1988). For their part, officers interviewed by Baldwin perceived one of the main advantages of videoing as being to protect them against accusations of impropriety by making interviewing practices transparent.

It appears that video-taping has had relatively little impact on the courts. Baldwin found that it was extremely rare for tapes to be played at court or for the defence to mount any challenge to interviewing techniques and methods. He points out that, in large measure, this is due to the fact that over 90 per cent of defendants pleaded guilty,[25] so that the way interviews were conducted was rarely an issue at court.

Baldwin was unable to judge whether cases in which interviews were videoed were more likely to produce guilty pleas than those where audio-taping was employed because his two samples were not directly comparable. It was also not possible to say whether videoed interviews were challenged in court more or less frequently than audio-taped ones because both were challenged so rarely that far larger samples would have been needed to establish reliable data.

It might be thought surprising that videoing does not produce more challenges. The potential is there for defence lawyers to use the dramatic impact of video pictures to highlight oppressive or threatening behaviour by interviewers. There may be several reasons why this does not occur. The most straightforward is that the existence of videoing may deter officers from acting improperly: in effect, there is little to challenge. This possibility is unlikely because, as Baldwin (1992c) has noted, there are no clearly laid down rules in English law about where the boundary between proper and improper behaviour lies. This being the case, there will always, in theory, be scope to challenge police actions. Another reason relates to the passive stance of legal advisers during police interviews (Baldwin, 1992b; Evans, 1993; McConville *et al*, 1994).[26] If they have not objected to the manner of questioning at the time of the interview, it may be difficult to do so later. Yet another factor to be taken into account is that, despite the existence of the video record of the interview, lawyers continue to place considerable reliance on the written record of interview prepared by police officers (Baldwin, 1992c). The deficiencies of these records have already been noted

25 The question of why the guilty plea rate is so high is one which is outside the scope of this review to address. This issue is considered more generally at length by McConville *et al* (1991 and 1994), who argue that the organisational and working practices of defence and prosecution laywers are a major factor in producing guilty pleas in the bulk of cases.

26 See Chapter 6 for a discussion of the reason for this.

above. However, as McConville *et al* (1994) have noted, defence lawyers are unwilling, for a variety of reasons, to engage in more time-consuming reviews of the evidence in the hope of spotting potential weak spots. Baldwin (1992c) contrasts the situation with that prevailing in the United States, where lawyers are more orientated to challenging interview evidence. Videos have been used there to raise issues of physical or psychological coercion by interviewers.

Supervision of interviews

It is implicit in the more accurate recording of interviews under PACE, whether by contemporaneous notes, audio-taping or video-recording, that supervisors are better placed to monitor them. This may, for example, serve the purposes of improving interviewing techniques or identifying evidential problems and instances of malpractice (Stockdale, 1993).

Several studies have considered the supervision of police interviewing.[27] Two, by Maguire and Norris (1992) and Baldwin and Moloney (1992), were conducted for the RCCJ and considered interviewing in the context of a broader examination of supervisory practices. The latter study was confined to more serious crime and included an examination of 45 cases, drawn from three forces (including the Metropolitan Police), and interviews with supervisory officers about their practices and procedures. More recently, Stockdale (1993) has examined the management and supervision of police interviews in a study set in five police forces (again including the Metropolitan Police). Evans (1992) has also touched on the issue of supervision in a study of the interviewing of juveniles carried out for the RCCJ.

Baldwin and Moloney (1992) found that supervisory responsibility rested at a relatively low level, even in serious cases, with only 20 per cent of investigations being overseen by an officer of inspector or higher rank. One consequence was that in nearly 60 per cent of cases, supervisory officers were also involved in the interviewing of suspects and there was therefore little scope for external scrutiny. The need for such scrutiny has been attested to by Baldwin (1992c) who, in a separate report, noted deficiencies worthy of attention by supervisors in the conduct of around 40 per cent of interviews. Although it should be stressed that his evaluation was a subjective one, he found that officers were often ill-prepared, conducted laboured or repetitive questioning, or adopted sloppy practices such as providing incomprehensible renditions of the caution. These criticisms are echoed by McConville and Hodgson (1993), in a study of custodial legal advice for the RCCJ. Many police officers agree with such criticisms: Stockdale (1993) found that a majority of over 200 officers she interviewed felt that standards of investiga-

---

27 Supervision of police work generally is considered in Chapter 11. Supervision of the preparation of ROTIs is discussed earlier in this chapter.

tive interviewing left much to be desired. One contributory factor cited was inadequate guidance and supervision.

Stockdale (1993) divides supervision of interviews into direct supervision (supervisors participate in the planning and/or conduct of interviews) and monitoring (supervisors check tapes and/or records of interviews). Other than during officers' probationary periods, she found that very little direct supervision was exercised in any of the five forces in her study in either CID or uniformed branches. Similar reluctance to supervise interviews was found by Baldwin and Moloney (1992). Direct supervision may have advantages. Baldwin (1992c) notes, for example, that supervisory officers can intervene to stop the interview if they feel this is necessary. On the other hand, he also points to dangers. It is possible, through use of a device known as an 'audio loop' to communicate directly with the interviewer during the course of the interview. While this may have advantages – for example, it enables officers outside the room to carry out enquiries to check statements made by the interviewee – it could also lead to unacceptable pressure being placed on suspects where colleagues of the interviewer outside of the interview were able to offer advice on questions and tactics.

Both Stockdale (1993) and Baldwin and Moloney (1992) found that supervisors were as reluctant to carry out retrospective monitoring of interviews as to supervise them directly. In the former study, it was found that only two out of five forces (neither were the MPS) had any clear policy on retrospective monitoring of tapes or interview records. Baldwin (1992c) suggests that many supervisory officers are reluctant to believe that a problem exists with interviewing standards. Stockdale (1993) found that officers gave a variety of reasons for not supervising or monitoring interviews including: insufficient time and resources; not part of their job; quality of interviews not an important performance indicator; lack of facilities for listening to tapes; and lack of the necessary supervisory training.

Baldwin (1992c) suggests that many of the more glaring errors in interviewing would surely have come to light if supervisors had been conducting any systematic check on interview quality. Stockdale (1993) found that two forces in her study had instituted formal procedures for monitoring interview quality, placing a responsibility on senior officers at divisional or subdivisional level for ensuring that samples of tapes were routinely examined. In one of these forces, however, it appeared that this instruction had had little impact. Where tapes were monitored, there was little consistency in the way this was done or in the evaluation criteria used. The content of the interview was not always compared with the summary, for example.

Even where problems with the quality of interviews do come to the notice of supervisors, they may be reluctant to intervene. This appears to be the product of engrained attitudes among detectives that officers need to be trusted with considerable autonomy in the way they work and that giving advice on how to interview breaches this trust and upsets professional pride (Baldwin and Moloney, 1992; Baldwin, 1992c). Baldwin and Moloney (1992) point out too that lower-ranking officers tend to believe that more senior officers are out of touch with the practical skills required. This picture is confirmed by Stockdale (1993), who notes that many supervisory officers have received little or no formal interview training and may have conducted few – if any – interviews under PACE conditions. She found that interviewing officers preferred to go to other, more experienced, officers of the same rank for advice rather than turn to supervisors. The latter course might be perceived as a sign of weakness.

The research described above, and particularly the work of Stockdale (1993), points to the following conclusions. Firstly, for there to be effective supervision and monitoring of interviews supervisors need to be more aware of the value of this exercise and, in particular, that the quality of interviews is just as important a performance indicator as, for example, response times. Furthermore, resources need to be made available to allow effective monitoring of interviews to become a reality.

Secondly, supervisors need to be equipped with the appropriate competencies for carrying out such monitoring. This does not necessarily mean that they should all be expert interviewers themselves but, rather, that they should be able to assess whether interviews by others have been well conducted and whether records of interview accurately reflect the content of the interview.

Thirdly, there is a need to develop clear criteria for supervisors to use in assessing interviewing. Stockdale (1993) suggests that these should distinguish between the interviewing process and the end product. In relation to the former, supervisors might, for example, assess the degree of planning involved, the appropriate use of questioning skills and compliance with PACE. Regarding the latter, feedback should be obtained from those whose concern is with the evidential value, reliability and fairness of the interview, as presented in written form (primarily ASUs, the CPS and courts).

Fourthly, there is a need to make inroads on the culture which militates against supervision of interviewing. Thus, interviewing officers need to learn that seeking advice on interviewing is not a sign of weakness; officers should be encouraged to assess their own performance critically; and positive feedback should be provided, where appropriate.

Lastly, there is a need to ensure that the information derived from supervisors' monitoring of interviews is collated, analysed and disseminated in order that it can be put to wider use.

Stockdale (1993) stresses that it is as important for senior managers to take these lessons on board as immediate supervisors of those carrying out interviews. For unless their support is forthcoming, supervisors will not be motivated – nor be given the resources – to fulfil their responsibilities in relation to interviewing.

Questioning outside the police station

Questioning of suspects outside the confines of the police station raises a number of concerns (Justice, 1994). Firstly, although attempts have been made to tighten up the safeguards relating to such interviews (e.g. in revised PACE Code C), they cannot be conducted under the same stringent conditions as those at police stations. Conversations are rarely tape-recorded, and this may lead to disputes about what was actually said. There is no means of verifying whether admissions made in such circumstances stem from the application of unacceptable physical or mental pressure by the police. There is also the issue of whether statements made by suspects who have not had the opportunity to seek independent legal advice and who may sometimes be in a state of shock are necessarily reliable. It is perhaps inevitable, given these concerns, that allegations of miscarriages of justice sometimes arise in cases where the main evidence comes from confessions made under such conditions.

Pre-PACE research suggests that a considerable proportion of suspects were questioned by the police prior to arrival at the police station. Both Softley *et al* (1980) and Irving (1980) refer to this practice. In the former study, 43 per cent of all suspects had either been questioned or, less commonly, had given unsolicited information away from the police station. Of this group, 60 per cent had provided information the police considered would assist with the case in some way. It is difficult to deduce from the available pre-PACE data what proportion of questioning would amount to interviewing within revised Code C's definition of the term (C 11A: "… questioning of a person regarding his involvement or suspected involvement in a criminal offence or offences").[28]

The original version of PACE Code C did not prohibit out of station interviewing. However, it stipulated that an accurate record should be made of any such interviews (11.3), but did not define what amounted to an interview, other than in relation to questioning at the police station (12A). The revised Code contains much tighter provisions: it restricts the circumstances in which interviews may be carried out away from the police station (11.1), applies a revised definition of an interview to such questioning (11A), contains more demand-

---

28   The further revised Codes of Practice, effective from 10 April 1995, add to this definition, making it clear that questioning can only amount to an interview where it is required to be carried out under caution. C 10.1 lists the circumstances in which a caution is necessary. The definition of an interview has also, for the first time, become a provision of the Codes rather than a Note for Guidance.

ing record-keeping requirements (11.5 to 11.12), and also requires a written record to be made of unsolicited comments that might be relevant to the offence (11.13).

Frequency of out of station interviewing

Of the relevant studies, only that by Irving and McKenzie (1989) appears to reject the possibility that interviewing away from the station occurs under PACE. It is questionable whether this study is either typical or accurate in this respect. There are several reasons to doubt its dependability. Firstly, the authors note that hardly any interviews at the station were conducted by officers who made arrests. If this is so, it runs counter to practice at many other police stations. It may reflect the fact that the study contained a disproportionate number of serious cases, in which arrests may have required the participation of a number of officers or the provision of assistance by uniformed officers to the CID. Secondly, they state that they would have expected any illicit interviewing to surface either at court or in a complaint. However, there is no reason why this should occur if the suspect voluntarily repeats an admission at the station and does not contest the case. Lastly, Dixon's (1992) criticism of the study (see above) that it may well have led to modifications in police behaviour is apposite.

Other research has drawn rather different conclusions about questioning away from the police station. The principal studies are those by Brown *et al* (1992) and Moston and Stephenson (1993). The former compared practice before and after the introduction of the revised Codes of Practice, which placed tighter controls on out of station interviewing. The latter, which was carried out after the revised Codes were introduced, examined the extent and purpose of interviewing away from the station, the records kept, and the effects of such interviews on the later progress of cases. There are similar limitations to both studies. They depend on the truthful completion of questionnaires about out of station interviews by police officers. This is a sensitive subject, as Moston and Stephenson (1993) acknowledge, although they do not discuss the extent to which the data may thereby have been flawed. Brown *et al* (1992) do discuss this issue, maintaining that the apparent ignorance of many officers about the Code's provisions on interviews outside the station may be one reason why their responses on this question could well be trustworthy.

A difficulty for both studies is that of gauging from the information provided what amounts to an interview and what is simply questioning in the normal course of an officer's duties.[29] The distinction is important, not least because

---

29   Further revised Code C clarifies that questioning in the normal course of an officer's duties includes that aimed at establishing a person's identity or their ownership of a vehicle or that which is necessary in furtherance of the proper and effective conduct of a search (C 10.1).

different record-keeping requirements apply. The studies adopt different approaches. Brown *et al* (1992) asked officers whether they had put questions to the suspect about the offence after arrest but prior to arrival at the police station and then sought to deduce from the nature of the questions whether they amounted to an interview. Moston and Stephenson (1993) attempted to predefine questioning and interviewing on officer questionnaires. The results were not entirely successful: they suspect that a considerable proportion of what officers categorised as interviews may not in fact have amounted to such under the Code C definition.

Both studies found questioning (i.e. whether amounting to an interview or not) in significant minorities of cases. However, Brown found that the frequency of out of station questioning had apparently declined with the introduction of the revised Codes, occurring in 19 per cent of cases in the first stage of the study, compared with 10 per cent in stage two. The report suggests that, under the original Code C, most questioning in stage one would have amounted to an interview; under the revised Code, very little (possibly around 15 per cent) would have amounted to interviewing.

Direct comparison with Moston and Stephenson's data is unfortunately not possible. Firstly, they separated interviewing and questioning; secondly, the data they obtained on questioning relates only to that which took place prior to arrest, while Brown looked only at questioning after arrest; and, thirdly, some of what Brown referred to as unsolicited comments by the suspect (and which are not included in the figures for questioning given above) may have been defined by Moston and Stephenson as interviewing, albeit begun at the instigation of the suspect.

Moston and Stephenson found that eight per cent of suspects were interviewed prior to arrival at the station. Most frequently, it appeared that it was the suspect who initiated the interview. The second most common reason for interviewing was to enquire about the suspect's involvement in an offence. Moston and Stephenson note that there must be some doubt about how many 'interviews' fell within the revised Code's definition and consider that well over half may not have done. They suggest that 'questioning' would have been the more appropriate category: for example, where the purpose was to establish whether a crime had been committed. They also query to what extent interviewing may have been justified according to the criteria set out in Code C. They note, however, that there is no requirement in the Code for the record of interview to state why the interview took place; this weakens the safeguards provided in the new provisions and opens the way for arresting officers to devise *post hoc* explanations that meet the criteria set out in the Code. Moston and Stephenson also found that 31 per cent of suspects were questioned prior to their arrest, primarily to establish whether a crime had been committed or eliminate a suspect from enquiries. A similar finding is reported by McConville (1993) who found that 'interviews of a significant character' occurred in nearly a third of cases prior to arrest. However, his sample of cases is not strictly comparable with Moston and Stephenson's as it consisted only of suspects who were subsequently charged. Moston and Stephenson also found that conversations unrelated to the offence occurred in two-thirds of cases, although in one-third they were restricted to 'the minimum necessary for politeness'.

Moston and Stephenson included race in their analysis and concluded that it was an important factor in relation to whether or not questioning took place outside the police station. Those they termed 'non-Caucasian' were more likely to be questioned prior to arrest than white suspects and more likely to be interviewed at home. They attribute this to racial bias, and suggest that 'police officers may be using questioning to develop pretexts for arresting non-Caucasian suspects'. However, it is submitted that this analysis is over-simplistic and the conclusion is unsafe without closer examination of the nature of cases involving 'non-Caucasian' suspects and the circumstances of arrest.

In addition to the two principal studies discussed above, several others have provided more anecdotal evidence about out of station interviewing. A significant minority of officers in Bottomley et al's (1989) Hull study admitted that obtaining 'some clarification of the suspect's account' was common before taking them to the police station. At the time of this study, this practice may have been influenced by the fact that police station interviews were still contemporaneously noted and pre-interview 'discussions' may have been seen as necessary to help the flow of the formal interview. Sanders et al (1989) also point to the practice of 'car-seat' interviews in their study of the duty solicitor scheme, using as their source solicitors' and suspects' accounts. Evans' (1993) study of the interviewing of juveniles also concludes, both on the basis of analysing tapes of police interviews and from the statements of interviewing officers, that pre-interview questioning of juveniles occurs in quite a number of cases (see too Evans and Ferguson, 1991). In their study of custody officers, Morgan et al (1991), although having no direct evidence that questioning occurred before arrival at the police station, point to the lengthy delay in a minority of cases between arrest and arrival. This was often unaccounted for, despite a requirement in PACE (s.30(11)) to do so.

Admissions

Brown et al (1992) and Moston and Stephenson (1993) put the proportion of suspects who admit their guilt prior to arrival at the police station at nine per cent and six per cent respectively. That Moston and Stephenson's figure is lower is probably because it is based only on interviews, while Brown et *al* also included admissions made during other questioning or in unsolicited comments.

Both estimates probably understate the real extent of admissions outside the police station because they do not take full account of those made prior to arrest. McConville (1993) found that more than a third of suspects who are later charged confessed during questioning prior to arrest, and a further 15 per cent made damaging admissions.

Moston and Stephenson (1993) found that those who had been interviewed outside the station were significantly more likely than other suspects to admit the offence during a subsequent interview at the police station. Where admissions had been made prior to arrival, they were invariably repeated at the station. Furthermore, where arresting officers had carried on *non-offence* related conversations prior to arrival, suspects were also more likely to make admissions at the station. The authors suggest that the latter finding may have innocent connotations and suggest merely that early rapport-building pays dividends later. Or it may reflect that some suspects are more prepared to 'chat' and that they are also those who are more likely to confess. More worryingly, the finding may suggest that things said during the conversation – perhaps about the possibility of bail – may have acted as later inducements to confess. However, the authors provide no direct evidence of the content of such conversations to back up this point. The authors conclude that there is a need for all conversations away from the police station to be recorded (on portable, hand-held tape-recorders). They point out that the taped record of police station interviews represents only a part of what is transacted between suspect and police officer. This fact hardly ever comes to light, however, because the police are generally reluctant for any indication to appear on the taped record of interview that any prior questioning or conversation has taken place.

Informal questioning at the police station

Informal contacts between investigating officer and suspect at the police station are not forbidden under PACE or the Codes. However, confessions made in an informal context raise the same concerns as those mentioned above regarding interviews outside the police station (Justice, 1994). The combined effect of various provisions in PACE Code C is to regulate access to interview very closely. Custody officers are responsible for deciding whether to deliver a suspect into the custody of the interviewing officer (12.1); as noted above, what constitutes an interview is defined in the Codes (11A); and there are precise requirements as to the way in which interviews are to be recorded (11.5). Unsolicited comments about the offence must also now be noted down (11.13). Custody officers may well be unwilling to risk disciplinary action by allowing investigating officers unregulated access to prisoners.

Irving and McKenzie (1989) argue that, as a result, the kind of informal sizing up of the prisoner which Irving (1980) had found to be common practice in his pre-PACE study, no longer exists. They note that custody officers afforded a wide definition to the term 'interview' to encompass any face to face contact between investigators and suspects. They do not deny that some informal contacts occur: instances were recorded in which investigating officers were allowed to 'have a look at' a prisoner. This usually involved a certain amount of conversation.

In contrast, other researchers have noted that the practice of carrying on informal discussions about the offence with the suspect persists although, with the exception of Bottomley et al (1989), they do not provide any quantification of its extent. In this study, it was found that informal discussions with suspects prior to interview were common practice: over half of officers interviewed admitted that they often or always had such informal discussions, most frequently on the way to the station but sometimes in the cells. However, the avowed intent of these discussions may not have been to pressurise suspects or gain access to them in a solicitor's absence but to clarify the account they were to provide during a formal interview. Similar practices have been referred to by Thornton (1989), who suggests that in some cases the substance of the interview is conducted informally prior to a formal repetition of the questions and answers for recording purposes.

Sanders et al (1989), in the course of observational work in custody blocks, also noted various occasions on which questions were asked about the offence during processing and in the cells. They argue that this practice is dubious since they believe that its intent is to circumvent the suspect's access to a solicitor. They also note that custody records present acceptable accounts of such practices, recording, for example, that the *suspect* asked to speak to the officer in the case.

Other evidence of informal access is provided by McConville et al (1991), who, on the basis of interviews with investigating officers, found evidence that they conducted off-the-record conversations with suspects in the cells or the interview room. Morgan et al (1991), in their study of custody officers, also refer to an increasing laxity in relation to controlling access to prisoners, and note many occasions' on which investigating officers had unregulated access to prisoners. Both they and McConville et al (1991) attribute custody officers' preparedness to allow this practice to their underlying commitment to crime clearance. This supposition has already been discussed earlier and subjected to a good deal of criticism (see Chapter 4 in particular). Morgan et al (1991) suggest that the worrying implication of uncontrolled access by officers in the case to prisoners is that they may be questioned or pressurised without those interviews in any way being recorded.

The studies referred to above are now somewhat dated and document police practice at a time when interviews were contemporaneously noted. As several commentators have noted, this practice was generally disliked as hindering the flow of the interview and stifling interviewing techniques (Brown, 1991; Williamson, 1990; Bottomley *et al*, 1989). Given the difficulties with conducting a normal interview under such conditions, there was therefore considerable incentive for case officers to talk informally with suspects before interviews began to clarify their accounts. The formal interview would then be shorter and more smoothly flowing.

With the introduction of taped interviews this practice may have declined, although it certainly appears not to have died out. A recent study by McConville and Hodgson (1993) of legal advice to suspects found that, in suspects' consultations with their lawyers, it was not uncommon for them to refer to prior conversations they had had about the offence with investigating officers.

Summary

- Far fewer interviews are now conducted with those who are unfit to be questioned, particularly intoxicated suspects. However, interviews do sometimes occur with those under the influence of drugs or suffering from psychological conditions and the latter may be especially difficult for the police to identify.

- Under PACE, suspects are interviewed less frequently and there has been some reduction in the average length of interviews. The frequency of night-time interviewing appears to have changed little.

- Securing a confession remains an important aim of interviewing suspects, although there is some support for the view that the reason for obtaining confession evidence is now more frequently to supplement other evidence.

- Interviewing officers continue to use a range of tactics designed to secure a confession, although it appears that some unacceptable tactics (for example, exploiting police control over bail and charge decisions) are now used less often. Interviewing styles are frequently accusatorial and inflexible and seldom produce an admission where the suspect has initally raised a defence.

- Around 60 per cent of those interviewed confess – little different from pre-PACE estimates. Confessions are less likely where suspects are legally advised or the evidence is weak; they are more likely in cases involving juveniles or strong evidence.

- Some forms of questioning raise concerns about false confessions, particularly in the case of suggestible suspects. They include leading and 'legal closure' questions and ones which feed information about the offence to the suspect. These concerns are mitigated – although not entirely removed – by the fact that in over 90 per cent of cases proceeded with by the police independent corroborative evidence is obtained.

- Audio-taping of interviews has led to fewer disputes in court about what was said and improved the flow of questioning. Problems have arisen with written records of taped interviews in terms of the omission of salient points, prolixity and prosecution bias. Recent research has shown that records prepared by civilians cost less, are more accurate and of higher overall quality that those prepared by police officers.

- Video-taping of interviews has raised technical problems. It appears to add value to audio-taping in a significant minority of cases – some very serious – in providing assurance that interviewing is fair. It also has worth as a supervisory and training tool. However, videos are rarely played in court.

- Little supervision or monitoring of interviewing takes place. One reason is that supervisory responsibility is often devolved to those who conduct interviews; another is supervisors' reluctance to risk injuring the professional pride of interviewing officers. One report points to the need to overcome cultural barriers to supervision, as well as to equip supervisors with the skills to assess interviewing competencies.

- Some questioning of suspects continues to occur outside of formal police station interviews. Up to 10 per cent of suspects are interviewed after arrest and prior to arrival at the station; one estimate suggests that around a third of suspects who are charged have made admissions prior to reaching the station. Once at the station, a certain amount of unregulated questioning by case officers still occurs.

8 The right of silence

Background

The right of silence[1] has attracted considerable attention in recent years in the context of the debate about where the balance should be struck between the rights of suspects and the public interest in convicting the guilty. The RCCP (1981: 84-7) argued against curtailing the right and PACE made no changes. However, in 1988, the Home Secretary announced the formation of a Working Group to examine ways in which the law might be changed to allow inferences to be drawn from a suspect's failure to answer police questions (Home Office, 1989a). This decision was taken in the belief that the balance had swung too far in favour of experienced and professional criminals. A major contributory factor was felt to be the strengthened right of the suspect to have a legal adviser present during police interviews. Proposals by the Working Group for curtailing the right of silence did not find their way into legislation at the time they were put forward. Subsequently, the RCCJ (1993) followed the approach of the previous Royal Commission by opting against altering the right of silence. The RCCJ feared that the possibility of adverse inferences being drawn from the suspect's failure to talk would create extra psychological pressure upon suspects to answer police questions and could lead to more wrongful convictions of the innocent. However, more recently, the Government has taken the view that this risk is outweighed by the likelihood that more convictions of the guilty, especially in serious cases, would stem from curtailing the right to silence. The Criminal Justice and Public Order Act 1994 (CJPOA) therefore provides for adverse inferences to be drawn in certain circumstances from the suspect's failure to answer police questions.[2]

---

1   This is taken here to refer to the right of suspects not to have adverse inferences drawn against them at court by virtue of their failure to mention during police questioning any fact on which they later rely by way of defence. The term is also sometimes used in the narrower sense to indicate the absence of any obligation on the part of suspects to answer police questions.

2   Under S.34 of the CJPOA, a court may draw such inferences as appear proper from the accused's failure, either during questioning under caution or on being charged, to mention any fact relied on in his or her defence, such fact being one which, in the circumstances existing at the time, the accused could reasonably have been expected to mention. Also, under S.36, inferences may be drawn from the accused's failure or refusal to account for objects, substances or marks or, under S.37, from the accused's failure to account for his or her presence at a particular place, where a constable reasonably believes that the presence at a particular place may be attributable to the participation of that person in the commission of an offence.

The purpose of this section is not to rehearse the debate for and against reform. This has been fully aired elsewhere.[3] However, it is clearly of interest to bring together the main research findings in this area, not least because any future monitoring of the CJPOA provisions will need to take account of the pre-existing situation. It is also relevant in a review of research on PACE to consider what impact the Act has had, for it is often contended that PACE has been associated with a considerable increase in recourse to the right, not least because of the large increase in legal advice to suspects.

This chapter therefore examines the frequency with which suspects exercised the right of silence before and after the introduction of PACE (but prior to the introduction of the CJPOA), the possible link with legal advice, and the implications of silence for the outcome of cases. First, however, some of the problems of research in this area and of making comparisons with the pre-PACE position are considered.

Research on the right of silence

Definitional problems

In a review of research on the right of silence, conducted for the RCCJ, Brown (1994) draws attention to differences between studies in their operational definitions of 'silence' and, consequently, in their estimates of its frequency in police interviews. The main difference has been in the way in which selective non-response to questions has been categorised. As the law stood prior to the CJPOA, the significance of a partial refusal to answer questions was that the interview became admissible as evidence and in some circumstances inferences could be drawn from the suspect's silence.

However, as Leng (1993) has pointed out, selective refusals to answer some kinds of question may have little legal significance, in the sense that neither under the pre-existing nor the present law would it be possible for a court to draw adverse inferences against the suspect. He and others (e.g. Greer, 1990; Baldwin, 1992b) maintain that their inclusion as exercises of the right of silence exaggerates the extent of its use. Among the kinds of questions at issue are ones unrelated to the suspect's own criminal involvement, including ones about his or her personal circumstances or about accomplices (Dixon, 1991b; McConville and Hodgson, 1993). Leng (1993) argues too that temporary refusals to answer questions should be discounted, since neither under the present or pre-existing law could these lead to adverse inferences being drawn against the suspect. Such temporary silences may occur, often on legal advice, where the police have been unwilling to reveal the extent or

---

3   For discussions which have been critical of proposals for reform see Dixon, 1991a; Dixon, 1991b; and Greer, 1990. For an opposing point of view see Zuckerman, 1989.

nature of the evidence (McConville and Hodgson, 1993). Moston *et al* (1992) have noted that it is not uncommon for suspects who have exercised their right of silence, perhaps in such circumstances, subsequently to admit the offence or make damaging statements. They suggest that this occurs in up to a fifth of right of silence cases.

Leng (1993) also argues that a refusal to answer questions to which the suspect has already provided an answer should not be treated as an exercise of the right of silence. Rather contentiously, McConville and Hodgson (1993) go further and suggest that a refusal to answer certain other types of questions also has little relevance to the drawing of adverse inferences against the suspect. Among these they include refusals to answer leading or abusive questions, as well as ones that are repetitious, relate to matters beyond the purview of the suspect, or stem from an arrest made on inadequate evidence.

Leng (1993) makes the further important point that studies have generally not categorised suspects' failures to mention matters on which they subsequently rely in their defence ('ambush' defences) as the exercise of silence.[4] This may be because they actually answered the questions put to them, albeit evasively or untruthfully. Equally, Dixon (1992) points out that studies have sometimes treated evasive replies as silence, although a trial court would not do so. Some studies (for example, Sanders *et al*, 1989; Leng, 1993; Moston and Stephenson, 1993) have treated denials of involvement in an offence without further explanation as exercise of the right of silence. In other studies it is not clear how such responses are treated.

These difficulties and inconsistencies in the classification of the right of silence mean that it is important to be clear, when comparing studies, what exactly was included within the working definition of silence.[5] For the reasons given above, there is a need for a particularly strong 'health warning' where refusal to answer *some* questions is included as exercise of the right of silence without further explanation.

Other methodological problems

Brown (1994), in common with Dixon (1991b) and McConville and Hodgson (1993), notes that, definitional differences aside, studies have counted the frequency of silence in different ways. On the one hand there are some, including those relied upon by the Home Office Working Group, which have used the interview as the unit of analysis (see Sanders *et al*,

---

4   Under the CJPOA, failure to mention such matters may, in certain circumstances, justify inferences being drawn. See footnote 2, Chapter 8.

5   See Brown (1994), Table 1, for a detailed comparison of the definitions of right of silence used in seven research studies drawn upon by the RCCJ.

1989; Williamson, 1990; Baldwin, 1992b; and ACPO, 1993). On the other hand, there are studies which have used the case (see Irving and McKenzie, 1989; Moston *et al*, 1990; Moston and Stephenson, 1993; Leng, 1993; McConville and Hodgson, 1993; Zander and Henderson, 1993; Phillips and Brown, forthcoming). Some (but not all) of the estimates of the extent of silence from this group of studies are lower than those of the former group, since multiple instances of silence in individual cases only count as one exercise of the right of silence.

Another issue to be considered is the reliability of the data. Brown (1994) notes that some researchers have depended on police officers to record and return information. These include studies by Moston *et al* (1990), Williamson (1990), Moston and Stephenson (1993), Zander and Henderson[6] (1993), ACPO (1993) and Phillips and Brown (forthcoming).[7] At the time that the studies were conducted, the police may well have had a vested interest in exaggerating the extent of silence in order to secure legal curtailment of the right. Brown (1994) notes that the highest estimates of silence have generally come from studies where police interviewing officers have been the source of information.

The size and representativeness of the samples of cases used in studies are also important issues. Brown (1994) found that in the research studies available to the RCCJ sample sizes ranged from less than 100 (cases) up to more than 3,000 (interviews). The number of forces included varied from one to seven and the number of stations from one to ten. More recently, a survey by the Association of Chief Police Officers (1993) has covered 3,633 cases in eight forces, while a study by Phillips and Brown (forthcoming) has drawn on over 2,000 cases at ten police stations. Brown (1994) draws attention to some of the dangers of drawing conclusions from limited samples. Firstly, refusal to answer all questions is relatively uncommon and fairly large samples are required to provide reliable information. Secondly, there is a need to be clear whether the sample is or is not intended to be representative of cases generally. If it is not, then it is difficult to make comparisons with other studies that are designed to be representative. He notes that a number of studies have only limited claims to representativeness. These include: Irving and McKenzie (1989) – mixed quota and random samples of CID cases; Sanders *et al* (1989) – non-random sample of legal advice cases; Moston *et al* (1990) – CID cases; Baldwin (1992c) – taped interviews (random sample) and video-taped interviews (non-random); and McConville and Hodgson (1993) – non-random sample of legal advice cases. Thirdly, use of the right of silence may vary between areas. In particular, there is strong evidence that far more suspects in London than elsewhere remain silent.

---

6   Similar information in this study was also collected from prosecution and defence barristers.
7   In the studies by Irving and McKenzie (1989), Sanders *et al* (1989), Leng (1993), Baldwin (1992) and McConville and Hodgson (1993), research personnel either sat in on interviews or scrutinised interview tapes or videos.

Caution must therefore be exercised in generalising from studies restricted to one or two areas. There is a particular need for care in aggregating data from several areas, particularly where the Metropolitan Police is included, without appropriate weighting to take account of differences in force size.

One last issue to note is the time at which data were collected. Research has not been conducted against a static background and intervening events may have influenced suspects' behaviour in interviews. Brown (1994) draws attention particularly to the national implementation of tape-recording of interviews and the growth in legal advice to suspects, especially the surge that occurred with the introduction of the revised PACE Codes of Practice in 1991 (see Chapter 6). To these must be added a possible growth in aware-ness of the right to silence among suspects, following the considerable publicity devoted to the proposed and, subsequently, actual curtailment of the right. It is relevant to note, therefore, that research in this area spans a considerable time period. Leng's (1993) data collection was carried out between 1986 and 1988, Irving and McKenzie's (1989) in 1986 and 1987 and Williamson's (1990) in 1987 and 1988. The most recent data are those collected for the ACPO (1993) study during September 1993 and for Phillips and Brown's (forthcoming) study during late 1993 and early 1994.

Use of the right of silence

Evidence of pre-PACE practices

Gauging the impact of PACE on suspects' exercise of the right of silence is impeded by the lack of pre-PACE information and problems of comparability between the pre- and post-PACE data that does exist. Only the study by Irving and McKenzie (1989) has attempted a direct 'before and after' comparison, drawing upon samples of cases from the same police station. However, this study is marred by its use of different classifications of silence in the 'before' and 'after' phases, its limited geographical scope, small sample sizes and sampling procedures.

A study by Softley *et al* (1980), drawing on interviews with 187 suspects at four police stations, found that four per cent refused to answer all questions 'of substance' and eight per cent refused to answer some questions, making a total of 12 per cent exercising their right of silence. Irving's study, based on a sample of just 60 suspects at Brighton police station, found that eight per cent refused to answer questions at all or refused to answer all questions of substance (Irving, 1990). Other pre-PACE estimates of silence are of more limited value because they relate to particular sub-groups of suspects. For example, Zander (1979) gives a rate of four per cent for a sample of those tried at the Old Bailey. McConville and Baldwin (1981) give figures of seven per cent and four per cent for defendants appearing in Crown Court cases in London and Birmingham respectively. The Birmingham figure is the same as that found by Mitchell (1983) in a study at Worcester Crown Court. The McConville and Baldwin figure excludes cases in which some questions only were refused, but includes ones in which there was no police interview.

Use of silence in PACE interviews

Studies since the introduction of PACE have provided figures on the proportion of suspects exercising their right of silence ranging from 6 per cent (Leng, 1993) up to 22 per cent (ACPO, 1993) and 23 per cent (Phillips and Brown, forthcoming). The review of studies by Brown (1994) attempted to reconcile the wide disparities in the figures. He concluded that, to a considerable extent, the wide variations were accounted for by differences in the definitions of silence used and in sampling methods. Studies varied considerably in terms of sample size, geographical spread and type of cases included. Brown's review does not include several more recent studies, notably those by ACPO (1993), Phillips and Brown (forthcoming), McConville and Hodgson (1993)[8] and Zander and Henderson's (1993) Crown Court study for the RCCJ. However, his conclusions may well be relevant to these studies, although with some reservations (considered below) in relation to the ACPO study.

He suggests that several points need to be taken into account if a dependable estimate of the extent of silence is to be arrived at. Firstly, studies in which independent observers have collected data have generally produced lower estimates than those where the police have undertaken the task. As Leng (1993) has noted, organisations representing all grades in the police service have campaigned for some time to curtail the right to silence. Consequently, they have some incentive to exaggerate the extent of silence. 'Independent' studies may therefore provide more reliable estimates. Secondly, the rate of silence may vary between areas and between categories of offence. Studies which have sampled a range of areas and offences are more likely to be dependable. Thirdly, there is good evidence that the rate of silence in the Metropolitan Police is considerably higher than elsewhere. It therefore makes sense to consider this force separately. Lastly, given the inconsistencies in the way studies have categorised partial non-response to police questions, the scope for data collection errors in such cases, and the likelihood that some selective refusals to answer questions will have little legal significance, it makes sense to consider these cases separately from those in which all questions are refused.

Taking all these factors into account, Brown suggests that a reasonable estimate is that not more than five per cent of suspects outside of the

---

8   This study sampled only suspects who had received legal advice; it is considered further below in relation to the link between legal advice and silence.

Metropolitan Police refuse to answer all questions, while within the capital the figure is probably somewhere between seven per cent and nine per cent. To these figures must be added the proportion of suspects who exercise silence selectively. The available figures here vary greatly for the reasons already mentioned. Brown suggests that a best estimate is that a further five per cent of suspects in non-Metropolitan forces may selectively refuse questions, while in the capital the figure is probably around seven per cent. These estimates of selective refusal are conservative ones which take into account, for example, that up to a fifth of suspects who refuse to answer some questions subsequently admit offences or make damaging statements (Moston *et al*, 1992) and cannot be said to have exercised their right of silence in any significant way. Similarly, they take account of those cases in which silence is purely nominal or incidental and does not prevent suspects answering questions about the offence for which they have been arrested. Taking the estimates for complete and partial refusal to answer questions together, Brown suggests that, in all, the right of silence is exercised in up to 10 per cent of cases outside of London and in up to 16 per cent in the Metropolitan Police area.

On the issue of whether PACE can be said to have led to any increase in the use of silence by suspects, Brown (1994) suggests that there is no clear evidence that this is so in the general run of cases. The pre-PACE estimates of the use of silence (see above) in the studies by Softley *et al* (1980) and Irving (1980) are not greatly at variance with the levels of silence found in the post-PACE studies reviewed by Brown. Thus, Softley gives a figure of four per cent refusal to answer all questions, while Brown estimates the post-PACE level at around five per cent outside London. Irving, who used the same station for his pre-PACE and post-PACE studies, actually found that rather fewer suspects in the post-PACE samples than in the pre-PACE sample refused to answer all questions (Irving and McKenzie, 1989). However, both Softley's and Irving's studies are based on relatively small samples of cases and it is doubtful whether they can be relied on as indicators of the extent of silence among suspects generally in pre-PACE days.

Since Brown's review was undertaken, three further studies have provided useful evidence of possible changes in the suspect's recourse to silence. Zander and Henderson (1993) carried out a national 'snapshot' survey of all Crown Court cases completed during the last two weeks of February 1992. The police and prosecution and defence barristers were asked about defendants' use of the right of silence in police interviews. The responses, which varied between the different sets of respondents, suggested that between 11 and 13 per cent of defendants had refused to answer all police questions and that between nine and 17 per cent refused some questions (although it is not specified whether this is taken to mean some questions *of substance*). Crown Court cases are generally at the more serious end of the spectrum and the findings cannot be taken to be representative of suspects generally. However, they may be compared with the findings of pre-PACE studies of Crown Court defendants by Zander (1979), McConville and Baldwin (1981) and Mitchell (1983). As noted above, these studies found rates of silence of between four per cent and seven per cent (presumed to be silence to all questions). There is some evidence, therefore, that in more serious cases, suspects are more often remaining silent than they did before the introduction of PACE.

The other two recent studies also provide some support for the view that, irrespective of whether there was any initial effect of PACE on the use of silence, there has been a much more recent rise in the rate at which suspects refuse to answer police questions. The study, conducted at the instigation of ACPO, was broadly based, with eight forces in the South East of England returning data on 3,633 suspects processed for recordable offences during the period 13 – 27 September 1993 (ACPO, 1993). The survey provides figures on the exercise of silence which are considerably higher than the estimates derived by Brown from the studies available at the time of his review. Ten per cent of suspects refused to answer all questions and 12 per cent refused some questions (no indication is given as to whether this includes temporary, incidental or nominal refusals). In Phillips and Brown's (forthcoming) study, carried out in late 1993 and early 1994, very similar results to the ACPO work were found. Ten per cent of suspects refused to answer all questions and 13 per cent refused some questions. At the two stations sampled in the Metropolitan Police, an average of 32 per cent of suspects refused some or all questions. Phillips and Brown's data are drawn from a sample of over 2,000 cases from ten police stations. Police officers completed a pro forma for each case in which they carried out interviews, providing details of the extent and nature of refusals to answer questions.

The implication is that more suspects are now exercising their right of silence than at the time the other post-PACE studies were undertaken. It is plausible that such a change may have occurred, given the lapse of time between the studies reviewed by Brown (none of which were based on data collected later than 1991 and some on considerably older data) and the ACPO and Phillips and Brown work. In the meantime, as was noted earlier, various developments may have affected the suspect's response to police questioning in a way tending to encourage reliance on silence. For example, the revised PACE Codes of Practice (introduced on 1 April 1991) have been associated with a substantial rise in the provision of legal advice to suspects.[9] It may also reasonably be argued that suspects may have become increasingly aware of their right of silence, following media attention to miscarriages of justice, the setting up and reporting of the RCCJ, and Government proposals for changes in the law in this area.

9   The link between legal advice and the suspect's silence is reviewed critically below.

Another reason for believing that silence is now exercised more often is that the ACPO and Phillips and Brown figure for refusal to answer *all* questions is, at 10 per cent, considerably higher than all previous estimates.[10] It is reasonable to suggest that there is less scope for error or differences of interpretation by those collecting data in relation to a complete refusal to answer questions. Therefore, irrespective of how partial refusal to answer was defined or of whether the figures on partial refusal are accurate, there are good grounds for believing that total silence in interviews has increased.

However, the ACPO figures in particular must be treated with some caution because there is insufficient information available about the study to assess the soundness of its methods. A brief résumé of the study, issued by ACPO (1993), states that data were collected about 3,633 suspects processed for recordable offences in eight South East forces during a two-week period in September 1993. It does not say whether this amounted to all suspects at all stations in the region or, if a sample, how this was selected. More importantly, there is no information on how silence was categorised, other than that refusals to answer all or some questions were separated. It is unclear how rigorously these categories were defined. Without clear instructions to those recording the data there is a danger of the figures being inflated. The danger is especially acute in this instance, since the police themselves collected the data and it was almost certainly common knowledge that the purpose of the survey was to provide further support for the case in favour of curtailing the right of silence. There are two ways (other than deliberate falsification) in which the figures might exaggerate the use of silence. Firstly, the figures on refusal to answer all questions might include cases in which incidental questions were actually answered. Secondly, the category of partial silence might include purely temporary refusals to answer questions. As was noted above, in up to a fifth of such cases suspects may in fact go on to admit the offence or make damaging statements. Partial silence may also include refusals to answer incidental questions, although questions about the offence were answered.

Use of silence by serious/professional criminals

A particular concern is whether the overlapping groups of those involved in serious offences or who offend repeatedly exercise their right of silence disproportionately (Home Office, 1989a). Looking first at those detained for serious offences, the available evidence suggests that more suspects in such cases do exercise their right to silence. In the study by Moston *et al* (1990), detectives rated offences according to their perceived severity as 'trivial',

---

10 The exception is a figure of 12 per cent in Williamson's (1990) study set in the Metropolitan Police. However, it has already been noted that silence is exercised more frequently in this force than elsewhere. Also, silence was measured on a per interview rather than a per case basis, and this tends to exaggerate its frequency.

'moderate' or 'very serious'. The latter included PACE serious arrestable offences.[11] Some or all questions were refused in 23 per cent of 'very serious' offences compared with 15 per cent of those rated 'moderate' and nine per cent of 'trivial' offences. This survey, as noted earlier, was confined to CID cases and under-represents less serious cases. The survey also covered only the Metropolitan Police, where the right of silence is used more frequently than elsewhere. However, similar findings are reported by Phillips and Brown (forthcoming) in their research set in a wide range of forces and sampling cases representative of all levels of seriousness.

McConville and Hodgson (1993) also rated cases according to seriousness in their study of legal advice and the right of silence. They found no apparent relationship between seriousness and exercise of silence. However, their sample was confined to cases in which suspects had received legal advice and these may not have been typical of right of silence cases generally. Furthermore, their sample of right of silence cases was probably too small (47) to draw reliable conclusions.

Other studies have simply categorised offences into bands of seriousness according to the offence label attached to them. This may be sound in the case of the most serious offences, such as murder or rape, but there are considerable margins of error in the case of some crimes, such as robbery, where offences of widely varying severity may be included under the same offence label.

The recent ACPO (1993) survey found that use of silence varied greatly between different types of offence. Thus, while on average 22 per cent of suspects exercised their right of silence, over half of robbery suspects and one-third of burglary suspects refused some or all questions.

Perhaps bearing in mind the difficulties of identifying serious cases, two studies have singled out only those at the most serious end of the spectrum and defined by PACE as 'serious arrestable offences'. Williamson (1990) found that silence was exercised in 26 per cent of interviews for serious arrestable offences in the Metropolitan area compared with 21 per cent of other offences; in West Yorkshire the respective figures were 17 per cent and 13 per cent. McKenzie and Irving (1988) also found that around 40 per cent of those detained for serious arrestable offences exercised complete or selective silence, compared with eight per cent of those held for other crimes. However, their figures are based on a small sample from just one station and are probably not generalisable.

---

11   It would appear from the fact that as many as 28 per cent of crimes were rated 'very serious' that this category cannot have consisted exclusively of serious arrestable offences.

Turning to the criminal experience of the suspect, there is a consensus that those with previous convictions are more likely to refuse to answer police questions and that this likelihood increases the more convictions the suspect has. The actual figures given by studies vary, in line with differences already noted in their overall estimates of silence. In the Metropolitan Police, Williamson (1990) found that 27 per cent of suspects with previous convictions refused some or all questions, compared with 17 per cent of those without a criminal record; in West Yorkshire the equivalent figures were 15 per cent and eight per cent. Phillips and Brown (forthcoming) found that refusals to answer questions among those with previous convictions ran at a level of 28 per cent, double the figure for those without prior criminal experience. More marked differences have been found by Moston *et al* (1990), again in the Metropolitan Police, and ACPO (1993) in their survey of eight South East forces. In the former study, 21 per cent of those with previous convictions exercised their right of silence compared with nine per cent of those without a crimnal record and, in the latter, 35 per cent compared with 12 per cent.

The ACPO (1993) and Williamson (1990) studies both relate silence to the number of previous convictions. The former suggests that those with five or more convictions are about 50 per cent more likely to remain silent than those with only one or two previous convictions (41% compared with 26%). Less pronounced differences are noted by Williamson, although he identifies the same trend.

The ACPO survey also ties together the themes of criminal professionalism and crime seriousness by relating the rate of silence both to number of previous convictions and the type of offence. It was found that those with previous convictions were more likely to exercise their right of silence in serious offences. For example, those with five or more convictions remained silent in over 47 per cent of serious offences compared with 35 per cent of other offences.

Impact of silence on interviews

There are conflicting findings on the effect of the suspect's silence on the course of police interviews. Moston *et al* (1990) found that it caused major problems and that interviews often disintegrated, with officers being uncertain how to proceed. In contrast, McConville and Hodgson (1993) found that interviews were rarely abandoned when silence was exercised; rather, they suggest that police officers saw this as indicative of guilt and as a reason to persist with questioning. Sanders (1988) argues that continued questioning once a suspect has indicated his or her intention to remain silent runs counter to the principle that confessions should be provided voluntarily.

Moston *et al* (1990) and McConville and Hodgson (1993) agree that officers have developed certain strategies for coping with silent suspects. A common technique was to increase the pressure by revealing more of the evidence against the suspect. Other strategies were: changing the conversation to a less stressful subject than the allegation; persisting with the existing line of questioning; or reasoning that silence is not constructive for the suspect or that it is the officers' duty to persist with questioning in order to arrive at the truth. McConville and Hodgson (1993) and McConville *et al* (1994) add a further three strategies to this list. Of these, the most frequent was for interviewing officers to tell silent suspects that they took their silence to mean that they were guilty (even though a court would not have been able to draw this inference). Another was to try to persuade suspects to speak by drawing attention to aspects of their body language (for example, nods of the head) which interviewers took to mean agreement with police questions. Lastly, in a few cases where silence was apparently the result of legal advice, officers attempted to undercut the position of the adviser.

A further response, noted by Thornton (1989) in an observational study of CID work carried out when contemporaneous notes were in use, was for detectives to move outside of PACE rules when they became frustrated with the suspect's silence. They might cease to record details of questions and answers and adopt more coercive strategies (although physical duress was never observed). It should be noted, however, that this option is probably not open to detectives now that interviews are tape-recorded and interruptions have to be accounted for. Leng (1993) found some evidence in a few cases of informal contacts between police and suspect after an initial refusal to answer questions, leading to a subsequent interview and admissions.[12]

Legal advice and silence

Before PACE was enacted, few suspects secured legal advice and lawyers are therefore unlikely to have had any significant impact on suspects' behaviour in police interviews. In Softley *et al*'s (1980) study, for example, only two out of 187 suspects received legal advice prior to interview. It is, of course, possible that some suspects remained silent because they had requested but not received legal advice and were uncertain of their position. However, the study provides no information about whether any suspects in this category exercised their right of silence.

Since the introduction of PACE, several studies have suggested that there is an association between receipt of legal advice and exercise of the right of silence. It appears that those legally advised are up to four times more likely

---

12   See too Chapter 7 under 'Informal questioning at the police station'.

to remain silent than those not advised. The actual figures given vary in line with different studies' estimates of the extent of silence (see above). The most startling finding is that of the recent ACPO (1993) survey which found that no less than 57 per cent of those legally advised compared to 13 per cent of those not advised refused to answer some or all questions. A wide discrepancy between legally advised suspects and others was also found in the recent work by Phillips and Brown (forthcoming). In their study, 39 per cent of the former group refused to answer some or all questions, compared with just 12 per cent of the latter.

By way of comparison, Williamson (1990) provides figures of 39 per cent (those advised) and 17 per cent (those not advised) in the Metropolitan Police and 23 per cent and eight per cent in West Yorkshire. Moston *et al* (1990) give figures of 33 per cent and five per cent, while Baldwin (1992b) provide rates of 22 per cent and eight per cent. McConville and Hodgson (1993), while not looking at cases in which suspects did not receive legal advice, found that 30 per cent of those who did obtain advice exercised their right of silence. At the lower end of the scale, Sanders *et al* (1989) found silence was exercised in 16 per cent of legal advice cases compared with just five per cent of other cases, while Moston and Stephenson (1993) found figures of 10 per cent and three per cent.

There has been a tendency to assume that there is a causal connection between receipt of legal advice and suspects remaining silent. Moston *et al* (1990) state that: "... the use of silence shows a clear cut pattern. Solicitors are routinely advising their clients not to speak to the police" (see too ACPO, 1993). Others have noted that it is a widely held view in the police service that silent suspects have been reinforced in their decision to remain silent by legal advice (Baldwin, 1992b; McConville and Hodgson, 1993). The apparent link between legal advice and silence was an important factor in calls for the curtailment of the right to silence (Dixon, 1992). However, some doubt has been thrown on the connection and its significance. Baldwin (1992b) refers to an 'elaborate and pervasive mythology' surrounding the subject among police officers.

The evidence reviewed in Chapter 6 indeed suggests that solicitors do not routinely advise silence or adopt an interventionist role in interviews. It is not intended to reiterate this argument here and the reader is referred to Chapter 6 ('Advice to remain silent'). However, it is relevant at this point to examine the correlation between the advice received by suspects and their actual behaviour during interview.

McConville and Hodgson (1993) found that in 60 per cent of cases in which suspects had received legal advice they remained silent during interview, although they had not received advice to this effect. In the majority of these cases legal advisers had not actively urged the opposite course (i.e. to answer questions), but simply went along with their client's desire to remain silent or preferred no clear advice. However, in a quarter of these cases suspects remained silent *despite* their adviser advising to the contrary or assuming that they would answer. Dixon (1991b) has noted that one explanation for silence in these circumstances may be that suspects sometimes see legal advisers as part of the system ranged against them and react adversely.

McConville and Hodgson (1993) also found that in 40 per cent of cases in which suspects remained silent they had actually received legal advice to this effect. However, judging from exchanges between suspect and adviser they consider that some of this group would have declined to answer questions even if this had not been explicitly advised. The presence of a solicitor at interviews may have done no more than stiffen their existing resolve. Sanders *et al* (1989) go further and argue that there are few cases in which silence is advised by legal advisers where this is not in line with the suspect's pre-existing intentions. However, their conclusions lack the empirical basis of those of McConville and Hodgson because they were unable to observe adviser/client consultations on as systematic a basis.

Further support for the view that legal advice is important in ensuring the suspect's silence in only a minority of cases comes from the Crown Court study conducted for the RCCJ. Zander and Henderson (1993) found that in nearly 80 per cent of cases in which suspects had received legal advice this did not lead to silence. Either the suspect had been silent prior to receiving advice or was not silent even after receiving it. In only 21 per cent of cases was the suspect silent after consulting a legal adviser where there was no prior indication of an intention to refuse to answer questions. These findings cannot be taken to be typical of suspects generally because they relate to Crown Court defendants. In particular, the rate of silence may be higher and the nature of the advice given by legal advisers different in view of the more serious nature of the cases involved.

This discussion of legal advice and silence may be concluded by briefly drawing attention to the point that a significant proportion of those who exercise their right of silence do not seek legal advice. In some studies this is the majority of silent suspects: thus, in Williamson's (1990) study nearly 60 per cent of those remaining silent had received no legal advice. More recent studies have put the figure somewhat lower, probably reflecting the growth in legal advice to suspects. In the ACPO (1993) study, for example, 35 per cent of silent suspects had not received legal advice. Coupling these findings with those discussed above, that the suspect's silence in cases where legal advice *is* received is frequently not the result of legal advice, this means that in the great majority of cases silence and legal advice are unrelated. There is, however, very little information available about what does prompt suspects to remain silent in the absence of legal advice to this effect. Perhaps the best explanation is offered by Dixon (1991b), who characterises most instances of silence either as an antagonistic refusal to co-operate by those hostile to the police or as an attempt to protect accomplices, but rarely as a reasoned strategy based on legal advice.

Silence and the outcome of cases

Moston *et al* (1990) considered the possibility of a link between exercise of the right of silence and whether suspects are charged. There appeared to be no significant association and they suggest that this was because, in just over half of the cases in which silence was exercised, it was mitigated by other factors. Most frequently, there was other strong evidence. Less often, suspects made some form of admission although they had refused to answer some questions. In only around eight per cent of cases – those in which the evidence was only moderate or weak and there was no admission – may use of silence have had some bearing on whether a suspect was charged. The authors suggest that in some cases in which the evidence was moderate and silence was used, this may have been a counter-productive ploy. Apparently, such suspects were more likely to be charged than if they had actively denied the offence and it is suggested that this may have been a form of retaliation against the suspect for refusing to co-operate with questioning.

Phillips and Brown (forthcoming) also explored the relationship between case outcome and exercise of silence. They found that those who exercised their right of silence were more likely to be processed, whether by way of charge or caution, than other suspects. The manner in which they were dealt with also differed significantly: they were much more likely to be charged rather than cautioned, and this probably reflects, firstly, that they were dealt with for more serious offences and, secondly, that where the offence was not admitted the option of a caution was not open.

Despite these findings, the belief that use of silence is instrumental in suspects being freed without charge has continued to be seductive. Responding to this concern, Leng (1993) has made a more detailed study of cases in which the police decided to take no further action (NFA). He found that, of the cases NFAed in his sample (268 out of 1,080), suspects had exercised their right of silence in only four per cent (9 cases). Generally, NFA decisions were made because the police were satisfied with the suspect's innocence or the suspect had denied the offence and there was no obvious scope for further investigation. Furthermore, where the right of silence had been exercised, the decision not to proceed was usually unrelated to this, but more bound up with the lack of other evidence.

Leng is sceptical about whether curtailing the right of silence would lead to more suspects being charged. He argues that, even if suspects did answer questions, they would tend to give replies which were of little evidential value: for example, denials of involvement or stories which were difficult to check. He found this to be the situation in three-quarters of the cases in his sample where suspects had answered questions and which were NFAed despite police doubts about the suspect's innocence. Without other independent evidence, the police cannot proceed. Conversely, if they have such other evidence, the suspect's silence would make little difference to a successful prosecution. It must be accepted that there is some logic to this view. However, the possibility must be considered that the extent to which suspects use their right of silence and the circumstances in which they do so, may have changed since Leng's data were collected (1986 to 1988). His estimate of silence was substantially lower than recent figures (see above). With more frequent exercise of silence, there could be more cases in which the drawing of inferences from the suspect's silence might tip the balance towards a successful prosecution, assuming a certain level of independent evidence is also available.

Several studies have looked beyond charge at the relationship between the exercise of silence and the outcome of cases at court. Zander and Henderson (1993) found that those pleading not guilty to all charges were more likely to have exercised their right of silence than those pleading guilty. The precise figures given vary, depending on whether prosecution or defence barristers' or police estimates are relied upon, but it seems that between 24 and 35 per cent of the former group had exercised their right of silence compared with 15 to 21 per cent of the latter. However, they also found that, contrary to what is often assumed, many of those who refuse to answer police questions plead guilty. Indeed, around half of silent suspects pleaded guilty to some or all charges, compared with just over 60 per cent of suspects who did not exercise their right of silence.

A rather different conclusion is reached by Moston *et al* (1992). They found that a much *higher* proportion of those who had exercised their right of silence pleaded guilty at court: 67 per cent compared with 49 per cent of other suspects. However, being based on a relatively small sample this finding may be less reliable.[13] Nevertheless, taking the findings at face value, they seek to explain this apparent anomaly by arguing that silence is initially used as a ploy by suspects knowledgeable of the legal system to secure tactical benefits, such as release. If this fails, then they may plead guilty because they know this will attract a lesser penalty than if they had pleaded

---

13   Moston *et al* base their conclusions on sub-samples of 52 silence cases and 52 non-silence cases. The conclusions of the Crown Court study are based on several different samples: 589 not guilty pleas and 643 guilty pleas in the prosecution barristers' survey; 597 and 693 respectively in the defence barristers' survey; and 578 and 595 cases respectively in the police survey. In the prosecution barristers' survey 337 suspects exercised their right to silence and 1,165 did not; in the defence barristers' survey the figures were 279 and 1,200; and in the police survey 387 and 971.

not guilty. In view of the findings of the Crown Court study, based on much larger samples, about the way in which silent defendants plead, it is doubtful whether the interpretation Moston *et al* place upon their findings is valid. While the Crown Court study found that a perhaps surprisingly high proportion of silent suspects do plead guilty, the proportion was lower than among other suspects. Moston *et al*'s assertions also do not accord with the views of other commentators who have argued that suspects rarely adopt such a rational model of decision-making. Dixon (1991b) notes that non-co-operation appears to be related less to criminal professionalism than to anti-police attitudes. From a police perspective, some suspects are just difficult and obstructive (rather than calculating). McKenzie and Irving (1988) also characterise exercise of silence in some cases as 'bloody-mindedness'. It should also be noted that in around half of cases silence is selective: Dixon (1991b) points out that suspects may not necessarily be choosing which questions to answer in order to secure tactical benefits for themselves but maybe to shield accomplices. He also makes the point that suspects appear ill-briefed about the possible adverse consequences for them at court of selective use of silence. This is hardly in tune with a calculating approach.

The Crown Court study found no evidence that, for those pleading not guilty, silence increased the chances of acquittal (Zander and Henderson, 1993). The estimates vary depending on which data source is used (see above), but it would appear that no more than 31 per cent of those acquitted had remained silent compared with a maximum of 40 per cent of those convicted. Looked at another way, around 45 per cent of those who remained silent were acquitted compared with around 50 per cent of those who were not silent. Moston *et al* (1992) also agree that fewer of those who exercise their right of silence are acquitted.

Whether silence has any bearing on the outcome of cases depends, of course, on what other evidence is available. Leng (1993) considered this question both in relation to discontinuance of cases by the CPS and in relation to acquittals at court. He found that suspects had exercised their right of silence in only 10 per cent of cases dropped by the CPS. These cases were generally discontinued on account of evidential weaknesses (i.e. other than the lack of a confession) which had either emerged since charge or been overlooked by the police. At court, 10 per cent of those acquitted following contested trials had also exercised their right of silence. Again, lack of supporting evidence largely explained these decisions. The view that exercise of silence has relatively little bearing on CPS decisions or on acquittal at court receives some support too from Moston *et al* (1992). They found no difference in the extent to which the CPS proceeded with cases in which suspects had and had not remained silent. And, at court, those who had exercised their right of silence stood less chance of being acquitted than those who had not.

There is reason to question the conclusion drawn by Leng (1993) that use of silence does not bear greatly on the outcome of cases. Firstly, as has been noted above, his study is based on quite old data which almost certainly do not reflect the present extent of silence nor, possibly, the circumstances in which it is now used. Secondly, the sub-samples of cases used are quite small and there is no guarantee that his findings are representative of practice at the time his study was undertaken.[14] Thus, his analysis of the circumstances in which discontinuance by the CPS or acquittal occurred in right of silence cases is based on just five and three cases respectively. Thirdly, it may be argued that where the other evidence is weak the suspect's silence does have a bearing on the outcome because, if he or she had been induced to speak and incriminated him or herself, a conviction might have been obtained. It is possible that the new provisions on the right of silence in the CJPOA 1994 may mean that suspects will increasingly be persuaded to answer questions.

'Ambush' defences

Linked with the right of silence is the issue of the extent to which defendants reveal defences at trial which they have not previously raised during police questioning (so-called ambush' defences). Such defences, it has been argued, may hamper the prosecution because it may be difficult to investigate them due to the time that has elapsed between the offence and the court hearing or because of the short notice provided (Home Office, 1989a). Where 'ambush' defences are raised, the suspect may have refused to answer questions during police interviews, but this is not necessarily the case. It is quite possible for the suspect to have answered all questions, albeit evasively or untruthfully. This means, as Leng (1993) has pointed out, that studies which have restricted their examination of the right of silence to suspects' responses during police interviews will not necessarily have identified cases in which suspects fail to mention a defence later relied on at court.

Leng's study for the RCCJ is the only one to have examined this particular aspect of the exercise of silence. His findings are based on an analysis of 113 cases which either were dropped by the prosecution (54 cases) or led to contested trials (59 cases, of which 25 led to acquittals and 34 to findings of guilt). Leng found no evidence of cases being dropped by the CPS because of new defences. In the sample of acquittals, he found that defences not previously mentioned during police questioning were raised in court in one-third of cases and in the guilty sample in around one-fifth. However, in his view, hardly any of these could be said to have involved 'ambush' defences. For example, they related to matters which the defendant could not have

---

14   These two criticisms may also be levelled at Moston *et al* (1992). Their data are drawn from 1989. Also, the sample of cases proceeding to court and the number of acquittals were small. The study only sampled CID cases.

raised, or was given no chance to raise, during police questioning or depended on evidence that was already in the possession of the prosecution. In only one case, in which the defendant was found guilty, was a new defence raised which could clearly be categorised as an 'ambush' defence.

Leng concludes that the problem is not so much one of 'ambush' defences but of unanticipated defences not amounting to an 'ambush'. Such defences sometimes involve challenges on points of law or procedure and, by their nature, are raised for the first time at court. Other defences are unanticipated because defendants are either not given an opportunity to raise them during interview or do so, but no attempt is made to investigate them further or no reference is made to them in the record of interview passed to the CPS. Leng argues that this problem is endemic in an adversarial system in which the police see their role as being to contruct a case for the prosecution.

Summary

- Because of differences in their methods, geographical coverage, definition of 'silence' and the date when they were conducted, studies have provided widely varying estimates of the use by suspects of the right of silence in police interviews.

- A review of many of these studies suggests that around five per cent of suspects outside the MPS and between seven and nine per cent in the MPS refuse to answer all questions, while around five per cent and seven per cent respectively refuse to answer some questions of significance. This probably represents little change from the pre-PACE situation, although comparative data is sparse.

- The most recent figures point to a possible change in the trend, suggesting that increasing numbers of suspects are having recourse to silence and that up to 10 per cent are refusing all questions.

- Those detained for more serious offences and suspects with previous convictions are more likely to decline to answer police questions.

- Suspects who receive legal advice are far more likely to remain silent. Only in a minority of cases is this a direct result of legal advice. More often, advisers either proffer no such advice, go along with their client's wishes or urge the opposite course.

- Some interviewing officers abandon interviews with silent suspects but others have various techniques – such as increasing the pressure by revealing further incriminating information – to elicit answers.

- Police decisions whether to take no further action are largely unrelated to whether suspects have exercised their right of silence. Those who exercise their right of silence are more likely to be charged than cautioned. There appears to be no link between use of silence and CPS decisions to discontinue cases.

- Those who plead not guilty at court are more likely to have refused to answer police questions than those who plead guilty. However, those pleading not guilty who have exercised their right of silence are less likely to be acquitted than other defendants.

- Significant minorities of defendants who plead not guilty raise defences not previously mentioned during questioning. However, few such defences genuinely amount to 'ambushes' because, for example, they relate to matters the suspect could not have raised during police interviews.

9 Juveniles

PACE makes particular provision for the treatment whilst in police detention of several 'at risk' groups: juveniles, the mentally disordered and mentally handicapped, the deaf, those with speaking difficulties and those unable to understand English. It was noted in Chapter 1 that concerns about the treatment of two of these groups – juveniles and the mentally handicapped – were an important stimulus for the setting up of the RCCP and, ultimately, for the enactment of PACE.

This chapter is concerned with juveniles. A number of studies have touched on the treatment of juveniles under PACE, although only two have had this as their primary focus. The first of these, by Evans (1993), was commissioned by the RCCJ and examined the interviewing of juveniles. The work is based on an analysis of a sample of interview tapes. More recently, Evans and Rawstorne (1994) have looked at aspects of the role, qualifications and training of appropriate adults.[1] Their findings are based on 140 interviews with custody officers and social work staff in the North West of England.

The issue with which this chapter principally deals is the operation of the safeguards which apply after the arrest of a juvenile. No special protections apply prior to arrival at the police station. Dixon (1990) has noted, however, that under-17s are over-represented in recorded figures for stop and search: over a quarter of stops and searches in the Hull study were among this age group. Other surveys have found similar concentrations of stops among the young (Painter *et al*, 1989; Skogan, 1990; Crawford *et al*, 1990). Thomas (1988) has also noted that those in care are more likely to be known to the police and this may mark them out for discrimination.

Appropriate adults for juveniles

Various studies suggest that juveniles constitute between 14 per cent and 19 per cent of those detained (Bottomley *et al*, 1989; Brown, 1989; Brown *et al*, 1992; Phillips and Brown, forthcoming) although numbers vary considerably between areas. The principal safeguard for juvenile detainees is the requirement for the police to secure the attendance of an appropriate

---

1   This study also looked at the same issue in relation to mentally disordered and mentally handicapped detainees.

adult. That person will normally be a parent, guardian or social worker (Code C 1.7), and their role is to advise and assist the suspect (C 3.12). A juvenile may consult the appropriate adult privately at any time. Other than in exceptional circumstances, police interviews may not take place in the absence of the appropriate adult. This last provision is intended to be an important safeguard. Code C (formerly in a guidance note but now in a provision of the Code – see 11.16) states the purpose of the adult's presence at interview as being: to advise the person being questioned and to observe whether or not the interview is being conducted properly and fairly; and to facilitate communication with the person being interviewed. The police are required to inform adults of their function.

Who is appropriate?

The presumption in Code C is that parents or guardians should generally act as appropriate adults (1C). Two studies, by Brown (1989) and Evans (1993), found that this indeed occurred in around three-quarters of cases, with social workers stepping into the role in most of the remaining cases. In the recent past, there appears to have been something of a shift towards social workers rather than parents acting as appropriate adults (Brown *et al*, 1992; Evans and Rawstorne, 1994). The former study, which compared practice before and after revised PACE Codes of Practice were brought in, found that parents attended in 60 per cent of cases[2] after the revised Codes were introduced, 10 per cent fewer than before, and that there was a corresponding rise in cases attended by social workers. The revised Code makes it clear that parents who are in any way party to the offence (as witness, victim or confidant of the suspect) are not appropriate and this, the study suggests, may explain the change. The Code also now makes it clear that solicitors acting in their professional capacity may not act as appropriate adults. The same research found that this was not a common practice under the pre-existing Code, but that it has now disappeared. Most recently, research by Phillips and Brown (forthcoming) has suggested a diminution in the demand for social workers services as appropriate adults. In this study, they were called upon in only 20 per cent of juvenile cases. While it is possible that the difference between this finding and those of previous studies may reflect variations in practice between the areas sampled, it may be related to a reduction in the number of children in care (Department of Health, 1995).

---

2   In another seven per cent relatives acted as appropriate adults.

The appropriate adult's role

Several commentators have drawn attention to the difficulties and conflicts attached to the appropriate adult's task, particularly where that person is a parent or relative who is unlikely to be aware of the law or police procedures. Dixon (1990) and Brown *et al* (1992) point out that parents may often be disorientated, scared and compliant with police requests. Parents of first-time offenders are particularly likely to be shocked, anxious and intimidated (Evans and Rawstorne, 1994). Few are articulate and well-informed enough to provide commonsense advice. A study of detective work by Thornton (1989) notes how CID officers may co-opt appropriate adults to their side against the juvenile. Thomas (1988) notes that the Codes give scanty guidance about how adults should fulfil their role, while Evans (1993) and Evans and Rawstorne (1994) are doubtful whether adults are actually told by the police what their role is, other than in very general terms. Some confirmation of this view is provided by Irving and McKenzie (1989), who observed no cases involving juveniles in their Brighton research in which such information was given. Where the adult is a social worker, the police may assume that he or she is aware of their role – an assumption that may not necessarily be justified (see below).

Dixon (1990) argues that the current provisions reflect an uneasy mix between a parent's right to be with their child when in trouble and the child's need for effective advice and support. Irving and McKenzie (1989) doubt whether a parent is likely to know that an interview is being conducted fairly. It is not surprising, therefore, that in 75 per cent of cases they make no contribution at all (Evans, 1993). Nor are they always supportive of their children: Evans (ibid.), with Dixon *et al* (1990b) and Fennell (1994), note that parents sometimes see their role as to extract a confession, using methods that would have amounted to contraventions of the Codes of Practice if used by the police. Evans and Rawstorne (1994) found that custody and interviewing officers tended to prefer parents rather than social workers as appropriate adults precisely because they were more likely to get the truth out of their child. They were also less likely to ask for a solicitor.

Evans (1993) and others (for example, Dixon 1990; Brown *et al*, 1992) point out that the adult's role in facilitating communication between police and suspect during interviews may detract from exercise of the juvenile's right to silence. Dixon (1990) notes too that, should adults take the more active role in advising juveniles which Code C envisages, they may rapidly come into conflict with the police who are content with the presence of adults only so long as they remain passive observers or assist the interview.

Brown *et al* (1992) and Evans and Rawstorne (1994) both make the point that the competence with which social work staff perform the role of appropriate adult may vary depending on how appropriate adult provision is organised by social services departments. Dedicated Youth Justice Teams, who often provided cover during office hours, have the advantage that they are conversant with police station procedure and PACE. Out of normal office hours, however, the quality of provision may vary, depending on the degree of specialism of the teams providing emergency cover. Evans and Rawstorne (1994) note that, in some areas, Emergency Duty Teams contain juvenile justice specialists while, in others, they consist of a range of staff performing the work on a rota basis or of relatively autonomous staff working from home. They found that the latter can sometimes feel isolated and unsupported by management.

Evans and Rawstorne (ibid.) found that members of Youth Justice Teams tended to have a reasonable knowledge of PACE and of issues arising from the appropriate adult role, but that this was less often the case with other social workers, some of whom had had no specific training in this area. Where training was provided there was often minimal police input. Nevertheless, they found some attempts by local social services departments to provide practical guidance. One, for example, provided a flow chart showing how the social worker should proceed when called to a police interview. Some guides to good practice for social workers have also recently become available.[3] However, busy professionals may have limited opportunity to absorb such information; moreover, theory and reality may be rather different where social workers are confronted with difficult situations at the police station. Not surprisingly, they may experience some of the same problems and conflicts as parents.

Evans and Rawstorne found that there was considerable variation within individual social work departments in the appropriate adult cover provided, there sometimes being a mix of specialised and emergency teams, as well as other fieldwork teams and various residential and care workers. They found that specialised teams had developed better practice, the principal components of which were; clear policies and procedures; multi-agency links; good organisation and training; a common culture and physical base; coherent understanding of the role of appropriate adult; prioritisation of this area of work; and institution of some form of monitoring and evaluation.

Some difficulties may persist, regardless of the form of organisation. Dixon (1990), Kay and Quao (1987) and Evans and Rawstorne (1994) refer to tensions between control and welfare ideologies in social work. Juveniles may view social workers as reflecting the former. Social workers who seek to look after the juvenile's best interests - perhaps advising silence during interview - may rapidly find themselves in conflict with the police. They may also, as

3   See, for example, Thomas (1994) and Littlechild (1994).

Thomas (1988) notes, experience difficulties in assessing what are acceptable interviewing tactics. These are not defined in PACE or the Codes and the question has by no means been settled in the courts. Since social workers have to maintain good working relationships with the police, they may find the easiest course is to act as passive witnesses to police interviews rather than to provide strong and confident intervention where required (Evans, 1993; Evans and Rawstorne, 1994). Evans and Rawstorne (ibid.) have suggested that the general acquiescence of appropriate adults, social workers included, suits the police well. For their presence gives police actions the gloss of legality and protects the admissibility of confession evidence, while allowing them to carry on with their work relatively unimpeded.

One key issue is that of potential conflict where social work professionals are also acting as appropriate adults for their own clients. A problem arises in relation to information about the offence confided by the suspect and whether this should remain confidential (RCCJ, 1993; Fennell, 1994; Evans and Rawstorne, 1994). Bean and Nemitz (1994) suggest that social workers' duty of care and control towards their clients may point towards disclosure, while the advocate/supportive role of appropriate adult may indicate the opposite. In law, it would appear that, unlike information passed to legal advisers, that imparted to appropriate adults is not legally privileged (Evans and Rawstorne, 1994). Another source of conflict arises where probation officers act as appropriate adults for their clients. The powers they possess, for example in relation to reporting their charges for breach, sit uneasily with the appropriate adult's supportive role (Bean and Nemitz, 1994).

In view of the difficulties with the appropriate adult's role, particularly those of finding suitable people and of resolving the contradictions attached to the role, it has been questioned whether the present mode of provision should continue. Fennell (1994) and Irving and McKenzie (1989) argue that the role of protecting juveniles from unfairness and oppression in interviews might be equally well served by the presence of fully qualified solicitors. However, as Fennell acknowledges and as others, notably Dixon (1990) have pointed out, this solution runs up against the problem that legal advisers seem generally unwilling to play an active part in police interviews, even in the face of oppressive questioning of the suspect (see Chapter 6). Furthermore, to stand any chance of success, it would probably be necessary to make the provision of legal advice mandatory in juvenile cases, for appropriate adults tend not to request legal advice on the suspect's behalf (although some social workers do as a matter of course in some areas). More recent research by Brown *et al* (1992) on the revised PACE Codes of Practice echoes these concerns, drawing attention to the large amount of variation in the rate at which solicitors advise in juvenile cases and the particularly low take-up rate in some areas (see below).

The problem of delay

Dixon (1990) draws attention to the danger that lengthy delays in securing the attendance of appropriate adults may increase the risk of juveniles saying what they think the police want to hear in order to get out of the police station. The problem may be greater than before PACE was introduced, since the police now have little leeway to conduct interviews without an adult present.[4] Typically, the police are able to contact adults within about half an hour and they then attend the station in just over a further hour's time (Brown, 1989; Brown et al, 1992; Phillips and Brown, forthcoming). This means, however, that most juvenile detainees spend around 60 per cent of their time in custody waiting for adults to attend. In some cases, the situation is far worse. Brown (1989) found that in 10 per cent of cases it took more than two hours to contact an adult (where, for example, parents were out at work), while, more recently, Phillips and Brown (forthcoming) found a delay of over four hours in seven per cent of cases. Brown et al (1992) found very lengthy waits for adults in a few cases where parents refused to come to police stations at night and the juvenile was detained for interview until next morning.

The same study, as well as Evans and Rawstorne's (1994) and Phillips and Brown's (forthcoming) research, points out that securing the attendance of social workers takes longer than parents. Moreover, Brown et al (1992) suggest that the situation has worsened, probably due to the increased demand being placed on members of the profession since the revised Codes of Practice clarified the situations in which the attendance of parents is inappropriate (see above; also, cf Phillips and Brown, forthcoming). Evans and Rawstorne (1994) note that, in a few areas, this increased demand has led social services departments to restrict the provision of appropriate adults to cases where juveniles are in local authority care. Some indication of the resource demands which calls for social workers entail comes from research by Knight and Giller (1986), which showed that, on average, each case involving a juvenile takes up over three hours of their time.

Rights of juveniles

Other than the right to have an appropriate adult in attendance, juvenile detainees have the same basic rights at the police station as adults (see Chapter 5 above). However, there are some special provisions, firstly concerning the way in which information about those rights is to be delivered. Thus, if an appropriate adult is with the juvenile on arrival at the station, rights should be given in the adult's presence. If the adult is not yet present, the same information should be given *again* when the adult arrives

---

4   In a large-scale study at 32 police stations, Brown (1989) found that interviews without an adult were authorised in only two out of 1,000 cases.

(Code C 3.11). Secondly, there are special provisions concerning the implementation of the juvenile's rights. Most importantly, if he or she wishes to exercise the right to legal advice before an adult arrives, action should be taken on this request straightaway and not delayed until the adult attends (NG 3G). Appropriate adults may themselves choose to exercise the right to legal advice on behalf of the juvenile (3.13).

Provision of rights

Despite the requirements noted above, there is some evidence that juveniles are not always informed of their rights. In their study of custody officers, Morgan *et al* (1991) found that juveniles accounted for most of the cases in their sample in which no rights were given and in which there were no extenuating circumstances (for example, suspects drunk on arrival), although this only amounted to around two per cent of all cases. Brown *et al* (1992) also report that it was more common for juveniles not to receive their rights than adults. Although some of these cases were missing person ones, in which custody officers may have felt provision of rights was not required under PACE, a significant minority involved offences. The reason rights were not given may have been due to misunderstandings about whether rights needed to be provided before the arrival of an appropriate adult. Brown *et al* (ibid.) also suggest that the requirement to provide rights could be overlooked where there was some delay in an adult arriving and investigating officers were anxious to proceed with an interview.

In the same study, practice was found to vary between police stations in relation to giving juveniles their rights. While it was invariably the case that some spoken explanation was given prior to the arrival of an appropriate adult, at some stations custody officers would wait until an adult arrived to obtain a signature to indicate rights had been given. Custody records could not therefore be relied upon to say whether juveniles were told their rights on arrival. Sanders *et al* (1989) and Bottomley *et al* (1989) also confirm that at some stations legal advice was not offered until an adult arrived.

Where information was given at the time juveniles arrived, Brown *et al* (1992) found that it tended to be sketchy, probably because custody officers often did not contemplate that juveniles would exercise their right to legal advice prior to an adult's arrival. Observers in this study characterised the giving of rights as unclear or too fast in a third of juveniles cases, compared with a quarter of adult cases.

When appropriate adults arrived, it was found that the information given to them was also often deficient. However, there appears to have been some improvement with the introduction of the revised PACE Codes of Practice.

Whereas almost half of appropriate adults were not told about the right to legal advice in the first phase of the study, after the new Codes came in, more than three-quarters were given such information. The study suggests that this change in practice does not appear to stem from any specific provision in the revised Code but may derive from generally heightened perceptions among custody officers of the need to follow correct procedure, encouraged by the revised Codes and internal force instructions.

Access to legal advice

Several studies suggest that juveniles do not always readily obtain access to legal advice. At some stations, custody officers may delay implementing requests for solicitors until an appropriate adult arrives at the police station. Irving and McKenzie (1989) found instances of this in their Brighton study. This could lead to considerable delay in taking forward requests for legal advice or to the cancellation of requests.

Sanders *et al* (1989) suggest that there may sometimes be a degree of intentionality behind such practices and that juveniles are particularly susceptible to 'ploys' which are calculated to deny the suspect legal advice. They remark on instances in which juveniles requested legal advice on arrival, but no action was taken until a parent arrived; the juvenile's request was then portrayed in a negative light, leading to its cancellation. Alternatively, the juvenile might not request advice. When a parent arrived, this was presented as a firm decision. Although the adult was asked if he or she wanted a solicitor, this was presented very much as a question presuming the answer 'no'.

Guidance in revised PACE Code C now states that action on requests by juveniles (and mentally disordered or mentally handicapped persons) for legal advice should be taken at once and not delayed until the arrival of an appropriate adult (GN 3G). The Code also forbids attempts to dissuade suspects from requesting legal advice (6.4). However, recent research by Brown *et al* (1992) suggests that custody officers' practices in relation to juveniles still sometimes depart from correct procedure. Requests for advice are not always implemented at once; and some juveniles are not told their rights at all or only in outline prior to the arrival of a parent. They are therefore effectively not given the chance to exercise their rights. For, as Dixon (1990) notes, legal advice is a less attractive proposition at the stage at which an appropriate adult arrives because securing it entails further delay.

Several studies have found that request rates for legal advice among juveniles are lower than for adults. Figures quoted include: 11 per cent (Brown, 1989); 16 per cent (Sanders *et al*, 1989); and 17 per cent (Bottomley *et al*, 1989). Brown *et al* (1992) comparing take-up of legal advice prior to and after the introduction of the revised PACE Codes found a substantial rise in requests among juveniles from 19 per cent in 1990 to 26 per cent in 1991. However, they remark on the tremendous variation between stations – far greater than for adults – with anything from seven to 58 per cent requesting legal advice. They suggest that differences in practice in relation to the provision of rights, as described above, may account for some of the variation. Much of the remainder may be due to local differences in juveniles' awareness of their rights (a factor also commented on by Dixon (1990) their criminal experience and social services' practice in relation to requesting solicitors when they act as appropriate adults.

Recent research by Phillips and Brown (forthcoming) suggests that as many as a third of juveniles now request legal advice, but this is still somewhat lower than the request rate for adults (39 per cent).

Outside contact

Juveniles have exactly the same right to have someone informed of their detention as adults (see above, Chapter 5). However, in their study of the revised PACE Codes of Practice, Brown *et al* (1992) found that juveniles frequently did not have a chance to exercise this right because contact with an appropriate adult was treated by custody officers as excluding the possibility of having anyone else informed. In fact, as they note, contacting an appropriate adult is compulsory; the right to intimation is an additional right which may be exercised at the suspect's discretion. Although revised Code C makes this clear (C 3.7), custody officers' practice does not reflect this clarification. Custody records were often found to record requests for an appropriate adult as requests for intimation, leading to misleadingly high recorded levels of take-up of this right among juveniles. The observational part of this study suggests that, in fact, no more than seven per cent of juveniles request intimation to someone other than an appropriate adult. It may well be that juveniles would not take up this right to any extent if they were genuinely given an opportunity to exercise it, since it is likely that they would not want anyone other than an appropriate adult contacted. The point is, however, that few juveniles are currently given any real option about exercising this right.

Interviews with juveniles

It has been noted by Evans (1993) that juveniles may be more vulnerable, by reason of their age, to the use of persuasive techniques by the police. Furthermore, they may not necessarily understand the implications of statements they make in interviews, and it is therefore important for the police to establish their degree of understanding.

The same study is the only one to have devoted attention solely to the interviewing of juveniles (interviewing more generally is dealt with in Chapter 7), although other studies have examined the relationship between age and confessions in police interviews (see, for example, McConville and Sanders, 1989; Moston *et al*, 1992). It is therefore worthwhile looking at the methods and conclusions of Evans' research in detail. The study is subject to certain limitations, mainly concerning the generalisability of its findings and the representativeness of the sample of cases used. Specifically, it was confined to one force (although six stations were sampled), and its analysis of police interview tactics was restricted to cases in which there was an admission or where this was unclear. The sample was drawn from earlier work on police cautioning by Evans and Ferguson (1991). The study aimed: firstly, to explore the factors associated with admissions or denials in interviews with juveniles, drawing for this purpose on a sample of 367 juveniles dealt with by the police; secondly, to provide a range of qualitative and quantitative data about such interviews, including the use of police tactics, using a sub-sample of 164 cases in which the suspect admitted the offence or where it was unclear whether there was an admission; and, thirdly, to examine how the outcome of interviews was related to case disposal.

The earlier work on cautioning had found that it was rare for juveniles to be interviewed other than under arrest and at the police station (Evans and Ferguson, 1991). This course may not be strictly required by the demands of the investigation; rather, Evans and Ferguson suggest, on the basis of their interviews with police officers, that the purpose of arrest is sometimes to act as 'frightener' and to raise the level of seriousness for the suspect. Set against this are Evans' (1993) findings that interviews with juveniles are generally fairly brief, on average lasting just under a quarter of an hour, and that there is little evidence of interviewing at unsocial hours when juveniles might be most vulnerable: only six per cent of interviews occurred between midnight and 6 a.m.

Evans (ibid.) found that 49 per cent of juvenile suspects made a full admission, 33 per cent denied the offence, while in 18 per cent of cases there was no clear outcome to the interview. Making comparisons with other studies, Evans suggests that the admission rate for juveniles is higher than for suspects generally or for adults. However, it is submitted that the evidence for this proposition from his own study is slight. In fact, as was noted in Chapter 7, different studies have provided statistics on admission rates for suspects generally ranging from 46 per cent to 59 per cent. There are difficulties comparing admission rates from different studies due to the use of varying definitions of what amounts to an admission. Evans, for example, uses a category of 'no clear outcome'; other studies have not always done so, and it is probable that these cases may variously have been coded as admissions or denials. Admission rates may also vary between areas according to

the characteristics of offender populations and offences and police interviewing practices. Only where the same study has compared admission rates
for juveniles and adults at the same police stations using consistent definitions is it possible to provide acceptable evidence of differences in admission rates for juveniles and adults. This was true of the studies by McConville
and Sanders (1989), which found that 61 per cent of juveniles made a full
confession compared with 42 per cent of adults, and Phillips and Brown
(forthcoming), which produced an admission rate of 62 per cent for juveniles, compared with 54 per cent for adults.

Evans (1993) reported that juveniles who admitted to their crimes did so
readily in over three-quarters of cases, leading to perfunctory and routine
interviews (a picture confirmed by the later work of Evans and Rawstorne,
1994). In the remaining 23 per cent of cases (i.e. where confession was
delayed or there was no clear admission), the police were more likely to use
persuasive tactics, particularly in more serious offences. Most frequently,
these consisted of confronting suspects directly with the evidence (for
example, where they had been found in possession of stolen goods) or
stressing that the truth would eventually come out or that the suspect would
feel better for making a confession. Interviewing officers also played on the
fact that juveniles tend to commit offences in groups by pointing out contradictions between the stories told by co-suspects. In some cases (the number
is not specified) Evans cites examples of questioning which he considers
oppressive, with juveniles being 'harangued, belittled or directly and indi-
rectly threatened that they will not be left alone until the police obtain
irrefutable evidence or the suspect confesses'. He also draws attention to the
dangers of certain other forms of questioning, which may lead the suspect
too readily to accept a police opinion and generate unreliable admissions.[5]

Despite his findings on the use of interview tactics, Evans maintains that
these appear to have little or no part in securing admissions. This is in line
with the conclusions of other studies, notably those by Irving and McKenzie
(1989) and Moston *et al* (1990). The latter study found that suspects were
persuaded to deviate from their initial response to questioning in remarkably
few cases. Evans' support for this conclusion is rather weakened by the fact
that he did not examine interview tapes for cases in which suspects clearly
denied offences and so was unable to say what, if any, tactics were used in
such cases. He also explored other factors associated with admissions by
juveniles and concluded that 'legal' variables – specifically, the strength of
the evidence, the suspect's criminal history and the seriousness of the
offence – are among the most significant predictors of the outcome of interviews (i.e. the suspects most likely to confess are ones against whom there is
strong evidence, those with no previous convctions, or those arrested for

---

5   See Chapter 7 for further discussion of the issue of false confessions.

less serious offences). These conclusions are in line with – although not identical to – those of Moston *et al* (1992) regarding suspects generally. In the latter study, legal advice was also found to be important. However, the number of juveniles who have legal advisers present at interviews is small and may explain why this did not feature as a significant factor in Evans' study. Both studies also found that the police sub-division in which interviews were conducted was important. Evans tentatively suggests that this may be a function of interviewing techniques varying between areas – although, as noted above, his general conclusion is that tactics are not a significant factor in producing confessions.

Turning to the safeguards for juveniles during police interviews, Evans' (1993) study considered the role played by appropriate adults. He found that they generally remained passive. It seems highly likely too that legal advisers have only a limited impact on interviews with juveniles, not least because they attend far fewer interviews with juveniles than with adults (Brown *et al*, 1992). In some areas, however, it appears that social workers acting as appropriate adults now insist on the presence of a legal adviser (Evans and Rawstorne, 1994). It is doubtful whether this is likely to have any significant effect, given that legal advisers appear to adopt as low a profile in police interviews with juveniles as in those with other suspects (Evans, 1993; Evans and Rawstorne, 1994). Evans (1993) remarks that the possibility of detecting malpractice during interviews with juveniles is limited by the fact that the majority of cases lead to a caution, and there is no public opportunity in court to examine or contest the evidence. In his study, he estimates from an examination of interview tapes that 13 per cent of suspects denied the offence or made no clear admission, but were nevertheless cautioned or informally warned.

Length of detention

The length of time juveniles are detained without charge is generally shorter than the time spent in custody by adults. Brown (1989), for example, gives an average length of detention for juveniles of just under four hours, compared with five and a half hours for adults. Dixon (1990) also cites times around one hour lower than for adults. The main reason detention periods are shorter is that juveniles are generally held for less serious offences than adult suspects. Thus, up to 35 per cent of juveniles are held for shoplifting, compared with nine per cent of adults (Brown, 1989). However, Phillips and Brown (forthcoming) found that juveniles spend slightly longer in custody than adults where they are not accompanied by an appropriate adult on arrival at the station.

There is some evidence that the length of time for which juveniles are held has risen since the introduction of PACE. A particularly sharp increase was reported by Brown (1991) in a study of burglary investigation. Precise figures vary from area to area. The increase probably stems from delays incurred by awaiting the arrival of appropriate adults. Also, the increase in requests for legal advice may be a contributory factor, since delays may occur in contacting solicitors and awaiting their arrival at the police station (Dixon, 1990). However, this is unlikely to be the main cause since the majority of juveniles do not request legal advice.

Summary

• Up to a fifth of suspects detained by the police are aged 16 or under.

• In around two-thirds of cases parents or relatives act as appropriate adults; social workers fulfil this function in up to a third of cases, although there is evidence of a recent decrease in this proportion.

• Parents are often not well-equipped to act as appropriate adults because they may know little about police procedures or what is acceptable in police interviews, may be emotionally upset at their child's predicament, or may take sides with or against the police. Their role is often not explained to them by the police. They tend to play little part in police interviews.

• Social workers also often lack training in the appropriate adult's role and may be oriented more towards welfare than justice issues. The quality of their response is related to the organisation of juvenile justice work in social services departments and the extent to which staff specialise in this area. Like parents, they generally remain passive during police interviews.

• Problems exist regarding the status of confidential information imparted to social workers acting as appropriate adults by clients who have been arrested.

• Around 60 per cent of juveniles' time in custody is spent waiting for an appropriate adult to attend. Demands on social services mean that waits are often longer for social workers than relatives. On average, however, juveniles are detained for shorter periods than adults.

• Juveniles are given full information about their rights less often than adults and in some cases information is either not given at all or not until an adult is present. There have been recent improvements in this situation.

- Juveniles are less likely than adults to request legal advice and there is far more variation between areas in request rates than for adults. There is evidence that the police sometimes delay or avoid taking forward requests by juveniles for legal advice.

- Juveniles are often given no opportunity to exercise their right to have someone informed of their arrest because custody officers, wrongly, take contacting an appropriate adult as satisfying this right.

- There is some evidence that juveniles are more likely than adults to provide admissions. Questioning is usually perfunctory and the tactics used are generally no more than persuasive; however, in a few cases interviewing is oppressive, although this appears not to be effective in producing admissions. Admissions are most often provided where there is strong evidence, the juvenile has no previous convictions and the offence is less serious.

10 PACE and the mentally disordered and mentally handicapped

Mentally disordered and mentally handicapped detainees[1] form a far smaller proportion of the arrest population than juveniles. They may present formidable difficulties for the police, not the least of which is that police stations are unsuitable places to house the acutely disturbed. However, as Robertson (1992) notes, the police have no wish to do so but, since they are responsible for public order they must respond where it is breached or where other offences are committed or threatened by mentally disordered persons. Only rarely are there arrangements whereby they may be taken directly by the police to local mental hospitals or units. In most cases, therefore, mentally disordered people are taken to police stations for assessment and for further arrangements to be made.

Another major difficulty for the police is that it is by no means obvious in some cases whether detainees are suffering from mental disorder or mental handicap. Many may have been arrested for offences the commission of which may demonstrate no obvious symptom of mental abnormality.

The PACE provisions relating to mentally disordered or mentally handicapped detainees are very similar to those relevant to juveniles. As with juveniles, the police are required to err on the side of caution and set the appropriate procedures in motion where an officer "has any suspicion, or is told in good faith, that a person of any age may be mentally disordered or mentally handicapped, or mentally incapable of understanding the significance of questions put to him or his replies ..." (C 1.4). In these circumstances, the custody officer must secure the attendance at the police station of an appropriate adult (Code C 3.9) and that person must be present at all police interviews (C 11.14). Preferably, the appropriate adult should be a relative, guardian or other person responsible for the detainee's care or custody, or someone who has experience of dealing with the mentally disordered or mentally handicapped (C 1.7). The adult's role at police interviews is the same as that described in Chapter 9 in relation to juveniles (see C 11.16).

---

1   The term 'mental disorder' is used in this section, as in the PACE Codes of Practice, to refer to mental illness, arrested or incomplete development of mind, psychopathic disorder and any other disorder or disability of mind. Mental handicap is different from mental disorder. However, both conditions are dealt with similarly in the PACE Codes of Practice. The terminology used in the Codes is also adhered to in this report.

A number of studies have considered the treatment of mentally disordered and mentally handicapped detainees. Two of these were undertaken at the request of the RCCJ. The first, by Gudjunsson *et al* (1993), tackled the difficult question of identifying those at risk. This subject was also touched on in the other RCCJ study, by Robertson (1992), which dealt primarily with the work of police surgeons. More recently, Bean and Nemitz (1994) and Evans and Rawstorne (1994) have examined the role, function, qualifications and training of appropriate adults in relation to mentally disordered and mentally handicapped detainees. The first of these studies is based on a large-scale survey of custody records, as well as interviews with custody officers and mental health professionals. The methods of the second study have been described in the previous chapter.

Identifying the mentally disordered and mentally handicapped

The scope of the problem

The PACE Code C provisions apply to both mentally disordered and mentally handicapped prisoners. Potentially, therefore, these provisions include a broader range of people than the former Judges' Rules, which related only to the mentally handicapped (Thomas, 1988). Exactly what this proportion is cannot be established with any precision because there is a considerable element of subjectivity in police assessments of the mental health of those in custody. There may also be variation between areas in the number of mentally ill people in the local population.

Several studies have provided figures on the proportion of persons treated as mentally disordered or mentally handicapped by the police. The lowest estimate is given by Bean and Nemitz (1994). They surveyed over 20,000 custody records drawn from police stations in Sheffield, Derby, Grantham and Skegness and found only 38 cases (0.2%) in which appropriate adults were called out of concern for the detainee's mental condition. Slightly higher figures of around one or two per cent have been found in studies by Brown (1989), drawing on custody records from 32 police stations nation-wide, Brown *et al* (1992) in a further custody record sample from 12 stations, Phillips and Brown (forthcoming) in an observational study of over 4,000 arrests at ten stations and Irving and McKenzie (1989), who observed procedures at Brighton police station. A rather higher figure of four per cent is provided by Gudjunsson *et al* (1993) in his observational study in London, carried out for the RCCJ. However, only two stations and a small number of cases (163) were sampled. It is arguable whether generalisations may be made from these figures either to London or to the country as a whole. It seems reasonable to assume that the population in some parts of the capital would contain higher than average numbers of mentally disturbed people.

A significant minority of those dealt with by the police as mentally disordered will not have committed offences but will have been brought to the police station as a place of safety under sections 135 and 136 of the Mental Health Act 1983. A study by Robertson (1992) in London for the RCCJ suggests the proportion may be around one-fifth,[2] although Phillips and Brown (forthcoming), who sampled a range of forces throughout the country, put the figure somewhat higher at one-third. The remainder will have been arrested on suspicion of offences. Robertson found that 27 per cent of mentally disordered suspects had been arrested for theft and 30 per cent for public order and criminal damage offences.

The 'dark figure'

The number of mentally disordered and mentally handicapped detainees would appear to be unduly low compared with the prevalence of these conditions in the general population (Dixon et al, 1990b), particularly bearing in mind that offenders typically have lower IQ scores and more associated learning disabilities than the general population (Gudjunsson et al, 1993). Persons with mental disorders or handicaps may also be more likely than others to come into contact with the police. This may suggest that the police are not interpreting Code C strictly by erring on the side of caution and treating detainees as mentally disordered or handicapped where there is any doubt about the matter.

Parker (1992) suggests that the police have a vested interest in not putting the PACE appropriate adult provisions into effect: firstly, they are effectively being asked to safeguard the rights of those with whom they have an adversarial relationship; and, secondly, the procedures may be time-consuming to implement. A less controversial explanation is that the police may experience genuine difficulties in identifying the mentally vulnerable – difficulties referred to by the RCCP and various commentators (RCCP, 1981; Tully and Cahill, 1984; Hewitt, 1986; Gudjunsson, 1992; Gudjunsson et al, 1993). Custody officers are not trained in identifying degrees or categories of mental abnormality. Robertson (1992) and Evans and Rawstorne (1994) found that they are usually alerted by more bizarre forms of behaviour (although there is some evidence from Irving and McKenzie's (1989) Brighton study and from Phillips and Brown's (forthcoming) research that this is not always the case). Bean and Nemitz (1994) found that custody officers often seemed to be sure of their judgement; so much so, that they did not always call the police surgeon to confirm whether their diagnosis was correct, as they are required to do under PACE Code C (9.2). Nevertheless, it is likely that police officers may not pick up on subtler manifestations of

---

2   Bean and Nemitz (1994) found that it was not always clear from custody records whether detainees were being held under section 136 or had been transferred to the section after initially being arrested for an offence.

abnormality (Robertson, 1992); indeed, many mentally handicapped people may actively - and effectively - try to disguise their condition (Gudjunsson, 1992; Parker, 1992). Sometimes, it may be a matter of chance that custody officers are alerted to problems: for example, by information from friends or relatives of the detainee or by medication found among the person's belongings (Bean and Nemitz, 1994).

Two studies provide evidence that the number of people who need some special help may be considerably higher than the proportion identified by the police. In research for the RCCJ, designed to test out a simplified version of the notice to detained persons, Clare and Gudjunsson (1992) found that as many as 15 per cent were suffering, or had suffered, from a mental health problem or had attended a special school, and over 40 per cent more had learning difficulties or were unable to read. Unfortunately, the study does not provide details of how the sample was drawn, although it is noted that the average intelligence level was similar to that of convicted suspects. It is unlikely that all of those with past or present difficulties would have need of an appropriate adult. However, the study does point to the need for caution in making judgements about the ability of ostensibly 'normal' people to cope with the experience of arrest.

Some abnormalities, such as an undue level of suggestibility, could probably only be detected by carrying out some form of psychological screening. This approach has been tested under 'live' conditions by Gudjunsson *et al* (1993). A range of psychological tests and a questionnaire were administered to a total of 163 suspects at two police stations in London in order to monitor: current mental state; intellectual functioning; reading ability; interrogative suggestibility; anxiety proneness; and understanding of legal rights. The sample comprised those who were due to be interviewed by the police, and is not necessarily representative of suspects generally. It also excluded cases in which there was insufficient time between the suspect's initial detention and interview to complete the tests (which took around one hour). The researchers adopted stringent criteria in making their clinical judgements. They excluded cases where the suspect was suffering from medical problems or drug addiction, even though there might be a link between these conditions and unreliable testimony.

On the basis of the researchers' clinical judgements, there was a need for an appropriate adult in 15 per cent of cases for the following reasons: mental illness (7%); mental handicap (3%); and language problems or illiteracy (5%). In contrast, the police called an appropriate adult in just four per cent of cases (all of which were ones where the researchers assessed that one was necessary), these being ones in which the suspect's difficulties were most pronounced. These included a third of the mental illness cases and half of the mental handicap cases.

The psychological tests administered in the same study also showed that a large number of detainees suffered from significant intellectual impairment, with one-third having an IQ of 75 or below. Around 20 per cent were found to be suffering from unusually high levels of stress and anxiety from being at the police station. Members of the sample were also more suggestible than members of non-offender populations, but suggestibility was found to be only weakly correlated with intelligence and level of anxiety. A small number of suspects (7%) were found to suffer from functional illiteracy. Taking the psychological tests in conjunction with their clinical assessments, the researchers suggest that the proportion of the sample requiring appropriate adults was as high as 20 per cent.

They acknowledge that proper identification of mental handicap, in particular, is a difficult task for the police and that it is inevitable that, for several reasons, some cases will be overlooked. Many persons with such handicaps are able to disguise their intellectual impairment and function reasonably normally; their difficulties may only become apparent on longer acquaintance.

Carrying out psychological assessments on all detainees is clearly impractical. Clare and Gudjunsson (1992) suggest that an effective way of identifying mental abnormality or other problems which impair the suspect's under-standing may be to ask suspects themselves a series of questions which enable them to draw attention to their difficulties. This approach was tried with some success in an experimental study of a revised notice to detained persons,[3] conducted for the RCCJ. While there is the risk that some suspects may incorrectly report that they have need of an appropriate adult and that others may prefer to keep their handicap private, they argue that this is outweighed by the number of people who are unlikely at present to secure assistance correctly reporting their difficulties. Gudjunsson *et al* (1993) suggest that this approach must be coupled with better training for police officers in identifying vulnerable individuals and the development of clearer criteria relating to the need for appropriate adults.

Where the police do pick up on the possibility of mental disorder or mental handicap this does not mean that they will necessarily call an appropriate adult. It is clear that custody officers sometimes suspect that a person may be suffering from a mental health problem but do not call an appropriate adult: Bean and Nemitz (1994) found this occurred in two per cent of detentions in their study. Furthermore, they also suggest, on the basis of interviews with custody officers, that doubts about the detainee's mental health are not always recorded on the custody record and that the scale of the problem may be larger than it was thought to be. They suggest two reasons

---

3   The notice to detained persons provides details of suspects' rights to legal advice, to have someone informed of their arrest, the right to consult the PACE Codes of Practice and the right to a copy of the custody record. The notice also explains the arrangements for obtaining legal advice. See Code C, 3.2.

why appropriate adults are not always called in possible mental health cases. Firstly, some custody officers are unfamiliar with the fact that the PACE appropriate adult provisions apply with equal force to juveniles and the mentally disordered. Secondly, custody officers sometimes appear to believe, wrongly, that the decision whether to obtain an appropriate adult is not for them but for the doctor.

Doctors are indeed summoned frequently where there are doubts about the suspect's mental condition (Evans and Rawstorne, 1994). In fact, under PACE Code C (9.2), medical assistance *must* be secured immediately if a person appears to be suffering from mental disorder. Arguably, custody officers should also call an appropriate adult in these circumstances, since Code C (3.9) requires such a person to be notified and summoned to the station 'as soon as practicable'. In practice, whether an appropriate adult is called tends to depend upon the surgeon's assessment. Bean and Nemitz (1994) suggest that the relative accessibility of police surgeons, who can generally arrive within the hour and make a quick assessment, may be a factor influencing custody officers against obtaining appropriate adults who can sometimes take a considerable time to attend. The result, as studies by Bean and Nemitz (1994), Gudjunsson *et al* (1993), Robertson (1992) and Phillips and Brown (forthcoming) all show, is that in many cases no appropriate adult is called. Robertson (1992) found that, of a sample of over 180 detainees initially referred by custody officers out of concern for their mental health, doctors confirmed as definitely abnormal only 38 per cent of those initially considered as such. Nearly 20 per cent were assessed as normal. Similar proportions were considered to be only possibly abnormal or as suffering principally from anxiety. Police surgeons may sometimes adopt a more robust attitude than the police in assessing the mental condition of detainees (Evans and Rawstorne, 1994). It is also likely that they may not have the appropriate expertise in mental health (Parker, 1992), a view confirmed by Evans and Rawstorne (1994), who found that social workers whom they talked to expressed some concern about the correctness of police surgeons' judgements on the detainee's fitness for interview. The important point is also made by Bean and Nemitz (1994) that the medical diagnosis of a detainee's fitness for interview should not be the determinant of the need for an appropriate adult. Fitness for interview does not necessarily imply that a person needs no special protection in the face of police questions.

The provision of appropriate adults in mental health cases

The RCCJ expressed some concern about the adequacy of the arrangements for ensuring that those at risk receive appropriate advice and protection while in police custody (RCCJ, 1993). In particular, they felt that a more systematic approach was needed to the question of which people are suitable to be called upon to serve as appropriate adults. Under PACE Code C (1.7), appropriate adults in mental health cases may be qualified professionals but, equally, they may be relatives or others who have little knowledge of police powers and procedures or of mental disorder or handicap.

Recent research by Brown *et al* (1992), Robertson (1992) and Evans and Rawstorne (1994) has suggested that there may be a trend towards the attendance of suitably qualified professionals as appropriate adults in mental health cases. The first of these studies found that, at that time, relatives acted as appropriate adults in less than a quarter of cases, and there was an increasing tendency for specialist and psychiatric social workers to be involved. More recently still, Bean and Nemitz (1994) and Phillips and Brown (forthcoming) have also found that various mental health and social work professionals are most frequently involved as appropriate adults and that relatives are only used in a minority of cases. Evans and Rawstorne's (1994) research suggests that the police often prefer mental health specialists to act as appropriate adults because they are likely to understand the detainee's condition and be more objective and less emotionally involved than relatives.

The demands made on mental health professionals raise the question of how well their organisations are geared up to respond. Evans and Rawstorne (1994) examined this question in relation to the work of local authority social services departments. They found that, during the day, Mental Health Teams were able to respond to calls to police stations. Outside of office hours, however, it was not always the case that a specialist social worker would be available, since Emergency Duty Teams sometimes consist of a range of personnel with different types of expertise. As is the case with juveniles, some social workers dealing with the mentally disordered have received little or no training on PACE.

Brown *et al* (1992) and Evans and Rawstorne (1994) found that the attendance of mental health specialists was generally achieved fairly quickly, and more speedily than was the case for duty social workers acting as appropriate adults for juveniles. The authors of the former study suggest that this promptness is in keeping with the spirit of the PACE Codes of Practice, which stress the need to assess those detained at police stations under s.136 of the Mental Health Act 1983 as quickly as possible.

The appropriate adult's role

Under PACE Code C (11.16) those acting as appropriate adults should be informed that during police interviews their tasks are 'first, to advise the person being questioned and to observe whether or not the interview is being conducted properly and fairly, and secondly, to facilitate communication with the person being interviewed'. The ultimate aim is to minimise the risk of unreliable evidence being produced (Haley and Swift, 1988). Bean and Nemitz (1994) found no documentary evidence from custody records that custody officers relayed such information, while Evans and Rawstorne (1994) noted that where any information is provided, it tends mainly to be given where relatives rather than professionals are acting as appropriate adults, and even then it is provided in very general terms. Nor does it appear that interviewing officers routinely advise appropriate adults of their role (Evans and Rawstorne, ibid.). Two reasons for these omissions are suggested by the Bean and Nemitz and Evans and Rawstorne research. Firstly, officers may assume that professionals are already aware of their role. This assumption may be misplaced, given that social work and mental health professionals often have only limited working knowledge of PACE (Parker, 1992). Secondly, custody officers and interviewing officers may tend to see the adult's role as being a limited one of looking after the suspect's 'welfare' and it is clear that they do not expect them generally to intervene in interviews to advise the suspect, for example.

A matter of particular concern is the duty of appropriate adults where suspects have admitted offences to them. Parker (1992) points out that social workers may have discovered this information from a position of trust and passing it on to the police breaches this confidence. On the other hand, if the appropriate adult's role is to ensure that evidence obtained is reliable, there is some pressure to reveal admissions to the police. This issue remains unresolved.

Research has pointed to further sources of confusion in this difficult area. Bean and Nemitz (1994) found that, while custody officers fully appreciated the need to have a third party present where there was concern about the suspect's mental condition, it was not always apparent from the custody record whether this amounted to a formal implementation of the appropriate adult provisions under PACE. A particular difficulty, noted in the same study and by Evans and Rawstorne (1994), arises in cases where persons have been detained under section 136 of the Mental Health Act 1983. In these circumstances it is not always clear whether social workers are acting as appropriate adults or as Approved Social Workers making an assessment under that Act. The two roles are distinct and there is the potential for conflict of interest, since advising and assisting the suspect may rest uneasily with the power to commit the detainee to a mental hospital against his or her will. However, Bean and Nemitz (1994) note that custody officers may not fully appreciate these issues and may therefore treat the two roles as synonymous, expecting them to be performed by the same person.

The rights of mentally disordered and mentally handicapped detainees

The mentally disordered and mentally handicapped have the same rights under PACE as other detainees, but ensuring that appropriate information is communicated effectively presents difficulties. Gudjunsson and colleagues at the Institute of Psychiatry in London have examined this issue in a series of studies (Gudjunsson, 1990 and 1991; Gudjunsson, Clare and Cross, 1992; Clare and Gudjunsson, 1992). Both the present and original notices to detained persons, which contain information about rights, were assessed for clarity and found to be deficient. Persons with a mild mental handicap were found to be the least able to understand their rights from the information given in the notice. In their most recent study for the RCCJ, Clare and Gudjunsson (1992) tested a simplified version of the notice, plus accompanying oral information about PACE rights, on a group of subjects, some of whom suffered from various degrees of mental handicap. It was found that show-cards setting out the suspect's main rights very briefly in everyday language were understood by nearly three-quarters of those with the lowest IQ scores, and nearly all of those defined as being of 'low average ability' (IQ 80-89) understood their rights. As yet, the approach adopted by the study has not been tested under 'live' conditions.

Even if the mentally vulnerable person is able to understand his or her rights, this is no guarantee that they will be implemented. As was noted in Chapter 6, there is some evidence that custody officers employ a variety of techniques to dissuade suspects from pursuing requests for solicitors in certain kinds of case (Sanders et al, 1989). Parker (1992) notes that mentally handicapped detainees may be particularly susceptible to such attempts to manipulate their decision making.

Interviewing mentally handicapped and mentally disordered suspects

Fitness for interview

The question of whether those believed to be mentally abnormal are fit to be interviewed appears to have generated some differences in practice. In a study for the RCCJ, Robertson (1992) found that it was rare for police surgeons in London to advise that detainees whom they had examined out of concern for their mental health were unfit for interview, but reasonably common for them to recommend that an appropriate adult be present. Elsewhere, less use appeared to be made of appropriate adults but detainees were more often assessed as being unfit for interview.

The suspect's response to questioning

A study in the Metropolitan Police suggests that, even where the correct action is taken and some kind of independent expert is summoned, difficulties of dealing with mentally abnormal suspects at the police station persist (Cahill and Grebler, 1988). Particular problems occur in assessing whether the suspect had the appropriate *mens rea* for the offence in question.

Tully and Cahill (1984), in a study of the interviewing of the mentally handicapped, have drawn attention to the varying response of this group of suspects to police questioning. In some cases, they may be extremely resistant, but in others they may perceive the situation as one demanding obedience and be over-ready to answer questions in a way which they believe will please the interviewer, irrespective of the truth.[4] They also draw attention to other features of interviews with the mentally handicapped which may render statements unreliable. Thus, questioning designed to portray the suspect in a bad light may lead the interviewee to respond in ways that avoid him or her looking foolish rather than representing the truth. Pressure to respond may also reduce the accuracy of replies. These problems would not be so significant if it were easy to identify and quantify degrees of mental handicap but, unfortunately, this is not the case.

The same study found that, while police officers recognised that there were problems associated with mentally handicapped suspects' responses to questioning, they consistently overestimated the reliability of information provided by them. Furthermore, officers took suspects' co-operativeness and confidence to imply reliability, probably because in normal cases these qualities are linked. They categorised a variety of ways in which erroneous responses to questions might be produced, a common element to which was that positive answers reduced the risk of the suspect appearing incompetent. Leading questions were important but not the most significant sources of error. Some of their categories are similar to styles of questioning which other researchers have identified as occurring under PACE interview conditions. McConville *et al* (1991), Moston *et al* (1990), Evans (1992) and Sanders *et al* (1989) all refer to styles of questioning which are designed to force responses in a particular direction or exploit the suspect's ignorance of the legal elements of offences.

The impact of appropriate adults and legal advisers

As with juveniles (see Chapter 9), it seems unlikely that the interests of mentally handicapped suspects are adequately safeguarded by the presence

---

4   The issue of suggestibility has been dealt with by a number of writers, most notably by Gudjunsson, 1983 and 1983a.

at interviews of appropriate adults. Firstly, they may not always have adequate opportunity to consult clients and assess their condition before interviewing begins (Justice, 1994). Secondly, their impact on interviews may be limited. Although Bean and Nemitz (1994) and Evans and Rawstorne (1994) disagree on whether social work professionals feel confident in asserting themselves in police interviews (the former found they were unconfident, the latter the opposite), the fact is that interventions are very seldom made (Evans, 1993). Those who would intervene face police disapproval: thus, Bean and Nemitz (1994) found that officers did not consider interruptions to be justifiable other than on 'welfare' grounds. Evans and Rawstorne (1994) report similar findings: interviewing officers commented that appropriate adults were primarily there 'as observers' or 'to oversee the interview' and they discouraged intervention unless it was helpful to the police.

Some mental health professionals make it their practice also to insist on the presence of a legal adviser (Evans and Rawstorne, 1994). However, given the passivity of legal personnel in police interviews (see Chapter 6) it is doubtful how much extra protection this affords. Parker (1992) also notes that legal advisers may have no special expertise in recognising or dealing with mentally vulnerable suspects. She notes that the Law Society's own guidance gives no special advice on this question.

The problem of unreliable confessions

Where the police have failed to appreciate the vulnerability of the suspect or where the appropriate adult provisions have failed to provide adequate protection, the risk arises that cases may be taken forward on the basis of unreliable evidence. A recent report by Justice (1994) documents various cases occurring since the introduction of PACE in which alleged miscarriages of justice turned upon the unreliability of statements provided by mentally handicapped suspects. In an examination of a number of cases revolving around confessions by such persons, Parker (1992) draws attention to the apparent reluctance of the courts to provide a consistent steer as to the way in which such evidence should be dealt with. It seems clear, however, that the lack of an appropriate adult during a police interview of a mentally handicapped person may not in itself be sufficient to warrant the exclusion of a confession. Drawing attention to the approach of the Court of Appeal and particularly that adopted in the case of McKenzie,[5] she notes that in order for the Court to be satisfied that a verdict is unsafe and unsatisfactory, stringent requirements must be met. Firstly, the prosecution evidence must depend wholly upon confessions; secondly, the defendant must suffer from a

---

5   R v. McKenzie (1992) N.L.J. 1162.

significant degree of mental handicap; and, thirdly, the confessions must be unconvincing to a point where a jury properly directed could not properly convict upon them.

Tully and Cahill (1984) suggest that there are ways of minimising the risk of unreliable evidence from mentally handicapped suspects. They include: establishing a good rapport with suspects prior to interview in order to assess their particular idiosyncrasies; sharing interviews, so that one officer may observe the suspect's reactions more closely; and conducting several interviews over a short period in order to cross-check information for reliability.

Irving and McKenzie (1989) raise the pertinent question of whether the events of the seminal Confait case could be repeated under PACE procedures. One suspect (Lattimore) in that case was mentally handicapped. It was not argued that he was subjected to oppressive interviewing tactics, but that due to his vulnerability he produced false confessions in response to the normal run of questioning. Furthermore, this was done in front of a parent. He did not request or receive legal advice. A doctor was called to examine him, because the police had some doubts about his mental condition, but this was after the confessions, and the doctor had no special expertise in mental handicap. Irving and McKenzie conclude that there must remain a lingering doubt that such events could happen again, although the risk has been reduced. Recording of interviews acts as one safeguard, while the PACE provisions requiring an appropriate adult and a doctor to be called where there is any suspicion that a suspect is mentally handicapped or mentally ill may help to ensure that a suspect's condition is assessed at an earlier stage and the appropriate safeguards set in motion.

The grounds for lingering doubts are, first, that Lattimore, despite his mental handicap, presented himself well, and there is room to doubt whether police officers would now consider that his condition justified putting the PACE provisions on mentally handicapped suspects into effect. The findings of research, reported above, that appropriate adults are relatively rarely summoned may be taken to support the view that police officers are still reluctant to treat suspects as mentally abnormal unless this abnormality is too obvious to be ignored. Secondly, even if an appropriate adult were summoned, there is no guarantee that they would provide any active support. As already noted, few are sufficiently confident to do so. Thirdly, Lattimore would have a statutory right to a solicitor, but it would be his election to request legal advice. The bulk of suspects still do not request solicitors. Nor do solicitors have any expertise in mental handicap. Lastly, while Irving and McKenzie are optimistic that PACE has reduced tactical interviewing, other researchers have pointed to the continuation of practices which may well lead to unreliable confessions (see Chapter 6). A coincidence of these factors could well lead to another Confait case.

Summary

- Up to two per cent of detainees are treated by the police as mentally disordered or mentally handicapped. In London, the figure may be nearer four per cent. Up to one-third are brought to the police station as a place of safety rather than on suspicion of committing an offence.

- The identification of detainees with mental health problems presents difficulties for custody officers. Studies estimate that up to 20 per cent of detainees may in fact need an appropriate adult. Asking those arrested whether they have need of such help has been found to be one way of identifying more of those with mental health problems.

- Custody officers often summon the police surgeon in the first instance and, acting on the doctor's advice, do not then call for an appropriate adult in many of these cases.

- There are difficulties in ensuring that detainees with mental health problems understand their rights. Experiments with simplified versions of the notices currently provided to all suspects have had some success in raising levels of understanding.

- Mental health and social work specialists are increasingly acting as appropriate adults where there are suspicions that the detainee is suffering from mental disorder or handicap. They are normally able to respond quickly to calls for their services.

- The role of the appropriate adult raises a number of problems in mental health cases. Firstly, there is sometimes confusion as to whether social workers are acting in this role or making an assessment under the Mental Health Act. Secondly, custody officers may not always be right in assuming that professionals know what is expected of them as appropriate adults. Thirdly, there is a lack of clarity about the status of information confided in appropriate adults by detainees.

- The interviewing of those with mental health problems raises particular dangers, including those of generating false confessions and over-ready compliance, leading to inaccurate replies. Police officers tend to over-estimate the reliability of the information provided.

- Appropriate adults seldom intervene during interviews with mentally disordered or mentally handicapped suspects and may not always constitute an adequate safeguard against the production of unreliable interview evidence.

11 Supervision and accountability

The theme of accountability runs like a thread through PACE and the Codes of Practice. This reflects the RCCP's concern that police procedures should provide satisfactory means of supervision and review, in order to allay suspicions about what takes place out of public view within police stations (Royal Commission, 1981: 20). The emphasis in PACE and the Codes on accountability takes several forms. First, there is accountability to those under investigation for offences in relation to decisions that affect them. This is reflected in various requirements to provide reasons for decisions and information about the statutory basis for actions: for example, in relation to stop and search and powers of entry, search and seizure. This aspect of accountability has been considered in earlier chapters.

Secondly, there is the issue of effective supervision within the police service. The RCCP considered this to be vital if police compliance with the rules they proposed was to be secured. PACE and the Codes reflect this supervisory requirement in specific procedures which are made subject to senior officers' authorisation: for example, delay of access to legal advice, and custody reviews.

The third aspect of accountability is external accountability. PACE introduced two important changes in this area. It provided for the setting up of a new independent body – the Police Complaints Authority (PCA) – to oversee certain aspects of the complaints procedure. This move was prompted by dissatisfaction with the effectiveness of the pre-existing arrangements and reflected the RCCP's belief that effective arrangements for the investigation of complaints against the police were an important component in securing public confidence in the police (Royal Commission, 1981: 111). The other avenue of accountability is rather different and concerned not with *ex post* review of police conduct but more with public input into the formulation of policing policy. Following the recommendations of the Scarman Inquiry into the Brixton disorders (Scarman, 1981), S.106 of PACE provides for arrangements to be made to obtain the views of the local community about policing in each area. The Police Consultative Groups (PCGs) which now exist throughout the country reflect this statutory requirement.

Police supervision

Particular aspects of supervision have been discussed earlier (for example, supervision of interviews). This section touches more generally on the role of police supervision. It provides information on the way in which supervisory officers approach their responsibilities and how this affects the compliance of their staff with PACE.

Relevant research

Despite the importance of these issues, they have been considered comparatively little by researchers until recently. Two studies carried out for the RCCJ were designed to remedy this deficiency. Maguire and Norris (1992) examined supervision in the context of the work of sub-divisional CID officers, Regional Crime Squads, Drugs Squads and other special squads, as well as that of major enquiries using the HOLMES[1] computer system. The researchers used a mix of interviewing and observation, as well as studying samples of case files and other documentary sources. Two main aims of the study were to ascertain the nature and degree of supervision exercised during different phases of inquiries, and to identify practical problems in managing and supervising investigations and ways of overcoming them. The second study, by Baldwin and Moloney (1992), concentrated on the supervision of investigations in serious cases. The study was less wide-ranging than that by Maguire and Norris, and examined just 45 cases, ranging from arson up to murder, drawn from three forces (including the Metropolitan Police). The data relied upon were also less extensive, deriving mainly from interviews with supervisory officers. The study was also biased towards investigations which were successful. All cases were ones in which interviews with suspects had been video recorded, which may have affected usual procedures. Nevertheless, the conclusions of both studies on the nature of investigative supervision coincide in important respects.

A further study for the RCCJ, by Irving and Dunnighan (1993), touches on the role of supervisors in maintaining quality control over CID investigations. In particular, the research focused on the part that human factors play in producing detective errors (for example, communication failures or mistaken deductions) and the extent to which these may be detectable by existing supervisory systems. The study draws on 60 cases in which detectives or CPS lawyers identified such failings. Interviews were conducted, in confidence, with the officers in the case and the relevant files were examined.

---

1   Home Office Large Major Enquiry System.

Training for supervisors

Baldwin and Moloney (1992) make the important point that detectives receive little formal training in how to supervise inquiries until they reach inspector rank or above, despite their heavy involvement in running investigations at lower ranks. Skills are mainly acquired on the job: this Baldwin and Moloney criticise as prone to perpetuate bad practice and dependent on there being mentors who are reliable models to copy.

Irving and Dunnighan (1993) point out that quality control issues are not dealt with in training for sergeants and inspectors. Yet, failings in this area are not uncommon and may have serious consequences (see below). It is therefore important for supervisors to be aware of the factors which are associated with investigative errors and of ways of assuring quality. Instead, courses concentrate more on the acquisition of professional skills (planning, leadership, performance management etc.).

The importance of supervision

Baldwin and Moloney (1992) note that the majority of investigations are straightforward and short, even in serious cases, but that it is nevertheless important to ensure that interviews are conducted fairly, evidence collected systematically and set procedures adhered to. Failure to do so may underlie miscarriages of justice. Maguire and Norris (1992) stress that it is not just in relation to interviewing suspects that supervision has a role; indeed, as interviews have become more closely regulated, the focus of attention has shifted to preceding events. They emphasise that it is important for the questioning of witnesses and victims to be subject to some form of scrutiny, because unreliable testimony from these sources may have as much potential to lead to wrongful convictions as unreliable evidence from interviews with suspects.

Some appreciation of the extent of the problems in this area is given by McConville (1993), in a study of corroboration for the RCCJ. In his assessment, the police overlooked important available evidence in 17 per cent of the cases which he examined. In a further eight per cent they were content to curtail the investigation once a confession was obtained. In part, he blames inadequate internal supervision for a failure to follow up other leads to strengthen the evidence in such cases.

Obstacles to effective supervision

Maguire and Norris (1992) point to specific features of CID work which lie at the root of malpractice and pose difficulties for effective supervision. One area, the cultivation of informants is, of necessity, an activity of low visibility to supervisors and carries the risk that detectives may be corrupted by too close contacts with criminals. Supervisors must also be alive to the possible conflict between the rights of suspects and the pressures on detectives to secure sufficient evidence to convict. Contributing to the difficulties of effective supervision are aspects of the CID working 'culture', which Maguire and Norris and others (for example, Smith and Gray, 1985; Hobbs, 1988; and Young, 1991) have all identified. Key elements of this are secrecy and defensiveness towards outsiders and, importantly for the prospects of internal supervision, close loyalties within small groups of detectives working together and a willingness to sail close to the margins of the rules in order to achieve results.

Irving and Dunnighan (1993) note that the CID working culture also predisposes officers towards secrecy about human error. The dominant ideology subscribed to by detectives is one of personal responsibility for their own work and supervisors mainly come into the picture where questions of morale, leadership or discipline are concerned.

Sometimes there is simply a refusal to acknowledge that there is a problem and a case in point is interviewing prowess. Baldwin (1992c) notes that supervisors tend to be unwilling to monitor the conduct of interviews, even though the technology to do so now exists. The reasons are probably complex, but there are probably issues of professional pride at stake, with many officers either being unwilling to admit their inadequacies in this area or failing to realise that they exist. By the same token, supervisors are unhappy about appearing to question individual competencies by conducting any close scrutiny of performance in this area.

Also relevant is the continued emphasis within the CID on assessing outputs in terms of numbers of crimes cleared up rather than in qualitative terms (Maguire *et al*, 1992), despite increasing efforts to devise other ways of measuring performance (see, for example, Audit Commission, 1990). Baldwin and Moloney (1992) note that one apparent criterion for judging the success of an investigation – the avoidance of problems – hardly encourages the achievement of excellence. Other than in major enquiries, they found it was unusual to conduct extensive post mortems into the way enquiries were conducted.

On the same theme, Irving and Dunnighan (1993) point out that quality control issues may usually only be expected to surface and be reviewed in undetected cases. Yet, they may be as apposite in detected cases. They also question whether senior officers are well placed to elicit information about investigative error. Detectives may not be frank with them because they may not believe assurances that the concern is more with the failure of systems rather than of individuals. Furthermore, they argue that it is artificial to separate the two for, in order to devise better systems, it is necessary to examine the correlation between human error and system error.

The nature of supervision

The nature and level of supervision has come in for criticism from studies in this area. Although, as Maguire and Norris (1992) note, the ratio of detective constables to sergeants is generally high compared with the uniform branch,[2] this has little significance for the degree of supervision exercised. Baldwin and Moloney (1992) found that up to half of those in charge of investigations were themselves constables. And, whether or not a constable or sergeant (or indeed an inspector) was in nominal charge, supervisors appeared reluctant to perceive their role in supervisory terms. While sergeants were technically above constables in the police hierarchy, their role was essentially that of *primus inter pares*; as Maguire and Norris (1992) also note, they performed identical work to detective constables, carried their own caseloads and exercised little directive supervision. Maguire and Norris draw attention to the frequent withdrawal of supervisory officers for a range of other duties and courses.

Maguire and Norris point out that the nature of detective work, involving as it does considerable autonomy and contact with known criminals, promotes the belief that supervision must be based on trust. Good detectives are seen as being those who can be relied upon to work on their own initiative. Baldwin and Moloney (1992) characterise the conduct of most enquiries as fluid, informal and democratic. Detectives' attitudes towards cases were typified by self-confidence and the view that investigation was generally a routine matter.

Supervision of interviews has been considered above (see Chapter 7). Baldwin and Moloney (ibid.) note that, frequently, the low level at which responsibility for investigations resides means that supervisors also conduct interviews. Where they do not, they play little part in monitoring them.

Baldwin and Moloney note that the ethos underlying detective work runs counter to more directive supervision by senior officers. They tend to be regarded by subordinates as too remote from operational police work and

---

2   Typically, CID establishments consist of four constables per sergeant, compared with nine uniform constables per sergeant.

too unfamiliar with the requirements of investigation under PACE procedures to be in a position to intervene. Active intervention is also regarded as a slight to professional pride. Senior officers therefore tend to prefer an 'open-door' policy, whereby case officers are free to come to them with any problems but little action is taken to pre-empt errors or misjudgement. Baldwin and Moloney point out too, that given the size of CID caseloads, more interventionist supervision is problematic. Maguire and Norris (1992) note that CID officers tend not to perceive supervision in terms of monitoring the quality of contacts with suspects, victims or witnesses or ensuring ethical standards are maintained. Rather, the emphasis is on ensuring that paperwork is satisfactorily completed and administrative rules are complied with, and generally on exhorting officers to be productive in clearing up crime. They characterise the dominant mode of supervision as 'charismatic' rather than 'bureaucratic'.

Shortcomings in supervisory arrangements

Baldwin and Moloney (1992) suggest that too great a responsibility for the supervision of serious cases is placed on the shoulders of junior officers. While in most cases this has no adverse consequences, breakdowns in standards of supervision in a few cases may lead to miscarriages of justice. The closed, cohesive nature of the groups in which detectives work also has the potential for incompetence or corruption to proceed unchecked.

Maguire and Norris (1992) examine the contention that PACE has impacted upon police culture and working practices sufficiently to make malpractice unlikely. They suggest that PACE has indeed had an impact on detective work: for example, detectives are no longer able to capitalise on the coercive conditions of custody by detaining suspects for lengthy periods (see too Irving and McKenzie, 1989). There have also been developments in working practices, not directly linked with PACE (for example, crime management systems), which have encouraged the systematic collection of evidence prior to arrest. However, they argue that the risk of malpractice remains despite these developments, partly because the values of PACE have not been internalised by detectives, but also because of deficiencies in supervision within the CID (see above) and continuing pressures on detectives to produce results.

They identify three particular areas, which are not amenable to supervision, where they consider that doubts about the reliability of evidence or the circumstances in which it was obtained may still linger. The first is dealings with suspects outside of the police station. While the revised PACE Codes have sought to specify closely the situations in which suspects may be questioned after arrest and other than in a formal interview at the station, it is difficult to be sure that off-the-record inducements have not been offered to suspects to confess. The second area is the taking of statements from witnesses. Practices here are not governed by PACE yet, as with interviews with suspects, there are equal risks of unreliable evidence. For example, witnesses are often involved in crime themselves and may provide the police with the information they think they want to hear in a bid to secure return favours. Another danger, noted too by McConville *et al* (1991), is that the police may convince themselves that they have caught the right suspect and, in questioning witnesses and suspects, will close their minds to lines of enquiry that would weaken their case. The third danger area is that of the police embroidering their own eyewitness accounts in order to bolster the evidence against suspects they 'know' to be guilty.

Maguire and Norris (1992) argue that there is little that may be done in the way of direct supervision to ensure against such malpractices. At present, prevention depends largely on supervisors setting the right 'moral tone' through their own personal integrity and strength of character.

Irving and Dunnighan (1993) suggest that a particular weakness of present supervisory systems is their failure to identify investigative errors that are the result of human factors. Among the examples they cite are detectives' failures to identify investigative leads, include relevant information in statements, obtain reliable information from suspects and witnesses and communicate adequately with colleagues and the CPS. These errors frequently involved breaches of PACE or CID procedures or led to breaks in the continuity of evidence linking suspect and offence. The types of evidence most affected were police identifications, statements from police officers and independent witnesses, and admissions by suspects. They argue that the nature of CID culture works against detectives admitting to such errors or supervisors putting procedures in place to identify them. Very few errors were first identified by supervisors, because they were not in close touch with cases. Most frequently, they did not come to light until cases reached court. Baldwin (1992c) argues that the same kinds of attitudes are responsible for supervisors' failure to acknowledge that standards of interviewing are deficient.

Supervision of major inquiries

In contrast to the picture of supervision painted above, the situation is apparently rather different in larger scale inquiries directed by senior officers. Baldwin and Moloney (1992) note that in the few such cases in their sample supervision was more directive and officers in charge played a fuller managerial role in the enquiry. Maguire and Norris (1992) were able to examine rather more such investigations (typically, of murder, rape or serious robbery offences) that were carried out using HOLMES. They note that such inquiries are not immune from weaknesses. As with conventional investigations, there may be problems associated with statements from unreliable witnesses; and it was not possible to ensure that detectives making enquiries did not put unacceptable pressure on witnesses.

However, they also draw attention to features of HOLMES-based investigations which militate against malpractice. Firstly, the regulatory system brought in by PACE and the Codes of Practice is most likely to be scrupulously observed in such cases (and major inquiries generally) because they are certain to be subject to detailed scrutiny later. Secondly, investigators are drawn from a range of different sources and do not form a ready-made team with pre-existing internal loyalties. Thirdly, there is a firm separation between managers of the inquiry and those making enquiries or inputting and analysing data. This helps managers to maintain a distance from the investigation and avoid closing their minds to specific lines of inquiry. Fourthly, team members have closely defined tasks (cf. the 'entrepreneurial' approach of detectives in traditional CIDs) and there are clear lines of responsibility and accountability. Considerable cross-checking and review of information generated by the inquiry takes place and there would be a high chance of fabricated evidence being discovered. The computerised systems for cross-checking evidence do not distinguish between that which is and is not 'convenient' for building the case. While, theoretically, the leader of the inquiry himself or herself could try to build a case on weak or improperly obtained evidence, there are internal quality control procedures (and sometimes external reviews by another force) which render this possibility liable to detection. Policy decisions relating to the course of the inquiry are also subject to discussion by senior officers leading investigations and are noted in a 'Policy Book', enabling them to be reviewed later. Lastly, all documents relating to the inquiry are held on a computerised database, one consequence being that the chances of deliberate or inadvertent non-disclosure of crucial evidence to the defence are minimised. Maguire and Norris conclude that, "[w]hile by no means eliminating problems caused by human fallibility, the HOLMES-based inquiry system encourages a much more thorough, professional and rational approach to major investigations, with inbuilt checks and balances".

Supervision in special squads

Maguire and Norris (1992) also looked at patterns of supervision in Regional Crime Squads (RCSs)[3] and Drugs Squads. These are dealt with separately because their work differs from the reactive pattern of much detective work, involving pro-active targeting of particular suspects. RCSs operate in syndi-

---

3   There are nine RCSs in England and Wales, spanning police force boundaries. Each is headed by a Detective Chief Superintendent, accountable to a management committee comprised of Chief Constables from each constituent force and an HMIC representative.

cates of 12 officers, based at regional branches; within each syndicate there are three teams of one detective sergeant and three constables.

The activities of both RCSs and Drugs Squads tend to be sparked off by intelligence reports from a range of sources about the activities of known offenders. Within each RCS, such intelligence is evaluated, reviewed and confirmed, leading to rational decisions about which offenders to target. Maguire and Norris (1992) note that this process is highly likely to weed out cases in which suspicions are erroneous or based on flimsy evidence. Some Drugs Squads follow a similar model, although intelligence gathering tends to be less systematised or subject to review. One key feature of both kinds of squad is their dependence on information from informants, both to identify target offenders and to specify when the target is likely to be engaged in criminal activity. Coupled with this strategy is the use of surveillance to establish evidence of criminal activity and information about criminal associates of the target offender, as well as to gauge the best time to move in to make an arrest.

Discussing supervision in RCSs and Drugs Squads, Maguire and Norris point out that there are some of the same weaknesses as those found in reactive detective work. Among these is the debasement of the sergeant's supervisory role. Although in RCSs there is a ratio of one sergeant to three constables, sergeants are very much team members carrying their own caseload. The predominant attitude is that formal supervision of day to day working practices is unnecessary because team members are high calibre individuals, able to work on their own initiative. The same applies in Drugs Squads.

Another major potential weakness is dependence upon informants. Maguire and Norris point out that detectives' dealings with them are of low visibility to supervisors, and often involve various kinds of 'deals' (for example, offers of favourable treatment to those who are themselves suspects), which carry the risk of generating unreliable evidence. They note that, due to a spirit of rivalry and competitiveness, detectives are traditionally reluctant to share information with other officers. Another danger area is the use of informants as participants in criminal enterprises to entrap target suspects. They note that, other than in RCSs, detectives receive little training in the handling and supervision of informants and may develop undesirable working practices by copying other officers.

As against these weaknesses, Maguire and Norris point out that there are certain strengths to supervision and control within special squads, which serve to reduce the risk of malpractice. The proactive nature of the work is the source of two of these. Firstly, evidence tends to be built up prior to arrest, often through surveillance, with less reliance on confessions and their attendant risks. Secondly, there is not the same pressure to generate high volumes of clear-ups, the emphasis being more on good quality clearances in a limited number of serious cases.

There are also control mechanisms other than formal supervision by sergeants. For example, the use of surveillance is subject to high level authorisation; and the risk of falsification of surveillance evidence is relatively low because it would require collaboration among several members of a team. Within RCSs there are tight guidelines and procedures regulating dealings with informants, particularly the making of payments. Thus, all informants must be registered, and contacts with them are supervised by a controller of senior rank. The essential elements of the RCS system have now been incorporated into a national set of guidelines issued by ACPO (1992) for the handling of informants generally.

Lastly, Maguire and Norris refer to the importance of the management information system within RCSs. Comprehensive indicators of activity are returned to regional co-ordinators each month. This, they argue, is a useful step towards engendering an ethos of strong managerial control and oversight. This could help to prevent the kinds of malpractice identified in the West Midlands Serious Crime Squad which were linked with the lack of such control.

Improving supervisory practices

Studies examining the issue of investigative supervision have made a number of suggestions for change, either to to reduce the risk of miscarriages of justice or to improve efficiency. Maguire and Norris (1992), concerned primarily with the former, have suggested that it is fundamental for supervisory officers to recognise the inadequacies of current supervisory arrangements. This means taking the monitoring of the integrity of investigations seriously and reducing reliance on outdated 'charismatic' modes of supervision. This must be coupled with a recognition of the negative consequences of the CID working culture and a change in emphasis from quantity to quality of crime clearances. Similar conclusions are drawn by Baldwin (1992c), specifically in relation to the supervision of interviews. It has been noted above that supervisors are reluctant to impugn officers' professional pride by scrutinising the way they conduct interviews. He argues that this aspect of police working culture must be overturned for, until supervisory officers are prepared to see the problems in this area at first hand, there will only be limited improvements in practice.

Irving and Dunnighan (1993) also lay emphasis on improvements in quality. Supervisors, they suggest, have a role to play here because they can take a broader view of the way in which particular investigative activities impact on the criminal justice process. They may be able to divert investigating officers from a way of thinking which assesses the quality of work in terms of its effects on promotion and career prospects towards viewing the quality of an investigation in overall terms.

There is general agreement that more effective supervision requires changes in supervisory practice and the relationship between supervisors and supervised. In this context, both Maguire and Norris (1992) and Baldwin and Moloney (1992) argue strongly for making the role of sergeants a genuinely supervisory one. To succeed, this would mean distancing them from day-to-day involvement in investigation by removing their own caseloads and thereby increasing their opportunities for effective supervision.

Maguire and Norris (1992) also argue for more scrutiny of investigations by officers unconnected with the enquiry. One suggestion is that an independent 'PACE Officer' should monitor and advise on the procedural correctness of inquiries. But their central recommendation is that, given the particular difficulties associated with supervising investigative staff in the field and the risks associated with certain kinds of evidence, systems of ensuring quality control should be introduced. The essential elements of such a system would be that staff not connected with investigations would carry out random checks of particular areas of detective activity, to see whether procedural, legal and qualitative standards had been met. The kinds of area they have in mind include: tape-recorded interviews; records of interview; victim and witness statements; and the progress of enquiries generally – particularly policy decisions made at key stages.

The police complaints system

The police complaints system is essentially concerned with members of the public's grievances about the conduct of the police and not with force policy or operational decisions. Complaints tend to be dominated by dissatisfaction with aggressive or uncivil behaviour, both verbal or physical. These account for over half of all complaints. The majority of other complaints involve allegations of irregular or negligent conduct (Brown, 1987; Maguire and Corbett, 1991; PCA, various years).

The complaints procedures established by PACE reflect the outcome of a long debate about the extent to which the police themselves should investigate allegations of misconduct by their own officers. The transfer of responsibility for complaints to an independent body was first considered by the Royal Commission on the Police (1962), but they opted instead for the tightening up of police procedures. The Police Act 1964 stipulated that all official complaints had to be fully investigated and the outcome reported.

Following the 1964 Act, waning public confidence in the operation of the system fuelled demands for an independent element and this was reflected in the creation of the Police Complaints Board in 1976, charged with monitoring chief officers' disciplinary decisions. Nevertheless, the system still continued to attract criticism. There was dissatisfaction abut the investigation of serious cases, the slowness of the procedure and its inflexibility in dealing with minor cases, and there were accusations of officers investigating complaints applying pressure on complainants to withdraw their allegations (Brown, 1987; Police Complaints Board, 1980 and 1983).

The Police Complaints Authority

PACE introduced a new and more substantial independent element into the investigation of more serious allegations and those of great public concern by providing for the supervision of complaints investigations in such cases by members of a new independent body, the Police Complaints Authority (PCA). The actual investigation is, as before, carried out by the police. In the most serious cases (where death or serious injury is alleged to have resulted from police conduct), the PCA must supervise. In a range of other cases they have discretion whether to do so.

In all cases which lead to the formal investigation of a complaint, a division of the PCA examines the full evidence and the final report of the investigation and decides whether they agree with its recommendations. They may direct that cases be referred to the Director of Public Prosecutions if they consider that an officer ought to be charged; and they may recommend or, as a last resort, direct that disciplinary charges be brought.

The informal resolution procedure

A new informal resolution procedure is intended to allow for the swift and speedy allaying of grievances in less serious cases. An officer may be appointed to seek to resolve a complaint informally, provided that he or she is satisfied that the conduct complained of, even if proved, would not justify a criminal or disciplinary charge. In addition, the complainant must be in agreement. The procedure is intended to be less rigid than formal investigation. Thus, an officer may admit fault and offer an apology to the complainant without the risk of disciplinary action or an entry on his personal record.

Research on the police complaints system

Some information on the pre-PACE complaints system is available from a study by Brown (1987). He interviewed over 100 complainants, including those whose complaints had been fully investigated or withdrawn, about their views and experiences of the complaints procedure. Since the introduction of PACE, only one study has been carried out on the new procedures. This was a wide-ranging piece of research conducted by the Oxford Centre for Criminological Research, which examined the police role in investigating and informally resolving complaints, as well as the functions of the PCA (reported in Maguire and Corbett, 1989 and 1991;[4] and Corbett, 1991). Maguire and Corbett undertook fieldwork in three forces, examined case files on complaints, and interviewed complainants, officers complained against, those involved in investigating complaints, members of the PCA (including those involved in the supervision of investigations), and representatives of police unions and Police Authorities. They also analysed samples of cases supervised by the PCA and sought the views of a sample of complainants in such cases.

The Maguire and Corbett study, while providing a valuable insight into the working of the complaints system at the time it was conducted, must now be regarded as dated. The complaints cases on which its conclusions were based were ones dealt with in 1986 and 1987. At the time, the PCA was in its infancy. Since then there have been many changes in the way it works, supervises investigations, deals with the media and communicates with complainants (PCA, 1995a). In reading the account of the research which follows, it must therefore be kept in mind that this is very much a snapshot of the system as it was at the time and that this now urgently requires updating.

Supervision of investigations by the PCA

The supervision decision

Maguire and Corbett found that a large proportion of cases supervised by PCA members related to complaints of assault. They note that such complaints tended to be very difficult to prove as there were rarely independent witnesses and, apart from medical evidence, it was often the word of the police against that of the complainant. They maintain that, because so many investigations in assault cases were therefore unpromising, PCA members tended to reject such cases for supervision at a greater rate than non-assault cases. They also make the point that inclusion of too many cases in which PCA supervision apparently showed no dividends in terms of a

---

4   This is the main report of the study and, unless otherwise stated, is the source of information drawn upon in this section of the review.

substantiated complaint may have lowered public confidence in the Authority. Where the decision made *was* to supervise the investigation of assault allegations, there tended to be some special factor present: for example, a particularly vulnerable victim, the suspicion of a police 'cover-up', or a greater than average prospect of the allegation being substantiated. Non-assault cases which were supervised typically involved allegations of corruption, serious arrestable offences, or cases that had a high public profile because of media or local community interest.

Maguire and Corbett draw attention to difficulties raised at the time of their research by the procedure for deciding whether the PCA should supervise complaints investigations. One was its inflexibility. In some cases alleging serious injury (which must be supervised), subsequent evidence revealed that injuries were not as grave as at first appeared. However, there was no provision to withdraw from supervision.[5] Sometimes, the involvement of the PCA was delayed while forces obtained more detailed evidence about the nature of injuries.

Nature of supervision

Maguire and Corbett found that the nature and extent of supervision varied. They identified three different forms: passive, active and directive. *Passive* supervision meant that PCA members largely restricted themselves to reading through all of the documentation from the investigating officer, only communicating if necessary. This was used in less complicated cases, where the police had developed standard practices in investigation. *Active* supervision involved frequent telephone conversations and sometimes meetings with the investigating officer. Members might make comments and suggestions on how the investigation should proceed. It was found more in high profile or very serious cases, particularly those where it was likely that the police officer would be prosecuted. Supervision was not constant but tended to occur in bursts at crucial stages of the investigation. *Directive* supervision was the most intensive and members might request or even formally direct investigating officers to follow specified lines of inquiry.

Effects of supervision

Maguire and Corbett found that the chances of some form of action being taken against an officer were greater in supervised cases than others. However, this may have reflected the process of selecting cases for supervision, whereby those with a greater prospect of substantiation stood a greater chance of

---

5   Schedule 5, para 31 of the Police and Magistrates' Courts Act 1994 now provides for the making of regulations to cover this point.

selection. They found some evidence of other benefits including: lower rates of withdrawn complaints; better quality reports; and speedier investigation.

The views of complainants and the public

A division of the PCA informs the complainant of the outcome of supervised cases by letter. Maguire and Corbett note that attempts have been made to ensure that letters are written in simple English and do not sound too bureaucratic. However, there were low levels of satisfaction with the outcome of supervised cases, with over 90 per cent of complainants interviewed expressing themselves to be fairly or very dissatisfied. Part of this dissatisfaction may have been attributable to the fact that complainants sometimes misunderstood the outcome of their complaint. But it may also have reflected the fact that complainants often wanted something other than a statement that their complaint had been substantiated. This echoes the findings of research on the pre-PACE complaints procedure (Brown, 1987). Complainants were also often hazy about what the role of the PCA was.

Nevertheless, Maguire and Corbett found some evidence that complainants in supervised cases had more favourable expectations and experiences of the complaints procedure than other complainants. They felt their case had been treated more seriously, that investigating officers had been thorough and that they had been kept well informed about what was happening. They were also less likely to experience pressure to withdraw their complaints. Maguire and Corbett argue, in consequence, that one effect of supervision may have been to sharpen up complaints investigations.

Maguire and Corbett draw upon evidence from the 1988 British Crime Survey (BCS) to suggest that the PCA has had only a limited impact on public consciousness (see too Skogan, 1990). The BCS found that less than 10 per cent of those interviewed knew of 'an independent organisation which supervises the way the police investigate complaints', only one in five of this subgroup could name it correctly, and even when the name was put to them, less than 40 per cent of the full sample claimed to have heard of the PCA.

The PCA itself has in recent years commissioned annual public attitude surveys to gauge public awareness of the Authority and of the complaints system. The findings appear to show rather greater public awareness than was found in the BCS. In the most recent survey, carried out in 1995, 65 per cent of respondents who were prompted with the name of the Authority claimed that they were aware of it (PCA, 1995b). It appears, however, that the Authority still has some way to go in persuading the public of its impartiality and independence from the police. Thus, less than half of respondents (45%) believed it to be impartial in its handling of complaints, although only

27 per cent felt that it inevitably came down on the side of the police. The proportion believing the PCA to be independent actually appears to have been declining: down from 51 per cent in 1993 to 41 per cent in 1995. Well under half of respondents – 43 per cent – trusted the police to investigate complaints against their fellow officers. Moreover, the proportion actually believing that they could not be trusted to do so has been declining and currently rests at 34 per cent.

Following concern about the perceived lack of confidence in the complaints system by those from ethnic minority groups, the PCA conducted special surveys of adults drawn from these groups in 1994 and 1995. Some of the findings were not reassuring: only 33 per cent of ethnic minority respondents were aware of the PCA's existence and only 27 per cent saw it as independent from the police – both figures far lower than for the general population (PCA, 1995b). However, the same surveys also found some signs of improvement in attitudes. For example, there was an increase in the proportions of ethnic minority respondents who believed that the PCA would take their complaints seriously and who saw it as impartial and not necessarily on the side of the police. There was also evidence that the loss of trust in the police investigating complaints against their own number has been stemmed.

The views of the police

Maguire and Corbett found that officers investigating complaints considered supervision by the PCA to have had little impact on the outcome of investigations, although it may have reassured the public or diverted media attention. However, there was a general view that the PCA had a good grasp of the system and could spot shortcomings in investigations. This therefore put investigators on their mettle in supervised cases.

Informal resolution

The most recent published statistics (for 1994) show that around one-third of all recorded complaints are now informally resolved (Home Office, 1995). The present position reflects a gradual increase in the informal resolution procedure since its introduction. In 1985 just eight per cent of complaints were informally resolved, in 1988 21 per cent and in 1991 25 per cent (Home Office, ibid.). Maguire and Corbett found that the informal resolution procedure was used most as a replacement for formal investigation. There was no evidence that use of the procedure resulted in more complaints being recorded, as might occur if duty inspectors had ceased to filter out some minor grievances at an early stage without recourse to the new procedure.

Maguire and Corbett point to various advantages of informal resolution: for example, it dispenses with the need for formal investigation in an adversarial setting in cases for which this is singularly inappropriate; it reduces administration and delays; complainants may receive an apology or explanation, which they might not if the complaint were investigated; and an officer can admit to the incident without risking disciplinary action.

Police views

Nevertheless, Maguire and Corbett's study found that informal resolution was not welcomed by the majority of officers complained against. They were concerned that accepting informal resolution was as good as admitting guilt and that they lost the opportunity that they would have had to clear their name if the complaint had been proceeded with. They were therefore reluctant to submit to the procedure where they estimated the chances of proving guilt as slim. Some regarded participation in informal resolution as a punishment in itself, since it put their behaviour under a spotlight. Furthermore, despite its nominally informal nature, officers appointed to resolve complaints could adopt over-formal approaches, thus limiting the free flow of information. Informal resolution was seen cynically by some as a way of saving Complaints and Discipline Departments' time.

On the other side of the coin, one advantage was that, if the complaint was likely to be substantiated, informal resolution allowed the officer complained against to admit to the complaint but receive no disciplinary action.

Both officers complained against and those conducting informal resolution were generally opposed to meetings with the complainant. The former objected as they felt that they should not have to defend themselves. The latter did not see meetings as conducive to agreement and felt that they could generate greater animosity between the two parties.

A common misunderstanding among those appointed to resolve complaints was that the officer concerned must agree to informal resolution. This is not the case.

The complainant's view

Most complainants interviewed stated that they were willing to accept the outcome of informal resolution, and only a few felt that they had been wrongly pressured into accepting this course. It is clear from complainants' responses that officers appointed to conduct informal resolution did sometimes push hard for complainants to go along this road, although this is not to say that the alternatives were not pointed out. Complainants were not obliged to accept the outcome and could have opted for formal investigation of the complaint. However, none of the complainants in the study could remember being offered this choice if they were unhappy with the outcome. Officers conducting informal resolution in fact admitted that they interpreted the regulations loosely in this respect and often persuaded the complainant to accept informal resolution whatever the outcome.

Complainants had various sources of dissatisfaction. About half would have wished for a meeting with the officer about whom they complained in order to obtain some form of apology. Complainants also felt that they were not given enough feedback during the course of informal resolution and, when it had been concluded, about matters such as the reactions of the officer complained against. Although complainants may apply for a record relating to their complaint, few were aware of this right and those that did apply were disappointed by how little information the record actually contained.

General views of the complaints system

A large proportion of complaints are neither supervised by the PCA nor informally resolved. Around 40 per cent are withdrawn. The remainder (about one-quarter) proceed to a full investigation (Home Office, 1995). Maguire and Corbett provide some general appreciations of the system, which are considered below.

Complainants' views

From interviews with complainants it was clear that a certain amount of tenacity was required to persist with a complaint against the police. A third of those interviewed reported various attempts to put them off complaining at the time they sought to register complaints. Similar findings are reported by Brown (1987) in his pre-PACE study. It is quite probable, in view of these findings, that some persons with legitimate grievances do not proceed beyond this stage and do not appear in the complaints statistics.

A majority of those who withdrew and of those who proceeded with complaints reported various efforts by the police to persuade them to with-draw. These approaches varied in acceptability and in strength of purpose. In some cases, investigating officers pointed realistically to the probable lack of success due to a lack of independent evidence or the triviality of the matter. Less acceptable approaches stressed the effect on an officer's career, possible repercussions for the complainant, and the (unlikely) possibility that the complainant would have to give evidence in court or at a disciplinary hearing. Again, this picture is remarkably similar to that reported by Brown (1987) in his pre-PACE work.

Satisfying the complainant is an important element in maintaining public confidence in the police. Maguire and Corbett found that complainants had a range of different aims, of which only a minority cited punishment for the officer complained against. Others wished to 'educate' the officer concerned, prevent repetition, secure an apology and express their anger (see too Brown, 1987).

Over two-thirds of all complainants were dissatisfied with the outcome of their complaints, and most very dissatisfied. These low levels of satisfaction are not a significant improvement on those reported by Brown (1987), prior to the introduction of the present procedures. In that study, 60 per cent of complainants were dissatisfied with the outcome. Maguire and Corbett found that those whose complaints were informally resolved tended to be the most satisfied, perhaps reflecting their wish for a speedy solution and an explanation or apology. A significant minority of those who withdrew were also satisfied: they may have received an apology or been promised that informal action would be taken against an officer. Those whose complaints were formally investigated were the most dissatisfied. Their criticisms were of delay, the absence of an apology, and the inadequacy of explanations for decisions reached. These negative views were unrelated to whether complaints were eventually substantiated. At the root of these criticisms was lack of communication with the complainant, both about the progress of the investigation and the outcome. Maguire and Corbett conclude that failures in this respect mean that the important aims of satisfying complainants and rekindling their faith in the police were not being met. These conclusions are depressingly similar to those reached by Brown (1987) on the pre-existing complaints procedures.

Similar points about the dissatisfaction experienced by complainants have also been made by Sanders (1988), in an examination of the remedies available to those aggrieved by the misuse of police powers under PACE. He argues that the relative weakness of the complaints procedure as a mechanism to redress such wrongs is of particular concern, given the lack of other remedies provided by PACE where procedures or powers are abused. Exclusion of evidence, for example, is at the discretion of the trial judge and is, of course, of no relevance where the police decide not to prosecute.

Police views

In common with complainants, officers complained against were critical of delays in the system, which placed them under a good deal of stress. Being subject to an investigation was described as an uncomfortable experience. However, the great majority of those interviewed claimed that complaints against them had not affected their subsequent behaviour.

Investigating officers, on the other hand, did see the complaints system as acting as a deterrent and as a way of identifying patterns of police misbehaviour. However, they laid relatively little emphasis on satisfying the complainant, probably because they realised the chances of substantiating complaints were so low. They considered that their main role in this respect was to give complainants a fair hearing and assure them that the investigation would be thorough. Where it was clear that the chances of a complaint being substantiated were slim or they sensed that a complainant was not committed to proceeding, most admitted that they would steer him or her towards a withdrawal.

Implications

Maguire and Corbett are pessimistic about the ability of the complaints system as it stood at the time of their research to achieve its main objectives. First, it cannot play a major role in maintaining police discipline. In order to do so, sanctions must be applied frequently and consistently, yet few complaints are substantiated and officers know that their chances of incurring discipline are slight. Secondly, the prospects of satisfying the complainant are also poor, again because of the low substantiation rate. They criticise the procedure's dependence on proof of a breach of the police disciplinary code. This runs counter to the philosophy of more 'consumer-oriented' organisations, where satisfying the complainant is a priority. Thirdly, they point to difficulties in fulfilling another important objective, that of winning public confidence. This depends on effective publicity in cases in which the PCA are closely involved in supervising investigations. However, they note that such cases were comparatively few. Also, the PCA's resources were spread too thinly to make closer supervision in more cases viable. However, they are more optimistic about the ability of the system to achieve a fourth objective, that of providing management information to improve police performance.

In considering what weight to attach to Maguire and Corbett's findings, it must, as noted earlier, be recalled that they relate to the complaints system as it was some eight or nine years ago. Since that time, the PCA has taken strenuous steps to improve its effectiveness and imprint itself on the public consciousness. It has, for example, vigorously asserted its independence and become involved at an early stage in many high profile cases, either following complaints from the public or on its own initiative (PCA, 1995). Some of these cases have attracted considerable media attention. It has also been forward in making recommendations for improvement in police practices and procedures where consistent patterns of malpractice have generated complaints. Another aim which it has pursued has been to improve the quality of communication with complainants. For the present, it is not known what impact these activities have had upon those who register complaints or on the police themselves, whether complained against or involved in investigating complaints. Further research would be required in order to establish this kind of information.

Police community consultative groups

Lord Scarman, in his report on the Brixton riots, recommended that there should be procedures to enable the police to consult local communities about policing in their areas (Scarman, 1981). The employment by the police of methods which did not command the support of local communities, and which were therefore inefficient and ineffective, was blamed on lack of communication. He felt that existing police authorities lacked the power to carry out the required consultation effectively. In consequence, administrative guidance was issued to the police in 1982 about the role and nature of local consultation arrangements, pointing to the need for a two-way flow of information and for membership of local committees to be flexible and wide-ranging. Section 106 of PACE strengthens these informal arrangements by putting them on a statutory basis, without specifying the form which they should take. They are to be developed by consultation between police authorities and chief constables (except in the Metropolitan Police, where they are made by the Commissioner in consultation with each borough). It has been noted that these arrangements fill an important gap in the apparatus of accountability. Courts, for example, can only rule on legal points where wrongdoing is at issue. Wider issues of the police role and objectives remain to be debated within a non-legal framework (Morgan and Maggs, 1985; Morgan, 1987).

Section 106 came into force on 1 January 1985. It was accompanied by guidance issued in a Home Office Circular (Home Office, 1985a) – the primary means by which the Home Secretary may influence the arrangements to be made. (He may also call for reports from police authorities or the Commissioner of the Metropolitan Police but he has no direct power over the arrangements.) The guidance refers to matters which might properly be the subject of local consultation. They exclude discussion of individual cases and certain operational matters, but include "discussion of the incidence of and the police response to both crime generally and specific types of crime" and "the operation of police procedures and policy in relation to law enforcement" (Zander, 1990). Guidance is also given on membership: this may include police, councillors, MPs and members of statutory agencies, but they should normally be fewer than the number of community representatives, who may be drawn from various voluntary agencies and local services. There should be regular turnover of the membership. In 1989, the Home Office issued a further Circular (Home Office, 1989b), following a review of existing consultation arrangements.

A recent development in the statutory background to police community consultation has been the introduction of provisions in the Police and Magistrates' Courts Act 1994 relating to the annual setting of objectives for the policing of each area. Objectives are determined by the police authority in consultation with the chief constable and are published in a local policing plan. Each police authority is first required to consider any views of the local community, obtained in accordance with the arrangements made under s.106 of PACE.[6]

The Home Office review, referred to above, is one useful source of information about the working of the consultation provisions. They have also generated a certain amount of research attention. The main study is one carried out at Bath University, which included a countrywide survey of the state of police community consultation arrangements in the mid-1980s (Morgan and Maggs, 1985). The survey is now rather dated and not necessarily representative of the current situation. However, in subsequent work, Morgan (1992) has continued to trace the progress of police community consultation. Attention has also been paid to the subject in studies by Fyfe (1992) and, more recently, Hughes (1994).

The Home Office review, referred to by Morgan and Maggs (1985) and Zander (1990), drew attention to the fact that, by the mid-1980s, consultation arrangements of some kind were in place in most parts of the country. Where they did not exist, pressure to put arrangements for consultation in place had been applied by Her Majesty's Inspectorate of Constabulary. The review drew attention to various failings of the consultation arrangements. It noted difficulties in attracting a membership representative of local communities. In some areas, membership was confined to representatives of local organisations; in others, individuals were allowed to join. However, it has proved difficult to attract members of ethnic minority organisations, and in some areas local Race Equality Councils or local authorities have distanced themselves from the consultation process. Consultative groups have also under-represented younger people. The membership has consisted predominantly of professional, middle-class, white people, aged over 40. Although meetings are generally open, allowing the public a chance to contribute, they have rarely attracted much interest. Meetings have been infrequent in some areas, sometimes only twice a year.

---

6   Initial indications are that most police authorities have relied heavily on Police and Community Consultative Groups to obtain views about policing objectives.

Agenda have apparently tended to be dominated by police authorities, who usually supply the chairmen of consultative groups. In some areas, the police have also contributed to the agenda and have been open with information. In others, they have been reluctant to share information. Morgan (1987) notes that the police see dangers in revealing operational details: they may be criticised both for low level police strategies and active enforcement. They also fear that information given may be wrongly used.

The conclusion reached by Morgan (1986) from the early part of his research is that police autonomy has largely been unimpaired by the existence of consultative groups. Offering accounts of what they are doing and propose to do operationally does not detract from their powers. Consultative groups have no formal authority and the police are not obliged to take account of what they say. He has also argued elsewhere that consultative groups have not been inclined to probe operational policies, since members tend to be those who are most satisfied with or not in conflict with the police (Morgan, 1987). He was pessimistic about the value of consultation as then organised. He argued that consultation groups had no practical effects where it really mattered: for example, on local administration or allocation of resources to the police. Committee members tended to be largely ignorant of issues of operational control over policy and of the basis for determining police priorities. The police revealed only superficial details of their organisation and operation, and the more important managerial and operational decisions were taken behind closed doors. The membership of consultative groups required stability so that policies might be followed through (although Home Office guidance points to the need for regular turnover of membership: Home Office, 1985a). However, he argued that consultative arrangements have the potential to define the boundaries of policing by consent. However, the failure by some community groups to use the committees and the absence of dispute at meetings could be taken, rightly or wrongly, as indicating that the public were satisfied with the way that the police were operating (Morgan, 1986).

The Home Office review of police/community consultation arrangements reached more positive conclusions (Home Office, 1989b). It maintained that there were enough groups playing active roles to demonstrate that such consultation could genuinely involve people in the policing of their area. For example, there was some recent anecdotal information to the effect that the holding of open meetings in some areas has met with success, nothwithstanding earlier experience to the contrary. However, there were also found to be many groups which were achieving very little. Further good practice guidelines have been issued for police/community consultation, but it is not clear what impact these have had.

A somewhat different message, albeit positive in a way, is contained in the research by Hughes (1994). In this study, police community consultation arrangements were studied over a three year period in a shire county. Although for the most part it was found that the status of consultation was similar to that which Morgan had described (see above), in the county's main connurbation in the research force the situation was rather different. Hughes found that there were powerful groupings of members drawn from political parties, local government and statutory and voluntary agencies. He points out that their representativeness of the local population is somewhat dubious. He characterises their effect upon the local police community consultation group as being to transform it into an inter-agency crime prevention forum rather than a public forum open to all. The influence of this coalition of members at meetings with the police was undeniable. To some extent this was due, in his view, to the fact that they spoke the same 'managerial' lanaguage as senior police officers. Also, they could be said to be broadly sympathetic towards the police, without necessarily supporting all police activities. In practical terms they had the effect of bringing to the fore specific local problems and of pressing for co-ordinated strategies for crime prevention in the area. While accepting that the style and impact of this particular group was atypical, he argues that the effect of having such a group in existence in close proximity to other, less dynamic, groups must not be under-estimated. Hughes suggests that it might be seen by other groups as a challenging 'model' to emulate.

Interestingly, Morgan's (1992) later work, which reviews the progress of police community consultation in the late-80s, suggests that the 'atypical' group described by Hughes may not be so unusual. He, along with Fyfe (1992), identifies a trend among the members of local agencies and political parties to become increasingly involved in local consultation arrangements with the police. A factor influencing this trend is, in Morgan's view, the increasing openness of the police to scrutiny, resulting in the provision of information to consultation groups which members may report back to their own agencies and institutions. These, in their turn, are sufficiently powerful to influence the agenda at the meetings with the police.

Summary

Supervision

- Detectives receive relatively little training in the supervision of investigations; in consequence, investigative errors or shortcomings may be overlooked.

- Effective supervision of investigations is impeded by the low visibility of much detective work, issues of professional pride (especially in relation to interviewing skills) and an emphasis on quantity rather than quality of clear-ups.

- The bulk of investigations are supervised by lower-ranking officers, who have their own caseloads to cope with. Senior officers generally carry out little proactive supervision of investigations. These supervisory arrangements carry the risk that malpractice or incompetence may pass unnoticed. Commentators have suggested the need for closer quality control over investigations and effective supervision.

- There is tighter supervision by senior officers in major inquiries and in special squads. In major inquiries, supervision is more directive, there are quality control procedures and teams are comprised of officers without established loyalties to each other. In special squads, there is rigorous scrutiny of the evidence before offenders are targeted and tight managerial control over dealings with informants.

Complaints

- No recent research has been carried out on the complaints system, although some information about public attitudes is available from recent surveys.

- In a study based on complaints cases dealt with in 1986 and 1987 the PCA was found to be less likely to select assault cases than others for supervision. Complaints of assault tend to be particularly difficult to prove and this may have had a bearing on the PCA's decision whether to supervise.

- PCA supervision varied from passive, active or directive, depending on how complex and how high profile cases were. Where investigations were supervised, action was more frequently taken against officers, complaints were less often withdrawn, reports were of better quality and investigation was speedier.

- Most complainants were dissatisfied with the outcome of supervised cases, although they were more likely than other complainants to feel their case had been treated seriously and receive good feedback and less likely to experience pressure to withdraw. Investigating officers felt that the PCA had little impact on the outcome of investigations, although its attention to the case put them on their mettle.

- A considerable proportion of the public (65 per cent) were aware of the PCA's existence, though rather fewer believe that it is impartial and independent from the police. Among members of ethnic minority groups these figures are considerably lower, although there is some evidence that confidence is improving.

- Informal resolution of complaints was generally not popular with officers subject to complaint since they felt that accepting it was seen as admitting guilt. Officers did not view meetings between officer and complainant as productive.

- Where complaints were informally resolved, most complainants accepted this outcome, despite persuasion to take this course in some cases. Complainants were dissatisfied at not meeting officers subject to complaint and with lack of feeedback.

- A third of complainants reported attempts to dissuade them registering a complaint. Of those withdrawing and proceeding, a majority reported attempts to secure a withdrawal.

- Over two-thirds of complaints were dissatisfied with the outcome of their complaint, usually due to the lack of an apology or of an explanation for decisions reached. Those whose complaints were informally resolved were the most satisfied.

- Officers subject to complaint criticised the slowness of procedures. Because of the low chances of complaints being substantiated, investigating officers doubted the chances of satisfying complainants, other than by treating grievances seriously.

Police community consultative groups

- Consultation arrangements now exist in most parts of the country. However, there have been difficulties recruiting members representative of local communities, particularly those from minority ethnic groups and younger people. Meetings are infrequent in some areas and, where public, have tended to be poorly attended.

- Agenda are sometimes dominated by police authorities. For their part, the police have not always been willing to share information, especially where it relates to operational matters.

- The effectiveness of consultative groups appears to be constrained by several factors including: lack of formal authority; absence of hard-edged information; ignorance of policing issues; pro-police orientation; and non-representativeness.

- However, there are groups which are very active and are genuinely involving local people in the policing of their area. In certain areas, groups appear to be dominated by influential coalitions comprising representatives from local political parties, statutory and voluntary agencies and local government, who are able to pursue their chosen agenda with the police.

12 Conclusions: the impact of PACE

From the considerable body of research on PACE which has been reviewed in this report it is possible to draw a number of broader conclusions about the impact of the Act. These are dealt with under three headings. First, consideration is given to the question of whether the rules contained in PACE and the Codes have in practice lived up to the standards of fairness, openness and workability viewed as so important by the RCCP. The second issue is that of the extent to which legal regulation has influenced police conduct. It has been argued by some that the potential of legal rules to affect what the police do was accepted too readily by the RCCP and by those who drew up PACE and the Codes (see, for example, Dixon *et al*, 1989). Lastly, this chapter attempts to answer the question of whether PACE has produced a satisfactory balance in the investigative process between the public interest in bringing offenders to trial and the rights and liberties of the suspect.

Fairness, openness and workability

Fairness

The concept of fairness, as was noted in Chapter 1, applies to both suspects and the police. From the point of view of the former, the essential elements are that suspects should be made aware of their rights and given the chance to exercise them; if rights are to be withheld, they should be told this and the reasons. Those under investigation should also be told the basis for the exercise of police powers. Rules should also be applied equitably across different groups of people and different parts of the country.

PACE has undoubtedly led to a significant improvement in fairness for the suspect as judged by these criteria. The most marked change has been in suspects' awareness of the right to legal advice and in the implementation of this right. Before the introduction of PACE, suspects enjoyed a right to legal advice but many were not given the opportunity to exercise it, either because they were not told about it or access to a solicitor was delayed or denied. A large body of research shows that the overwhelming majority of suspects are now told about this right; furthermore, the amount of information provided about it has increased, enabling them to make better informed decisions. Where legal advice is requested, it is successfully provided in the great majority of cases. The police only resort to the power available in serious arrestable offences to delay access to legal advice on increasingly rare occasions.

While there has been an improvement, there are still shortcomings. In a minority of cases, custody officers do not provide suspects with adequate information about their rights or do so in ways which, intentionally or unintentionally, prejudice suspects against taking advantage of them. More rarely, they fail to provide any information at all. Furthermore, there are considerable variations between areas in these respects. And some groups of suspects, particularly juveniles, are more likely to suffer from shortcomings in the way rights are conveyed and implemented. It has been argued by some that inequitable treatment of suspects stems from coherent strategies designed to deny certain groups access to their rights (see, for example, McConville *et al*, 1991). This view has been contested in this report. It has been pointed out that custody officers have developed a considerable degree of independence which makes it unlikely that they will connive with investigating officers to deny suspects their rights; they will not risk the possibility of discipline simply to assist investigators to secure admissions. They will, however, assist within the law, and this may sometimes mean that information about rights is pared to a minimum.

There are other reasons why suspects are effectively denied equal access to their rights. What is to the custody officer a highly routinised procedure, the provision of rights, may not be so to suspects, some of whom may fail to take in the information they are given. Not all suspects are in a reasonable frame of mind on arrival at the police station, but custody officers may not fully appreciate this and adjust their approach accordingly. Importantly, they may develop their own working rules about the best way to deal with particular groups of suspects, which conflict with the requirements of the PACE Codes. For example, the reason why juveniles are not always told their rights on arrival or why implementation of those rights is sometimes delayed until the arrival of an adult may be that custody officers regard juveniles as incapable of making unaided decisions about what is in their best interests. They may also make judgements about the utility of advice in particular cases – particularly trivial ones – or about suspects' pre-existing knowledge of their rights which influence the way in which they convey information about rights and their enthusiasm for putting them into practice.

PACE may also have had mixed success in achieving fairness for the suspect by ensuring that those under investigation are aware of the basis for police actions and that powers are exercised equitably. This view applies particularly to discretionary police actions outside the police station and exercise of the powers to stop and search persons or vehicles, and to enter and search premises. The research suggests that the police rely on the consent of the person concerned where possible, in order to take the search outside of the statutory requirements and minimise the risk of later repercussions if it turns out not to be justified. There are severe doubts about how often consent is genuinely given, in the sense that the person to be searched is aware that he or she may refuse. Where a power is used, there is evidence that the person concerned is not always given adequate information about the basis for its exercise. Powers of stop and search are also still open to the criticism which was made of pre-PACE powers that they are used discriminatorily against different groups. Young black males who are stopped are far more likely to be searched than their white counterparts.

For the police, fairness means, in essence, that rules should be part of a clear and understandable framework and not liable to arbitrary reinterpretation at a later stage. Failure to meet these criteria was an accusation justifiably levelled at various aspects of the pre-PACE rules: for example, those relating to length of detention, powers to search premises, the interviewing of suspects and denial of suspects' access to legal advice. In many areas it may be argued that the rules are now clearer and easier to work with. A common police contention is that they know where they stand once a suspect is in police detention. PACE and the Codes lay down precise rules about the length of time for which someone may be detained, the conditions of deten-tion, suspects' access to legal advisers and the basis on which this may be delayed. The rules may not always be popular but they are certain.

However, there remain areas, identified in this review, in which a lack of clarity remains. One is the grounds of suspicion required to justify stop and search. Attempts to lay down guidelines in the first edition of the PACE Codes of Practice have not been entirely successful. The distinction between reasonable grounds and mere suspicion has been found to cause confusion, as has the requirement that it should be no less than the standard of suspi-cion required to arrest. Attempts to individualise the basis for suspicion have also not always been found helpful. Confronted by these uncertainties, the police preference has been to work outside of legal constraints by stopping and searching with consent. Attempts have been made in revisions to PACE Code A to remove these confusions, although there is little available evidence as to whether this has had the desired effect. Another area in which the police have found there to be a lack of clarity is in the procedures for authorising and recording details of searches of premises. Several powers are available in this area, depending upon the circumstances. In certain situa-tions prior authorisation from a senior officer is not required. The different requirements for authorisation and recording have caused confusion and, again, a common response has been to operate with consent (not necessarily freely given) and to under-record searches.

A further and perhaps more important area in which the rules are less than certain is in the interviewing of suspects. PACE and the Codes of Practice reflect the RCCP's concern to reduce the risk of unreliable confessions. The emphasis is placed on ensuring that there are appropriate safeguards: for example, that suspects have access to legal advice; that interviewing is not inordinately lengthy; and that those at risk have a third party present to assist them. But there is no definition of what tactics are and are not admissible during interview. The RCCP had considered it impossible to define with precision what was and was not prohibited. The decided cases have pointed to extremes of police behaviour which may lead to evidence being excluded: for example, inducing the suspect to confess through claims that the police had evidence that they did not in fact have. It is also clear that flagrant breaches of the PACE Codes will lead to evidence being excluded. Short of this, however, there is less certainty about the point at which the acceptable shades into the unacceptable. Research has shown that questioning is sometimes coercive in nature and that various inducements to confess are offered. The RCCP had recommended that police officers should receive better training in interviewing which pointed to the psychological effects on the suspect of particular interview techniques. This would help enable them to assess what is within the bounds of acceptability. However, this need has only recently begun to be addressed.

Openness

The criterion of openness requires that the basis for police actions should be clear to the suspect, and that decisions should be written down and therefore open to review by others. There must be some doubt about the extent to which this standard has been achieved by PACE and the Codes. This criticism applies both to the exercise of powers outside the police station and to events during custody.

It has been noted earlier in this review that the police prefer to operate on a basis of consent, where possible, in conducting stop/searches and searches of premises. Whether the decision is made to record the search as one conducted under a PACE power may depend on a number of contingent factors (for example, whether stolen property is found or whether later repercussions are anticipated). Furthermore, searches sometimes occur as a logical development of a continuing encounter with members of the public and there is not always a clear point at which suspicions reach the required level to enable officers to state clearly when exercise of a PACE power is justified. In many situations, therefore, it may not be clear to those subject to searches on what basis the police are acting. To explain the real grounds may also run the risk of antagonising the person to be searched. Even where it is clear that the police are acting under a statutory power, as in searches of premises under warrant, it would appear that householders are not always given adequate opportunity to scrutinise the warrant prior to the search (although steps have been taken in the first set of revisions to the Codes of Practice to deal with this problem).

The extent to which decisions to search persons or property can be reviewed after the event by reference to written records is also questionable. First, the research has pointed to inadequate recording of the grounds for searches, so that it is very difficult to tell from stop and search records whether suspicions were reasonable. Similarly, where property not covered by a warrant is seized during a search on warrant, the basis for doing so must be recorded but this is not always done. Secondly, it is very difficult after the event and usually with no independent information to question whether decisions presented as reasonable by police officers were in fact so. Thirdly, there is evidence of considerable under-recording of searches by the police. There are several factors at the root of this problem: confusion surrounding procedures where searches of persons or premises are carried out with consent; misunderstandings about recording of searches or premises carried out under PACE powers without prior authorisation by a senior officer; and non-recording of searches where nothing incriminating is found or where there is no prospect of later comebacks. The effect is the same, that review of the basis for such searches is made very difficult.

On the surface, there is less discretion about the recording of events at the police station and there are various requirements to inform suspects about the basis for police decisions. Custody records, available for inspection by supervisors and outsiders, readily indicate whether items of information that must be recorded under PACE and the Codes have been missed out. In practice, the situation is unfortunately not so clear-cut. A convincing body of research has drawn attention to the way in which key police decisions to authorise initial detention and extend detention at reviews are often routinised affairs, devoid of any substantial enquiry into the circumstances. There are good reasons for this deficiency which have been discussed in the report. The effect is that suspects will not always be clear why they are being detained (or further detained), nor does the custody record provide any real clue. Typically, all that will be recorded is the offence (which is sometimes the only grounds for detention presented to the custody officer) and the remarkably opaque 'detention necessary to secure evidence or preserve evidence/obtain evidence by questioning', which could be taken to apply to all detentions.

Whether more detailed recording of the circumstances in relation to such discretionary decisions would aid reviewability is, as was argued in relation to search powers, a matter of debate. It is up to the custody officer to decide whether he or she has reasonable grounds for believing that detention without charge is necessary or whether there is sufficient evidence to charge. Ultimately, it may be difficult later to question subjective estimates of reasonableness.

The reviewability of other aspects of detention may also create problems. It has been noted by several studies that custody records may not accurately represent what occurred during periods of custody. The evidence is that, for the most part, this is a matter of unimportant slippage in recording at times when custody officers are busy. The allegation is not generally of non-record-ing (custody records on the whole tend towards over-inclusion of often extraneous information) but mis-recording. Checks on prisoners or reviews may be delayed, but entered at the time they should have taken place, for example. However, some entries on custody records may reflect police pref-erences for surface compliance with the rules, when the substance of what occurred is somewhat different. It has been found, for example, that custody records over-represent the extent to which suspects are given information about their rights. Drunks, for example, should be given their rights when sober but often are not. An entry on the custody record of 'refused to sign' demonstrates that the rules have apparently been complied with.

For the most part, this kind of slippage does not have serious implications (despite the contentions of some research) and would not appear to stem from any ulterior intent systemically to deprive suspects of their rights. However, one practice raises more concern and that is in relation to allowing investigating officers access to suspects in the cells. Several studies have drawn attention to the existence of this practice, although it has been noted earlier that there are good reasons to believe that it has declined. It is not necessarily in contravention of PACE, although in some circumstances it may be (where, for example, the intent is to ask questions about the suspect's involvement in an offence without recording the questions and answers). Such visits raise concern because what occurs during them is of low visibil-ity, even to the custody officer, and not readily open to review. While it is a matter of good practice that all visits to the prisoner should be recorded on the custody record, such entries may sometimes obfuscate rather than aid review by referring to visits in the cells as 'welfare' visits. Research has pointed to cases in which, following such visits, suspects agree to proceed with an interview without a solicitor, suggesting that the purpose of the visit was something more. The value of custody records as an aid to review is seri-ously undermined if they contain information which custody officers base on hearsay.

Workability

The criterion of workability implies that the police should have sufficient powers to investigate and detect crime, and that these powers should be clear and certain and take account of the practical circumstances in which they are likely to be used. At the same time, they should enable the police to respect the rights of the suspect. There is a fair measure of agreement that

PACE has gone a long way towards meeting these goals. The codification and clarification of police powers on the street has generally been viewed as a helpful advance in enabling the police to recognise what they are and are not able to do. Prior uncertainty, particularly in the law on search of premises, meant that many searches were probably illegal. The police carried out searches on warrants obtained from magistrates – a time-consuming procedure – far more frequently in view of inadequacies in the law. The swinging of the balance towards police authorised search powers demonstrates the accessibility of the new powers in this area.

However, there are difficulties associated with police powers on the street. Some of these have been discussed above in relation to the concept of fairness. Putting the concept of reasonable suspicion into practice has caused some problems in relation to stop and search, for example, as have procedures for authorising searches of premises. It has been argued that the legislation does not take adequate account of the practical situations in which the police are required to exercise their discretionary powers. However, an important aspect of workability from the point of view of the police is that they are able to operate outside the legislative powers in problematic situations if consent is obtained. This is a source of the statutory powers' strength for the police. But it is at the same time a source of weakness for the suspect. For consent is, as has been noted, not always informed by awareness of whether a statutory power is being exercised or not and whether there is an option to refuse. Unwitting consent will deprive the suspect of various safeguards afforded by PACE and the Codes.

There is general agreement that the police find their powers of investigation clear once a suspect has been detained. The time for which a person may be held and the scope for delaying the exercise of the suspect's rights are closely regulated, for example. There is less agreement that the police always find their powers at this stage of an investigation adequate. Some argue that the limits on the length of detention do not take account of the practicalities of police work. Others suggest that the criteria for delaying suspects' exercise of their rights are too exacting and that, for example, informing others of the suspect's detention leads to evidence being lost. The recent changes in the law on the right of silence (discussed further below) may be taken as recognition that the police have been at a relative disadvantage when questioning silent suspects. Further support for the view that PACE did not always provide the powers that the police needed is provided by attempts, documented in the research, to evade the Act's restrictions. Reference has been made in this review to the practice of voluntary attendance of suspects as a way of overcoming the necessity principle governing police detention. And, contact requested by suspects with friends and relatives is sometimes informally delayed where no power to do so exists.

However, workability requires a balance between the powers the police need and the protection of the rights of the suspect. Few police would disagree that in the great majority of cases the rules on length of detention are adequate. The vast majority of suspects are released well within the statutory time limits. Similarly, in the bulk of cases problems of undesirable consequences from notifying those outside do not arise. In both instances, the relative advantages to the police of providing more powers has to be weighed against the detriment to the rights of the suspect. One further point should be made. The statutory framework of powers PACE provided was not designed to be grafted onto pre-existing methods of working. If this had been the case, it would not have been viable. It was intended to change the way the police work in various ways. This issue – the effect of legal rules on police behaviour – is discussed in the next section.

The legal regulation of policing

It is implicit in PACE and the fine level of detailed rules and guidance in the accompanying Codes of Practice that those who drew up the legislation placed faith in the capacity of legal rules to influence police conduct. Considerable debate has surrounded this issue, an understanding of which is clearly relevant to any further reforms in the statutory context of policing. At one extreme are those whose view of policing might be described as mecha-nistic, who believe that the police will act in accordance with clearly formu-lated rules. The report of the RCCP (1981) may be taken to reflect this view. At the other extreme are those who maintain that legal reform is largely irrelevant to what the police actually do, because their actions are governed so strongly by cultural norms and imperatives that the influence of the law is peripheral (McConville *et al*, 1991). Indeed, legal reform may actually encourage the police to avoid using statutory powers (Baldwin and Kinsey, 1982).

In between are those who argue that legal rules may influence police conduct, but that the nature of this impact varies according to a number of factors: for example, the relationship of the rules to existing working practices and the way that the rules are enforced. This view has been argued by, among others, Smith and Gray (1985), Bottomley *et al* (1989) and Dixon *et al* (1989 and 1990b). On the basis of the large body of research evidence now available, it is suggested that this view provides the best explanation of the response of the police to PACE and the Codes of Practice. As has been demonstrated at various points in this report, it is clear on the one hand that compliance with the provisions of the legislation is by no means complete. On the other, it is equally clear that PACE has had an impact, sometimes considerable, on various aspects of police work. In the remainder of this section it is therefore proposed to examine this view of the variable impact of PACE in a little more detail and to suggest what factors are important in determining compliance or non-compliance.

A broad dichotomy may be drawn between police actions inside and outside the police station. The weight of evidence suggests that PACE rules are followed to a lesser extent outside the police station than inside. Earlier in this review, attention was drawn to police reliance on consent to conduct stop/searches and searches of premises, often where it was arguable whether consent was genuinely given. The grounds for suspicion to conduct searches of persons or vehicles may not always have been reasonable, and searches of premises were sometimes suggestive of 'fishing expeditions'. There are grounds to believe records of searches were not always completed when they should have been, and those that were submitted by no means always recorded the grounds for suspicion adequately. Practice at the police station is also open to various criticisms, however. Decisions about detaining suspects tended to be ritualised and to lack any real element of enquiry. Custody records sometimes misrepresented what occurred: for example, in relation to providing the suspect's rights or allowing investigating officers access to the suspect in the cells. Implementation of the right to outside contact was sometimes informally delayed. Suspects were sometimes discouraged from seeking legal advice. And tactics used during interviews were sometimes open to the criticism that they were coercive or manipulative.

What determines whether legal rules are obeyed? There is a convincing body of opinion which suggests that this is a product of a complex interaction between the nature of the rules, the way in which they are expressed, methods of implementation and enforcement, and their relationship with existing methods of working (Dixon *et al*, 1989). This last consideration provides a useful starting point. Various commentators have drawn attention to the way in which informal rules are extremely important in governing what the police do (Reiner, 1985; Smith and Gray, 1985; Bottomley *et al*, 1989; McConville *et al*, 1991). They are particularly relevant in situations in which the police have considerable discretion and their actions are of low visibility to supervisors. Exercise of search powers outside the station provides a good example. (So did interviewing of suspects prior to PACE, when methods of recording were less closely regulated.) Actions tend to be guided by a variety of non-legal criteria: the stereotyping of particular categories of person as a basis for stop and search provides one example (Willis, 1983). Those who point to the importance of such working rules do not necessarily argue that the law is irrelevant. Sometimes, its very breadth is permissive of actions undertaken according to non-legal criteria (McBarnet, 1981). And various other constraints apply: for example, moral and practical ones (McConville *et al*, 1991).

The introduction of legal rules which conflict with working rules is not necessarily doomed to failure. Commentators have suggested that there are several preconditions for success, without all or some of which their impact will be variable. First, new rules must be clearly expressed. Secondly, implementation must be accompanied by training which is adequate to assert the importance of the rules and to counteract the strength of existing working rules. Thirdly, the rules must be backed up by effective sanctions and supervision which raise a real possibility that breaches will be detected and acted upon. Lastly, public awareness of rights and of police powers may also be an important constraint upon police action. The extent to which each of these conditions needs to be satisfied and in what way will depend on the nature of the changes which are being introduced, the extent to which they impinge upon existing working practices, and the visibility of the area of police work concerned.

The evidence from research suggests that variability in the impact of particular PACE provisions stems largely from differences in the extent to which these conditions are met. Dixon *et al* (1989) have drawn attention to the failure of the stop and search provisions to match up satisfactorily to any of them. The police do not perceive the rules as clear, insufficient training was given to stress that the rules were intended to mark a change in the ethos underlying police practice, officers feel relatively safe that their actions are protected from scrutiny and that discipline is not generally a real possibility, and members of the public are largely unaware of police stop and search powers.

The situation may be contrasted with the operation of many of the rules applicable at the police station, particularly those which fall to the custody officer to implement. They are, on the whole, characterised by clarity, and supervision within the station is more apparent and significant than on the streets. Important elements in the context of supervision are the availability of the custody record for later inspection and the success, acknowledged by some studies, in instituting the post of custody officer as independent overseer of the treatment of the suspect. Procedures at the station are also far more visible than before to outsiders such as solicitors, appropriate adults, doctors and even researchers. Discipline is seen as a very real threat by custody officers themselves, as well as by other officers, for breaches of PACE provisions on detention (Dixon *et al*, 1990b). It is less clear that training or public awareness of police procedures have been important elements in securing compliance with PACE procedures at the police station. However, the other influences described are probably so strong that they have been sufficient in themselves.

One clear message from the research is that, in some circumstances, legal rules will be obeyed in form but not in substance. This may occur where there are clear requirements to carry out particular procedures, with recording requirements to show whether this has occurred, but where working rules or practical considerations make compliance problematic. Examples are the procedures for authorising detention and for the provision of information about rights. It was noted earlier in the report that detentions are authorised largely as a matter of routine, not least because of the lack of an established procedure for not authorising detention and to avoid conflicts in front of suspects. Provision of information about rights is sometimes minimal because custody officers may feel that some suspects do not need advice or are incapable of making a valid decision. These are examples of circumstances in which essential conditions for compliance are again lacking. A combination of better training, more effective oversight and clearer procedures might effect improvements in both areas. However, the procedures as they stand allow the appearance of compliance.

Balance in the investigative process

In the introduction to this report it was noted that the RCCP's report called for a balance in the investigative process between the public interest in bringing offenders to justice and the rights and liberties of suspects. In as much as legislation may be said to have any unifying 'intention' (Dixon, 1992), this was the aim which underlay PACE. In this concluding section of this review the question is addressed of whether it is possible, on the basis of the research evidence, to provide any answer to the question of whether such a balance has been achieved.

There must be considerable doubt about whether such a question can satisfactorily be answered and, if so, how. It assumes that a desirable balance is objectively verifiable in some way. In fact, what is a satisfactory balance must be largely a matter of subjective judgement and judgements will inevitably vary, particularly as the various parties with a stake in the criminal justice system will have different standpoints and will interpret the same data differently. Moreover, some data which are required in order to arrive at a view are effectively unknowable. There must be an assumption, for example, that the preservation of the rights and liberty of the suspect dictate that a certain percentage of guilty people are released without proceedings because the solution of crime does not justify unlimited detention or over-invasive investigative methods. But there is no way of knowing what proportion of those released without proceedings are guilty.

Another way of looking at the question is to draw up a kind of profit and loss account, which assesses whether or not any benefits which the police have derived from new or clearer powers outweigh the advantages to the suspect of more adequate safeguards. However, it is meaningless to weigh the acquisition of powers in one area of police work against the introduction of safeguards for the suspect in quite another. The fact that adequate safeguards may exist in relation, for example, to the seizure of special procedure material is of little comfort to the suspect stopped and searched on flimsy grounds. A more realistic approach, therefore, is to examine the equivalence of powers and safeguards in specific areas: for example, in relation to stop and search, the treatment of juveniles and the interviewing of suspects. If powers and safeguards appear to be out of kilter in a significant number of different areas, the conclusion could be drawn that the system as a whole is out of balance.

Viewed from this perspective, it would be difficult to argue that PACE has produced a system that is in a state of balance. However, two qualifications must be made straightaway before expanding on this view. Firstly, the position is not a simplistic one of the balance now being entirely in favour of or against the interests of the suspect. There are areas in which the suspect is at a disadvantage and others in which the opposite is arguably the case. But, in view of the position argued for above that gains in one area cannot be traded off against losses in quite another, it cannot be maintained that this constitutes a system in balance. Secondly, the picture being examined is a moving one. The way in which safeguards have been applied and powers exercised has changed over time, partly in response to changes in the PACE Codes of Practice but also in response to other trends in the criminal justice system. The answer to the question of whether there is a state of balance might receive a rather different answer now to that which would have been given after PACE was first introduced.

Turning then to specific areas dealt with by PACE and the Codes, it might be argued, on the evidence presented in this review, that suspects are at a disadvantage relative to police powers in several key areas. Among these may be included stop and search, search and seizure, and the treatment of at risk groups. Readers are referred to the relevant chapters of this report in order to understand fully the rationale behind this view. In short, however, the first two of these areas have, inter alia, presented problems in relation to: controlling the exercise of police discretion in relation to areas of police work of low visibility to supervisors; clarity of the legislative and Code provisions; and recording requirements. As regards at risk groups, the major problems have related to the provision of effective appropriate adult arrangements for juveniles, the mentally disordered and the mentally handicapped, and ensuring that rights are conveyed and implemented as effectively as for suspects generally. The attention given to this subject by the RCCJ (1993) and its recommendation that a comprehensive review should be conducted of the appropriate adult arrangements are factors which further support the view that suspects in these groups remain at a relative disadvantage.

The areas which have generated the greatest debate are the related ones of the interviewing of suspects, the provision of legal advice and the suspect's exercise of the right of silence. Important safeguards for the suspect exist in that almost all interviews at police stations are now tape-recorded (and some video-recorded), interviewing outside the police station is only possible in limited circumstances, and all suspects have the right to legal advice prior to and during the course of police interviews. Suspects also have the right to remain silent in interviews. Heavy-handed tactics are used relatively rarely in interviews compared with pre-PACE days.

A view has gained currency that the safeguards for the suspect in relation to legal advice and interviewing have been pitched too high. This has been expressed most often in relation to the debate about the curtailment of the suspect's right of silence and is reflected in a lecture which the then Home Secretary gave to the Police Foundation in 1987:

> "*A few forces have suggested that the strengthened right for an accused person to have a legal adviser present may have increased their difficulties in bringing the guilty to book ... [I]t is right to consider whether the balance being struck between the interests of a person suspected of crime and the interests of society as a whole in bringing criminals to justice is being struck at the right point*" (quoted in the report of the Working Group on the Right of Silence: Home Office, 1989a).

It is undoubtedly correct to argue that suspects in police custody are better protected than was the case under the pre-PACE Judges' Rules, although the evidence from the research is that the safeguards both at the station and outside are not always as watertight as might appear. For example, some interviewing still does take place outside the police station, while interviewing at the station is supervised only loosely by senior officers Also, custody officers have been found to influence suspects against requesting legal advice.

However, the area of legal advice, interviewing and right of silence is one in which practice appears not to have stood still since PACE was introduced. The research provides evidence that, over time, suspects have increasingly taken advantage of their rights in relation to legal advice and silence in interviews (although there is considerable debate about the extent to which these trends are linked – see Chapters 7 and 8). Requests for, and receipt of, legal advice, have risen significantly since the introduction of PACE. The most recent figures show that nearly 40 per cent of suspects now request a legal adviser (Phillips and Brown, forthcoming), compared with one-quarter when PACE was introduced. There also appears to have been a rise over time in the proportion of suspects exercising their right of silence during interviews. Recent figures suggest that around 22 per cent of suspects now refuse to answer some or all police questions (ACPO, 1993; Phillips and Brown, forthcoming) compared with around 10 per cent in the late1980s.

In response to these concerns, the Criminal Justice and Public Order Act 1995 contains provisions which allow courts or juries in certain circumstances to draw appropriate inferences from the suspect's refusal to answer police questions or raise a defence that he or she might have been expected to raise during police questioning. The new provisions, it must be emphasised, do not withdraw rights which the suspect formerly had. Nor are they intended to work to the disadvantage of the innocent. However, they put guilty suspects on notice that they do not necessarily put themselves on the same footing as the innocent by having recourse to the right to silence.

The CJPOA provisions have been perceived by some as a major incursion on the presumption of innocence (see, for example, O'Reilly, 1994). It is not intended in this review to enter this debate. However, the introduction of the Act's right of silence provisions illustrates how achieving balance between the suspect's rights and the public interest in convicting the guilty is a continually shifting process of adjusting to circumstances as they change or as weaknesses in the existing provisions become apparent. Nor is this process a one-sided one of increasing police powers. Reference has been made to the recommendations of the RCCJ for a review to be conducted of the appropriate adult arrangements in relation to 'at risk' groups of suspects. This review, aimed at improving the safeguards in this area, was completed only recently. The PACE Codes of Practice are also subject to continuing review. The most recent version, issued in April 1995, contains new provisions aimed both at strengthening protections for the suspect, where deficiencies have come to light, and at bolstering police powers where needed. While, for the present, the conclusion might be drawn that the balance intended by PACE has not yet been achieved, the state of play must be regularly reviewed in order to take account of the effect of new initiatives affecting the pre-trial process.

References

Allen, C.J.W. (1990). 'Discretion and security: excluding evidence under s.78(1) of the Police and Criminal Evidence Act 1984'. 49 Camb. L.J. 80.

Association of Chief Police Officers. (1992). *National Guidelines on the Use and Management of Informants.* ACPO Crime Committee Working Party on the Management of Informants (unpublished).

Association of Chief Police Officers. (1993). *ACPO Right of Silence Survey* (unpublished).

Audit Commission. (1990). *Effective Policing - Performance Review in Police Forces.* Police Papers Number 8, Dec. 1990. London: Audit Commission.

Baldwin, J. (1992a). *Preparing the Record of Taped Interview.* Royal Commission on Criminal Justice Research Study No 2. London: HMSO.

Baldwin, J. (1992b). *The Role of Legal Representatives at Police Stations.* Royal Commission on Criminal Justice Research Study No 3. London: HMSO.

Baldwin, J. (1992c). *Video Taping Police Interviews with Suspects - an Evaluation.* Police Research Series: Paper No 1. London: Home Office Police Department.

Baldwin, J. and Bedward, J. (1991). 'Summarising tape recordings of police interviews'. *Criminal Law Review*, 671-679.

Baldwin, J. and McConville, M. (1979). 'Police interrogation and the right to see a solicitor'. *Criminal Law Review*, 145-152.

Baldwin, J. and McConville, M. (1980). *Confessions in Crown Court Trials.* Royal Commission on Criminal Procedure Research Study No. 5 London: HMSO.

Baldwin, J. and Moloney, T. (1992). *Supervision of Police Investigations in Serious Criminal Cases.* Royal Commission on Criminal Procedure Research Study No 4. London: HMSO.

Baldwin, R. and Kinsey, R. (1982). *Police Powers and Politics.* London: Quartet Books.

Barclay, P.J. (1986). *Detained in Police Custody.* Bramshill Student's Paper. (Unpublished.)

Bean, P. and Nemitz, T. (1994). *Out of depth and out of sight.* Final report of research commissioned by Mencap on the implementation of the appropriate adult scheme. Midlands Centre for Criminology: University of Loughborough.

Birch, D. (1989). 'The PACE hots up: confessions and confusions under the 1984 Act'. *Criminal Law Review*, 95-116.

Bittner, E. (1967). 'The police on skid row: a study in peace-keeping'. *American Sociological Review.* (32), 699-715.

Bottomley, K., Coleman, C., Dixon, D., Gill, M. and Wall, D. (1989). *The Impact of Aspects of the Police and Criminal Evidence Act 1984 on Policing in a Force in the North of England.* Final report to ESRC. Unpublished.

Brown, D. (1987). *The Police Complaints Procedure: a Survey of Complainants' Views.* Home Office Research Study No. 93. London: HMSO.

Brown, D. (1989). *Detention at the Police Station under the Police and Criminal Evidence Act 1984.* Home Office Research Study No. 104. London: HMSO.

Brown, D. (1991). *Investigating Burglary: the Effects of PACE.* Home Office Research Study No. 123. London: HMSO.

Brown, D. (1993). *Detention under the Prevention of Terrorism (Temporary Provisions) Act 1989: access to legal advice and outside contact.* Research and Planning Unit Paper 75. London: Home Office.

Brown, D. (1994). 'The incidence of right of silence in police interviews: the research evidence reviewed'. *Research Bulletin*, No.35, 57-75. London: Home Office Research and Statistics Department.

Brown, D., Ellis, T. and Larcombe, K. (1992). *Changing the Code: Police Detention under the Revised PACE Codes of Practice.* Home Office Research Study No.129. London: HMSO.

Brown, D. and Ellis, T. (1994). *Policing Low-level Disorder: police use of section 5 of the Public Order Act 1986.* Home Office Research Study No. 135. London: HMSO.

Burrows, J., Morgan, P. and Henderson, P. (1995). *Improving Bail Decisions: the bail process project, phase 1.* Research and Planning Unit Paper 90. London: Home Office.

Cahill, D. and Grebler, G. (1988). *Vulnerable testimony.* Report to MENCAP and the Metropolitan Police. Unpublished.

Cape, E. (1993). *Defending Suspects at Police Stations.* London: Legal Action Group.

Central Planning and Training Unit. (1992a). *The Interviewers Rule Book.* Available from the Central Planning and Training Unit. Harrogate.

Central Planning and Training Unit. (1992b). *A guide to Interviewing.* Available from the Central Planning and Training Unit. Harrogate.

Chatterton, M. (1987). 'Front line supervision in the British police service'. In Gaskell, G. and Benewick, R. (eds). *The Crowd in Contemporary Britain.* London: Sage.

Clare, I.C.H. and Gudjunsson, G.H. (1992). *Devising and Piloting an Experimental Version of the 'Notice to Detained Persons'.* Royal Commission on Criminal Justice Research Study No. 7. London: HMSO.

Corbett, C. (1991). 'Complaints against the police: the new procedure of informal resolution'. *Policing and Society,* 2(1).

Cox, B., Shirley, J. and Short, M. (1977). *The Fall of Scotland Yard.* Harmondsworth: Penguin.

Crawford, A., Jones, T., Woodhouse, T. and Young, J. (1990). *The Second Islington Crime Survey.* London: Middlesex Polytechnic Centre for Criminology.

Cresswell, P., Howarth, G., Dolan, M. and Hedges, J. (1993). *Opportunities for Reducing the Administrative Burdens on the Police.* Police Research Series: Paper No. 3. London: Home Office Police Department.

Curtis, L. (1986). 'Policing the streets'. In Benyon, J. and Bourn, C. (eds). *The Police: Powers, Procedures and Proprieties.* Oxford: Pergamon.

Davison, S.E. and Forshaw, D.M. (1993). 'Retracted confessions: through opiate withdrawal to a new conceptual framework'. *Medicine, Science and the Law*, 33, pp. 285-290.

Dixon, D., Bottomley, A.K., Coleman, C.A., Gill, M. and Wall, D. (1989). 'Reality and rules in the construction and regulation of police suspicion'. *International Journal of the Sociology of Law*, (17), 185-206.

Dixon, D., Bottomley, K., Coleman, C., Gill, M. and Wall, D. (1990b). 'Safeguarding the rights of suspects in police custody'. *Policing and Society*, (1), 115-40.

Dixon, D. (1990). 'Juvenile suspects and the Police and Criminal Evidence Act'. In Freestone, D. (ed). *Children and the Law: essays in honour of Professor H. K. Bevan*. Hull: Hull University Press.

Dixon, D., Coleman, C. and Bottomley, K. (1990a). 'Consent and the legal regulation of policing'. *Journal of Law and Society*, 17(3), 345-362.

Dixon, D. (1992). 'Legal regulation and policing practice'. *Social and Legal Studies*, Vol 1, 515-541.

Dixon, D. (1991a). 'Common sense, legal advice and the right of silence'. *Public Law*, 233-254.

Dixon, D. (1991b). 'Politics, research and symbolism in criminal justice: the right of silence and the Police and Criminal Evidence Act'. *Anglo-American Law Review*, 27-50.

Evans, R. and Ferguson, T. (1991). *Comparing Different Juvenile Cautioning Systems in one Police Force Area*. A report to the Home Office Research and Planning Unit and Coventry Social Services Department. Unpublished.

Evans, R. (1993). *The Conduct of Police Interviews with Juveniles*. Royal Commission on Criminal Justice Research Study No. 8. London: HMSO.

Evans, R. and Rawstorne, S. (1994). *The Protection of Vulnerable Suspects*. A report to the Home Office Research and Planning Unit. Unpublished.

Fennell, P.W.H. (1994). 'Mentally disordered suspects in the Criminal Justice System'. *In Justice and Efficiency? The Royal Commission on Criminal Justice*. S. Field and P.A. Thomas (Eds.). Oxford: Blackwell.

Fisher, Sir H. (1977). *Report of an Inquiry by the Hon. Sir Henry Fisher into the circumstances leading to the trial of three persons on charges arising out of the death of Maxwell Confait and the first at 27 Doggett Road London SE6.* London: HMSO.

FitzGerald, M. (1993). *Ethnic Minorities and the Criminal Justice System.* Royal Commission on Criminal Justice Research Study No. 20. London: HMSO.

FitzGerald, M. and Hale, C. (forthcoming). *Ethnic Minorities and the British Crime Survey.* Home Office Research Study..

Fyfe, N. (1992). 'Towards locally sensitive policing? Politics, participation and power in community/police consultation'. In Evans, R. *et al* (eds.) *Crime, Policing and Place.* London: Routledge.

Gelowitz, M. (1990). 'Section 78 of the Police and Criminal Evidence Act 1984'. 106 L.Q.R. 327.

Gemmill, R. and Morgan-Giles, R.F. (1980). *Arrest, Charge and Summons: Current Practice and Resource Implications.* Royal Commission on Criminal Procedure Research Study No. 9 London: HMSO.

Greater Manchester Police Development and Inspectorate Branch. (1988). Solicitors and Interviews. Manchester: GMP.

Greer, S. (1990). 'The right to silence: a review of the current debate'. *Modern Law Review*, 53 (6), 709-721.

Gudjunsson, G.H. (1983a). 'Suggestibility, intelligence, memory recall and personality: an experimental study'. *British Journal of Psychiatry*, (142), 35-37.

Gudjunsson, G.H. (1983b). 'A new scale of interrogative suggestibility'. (Unpublished manuscript.)

Gudjunsson, G.H. (1990). 'The 'Notice to Detained Persons': how easy is it to understand?' *Law Society Gazette*, 87(43), 24-27.

Gudjunsson, G.H. (1991). 'The 'notice to detained person', PACE Codes, and reading ease'. *Applied Cognitive Psychology*, (5), 89-95.

Gudjunsson, G.H. (1992). *The Psychology of Interrogations, Confessions and Testimony.* Wiley.

Gudjunsson, G.H. and Clark, N. (1986). 'Suggestibility in police interrogation: a social psychological model'. *Social Behaviour*, 1(83).

Gudjunsson, G., Clare, I. and Cross, P. (1992). 'The revised PACE 'Notice to Detained Persons': How easy is it to read and understand?'. *Journal of the Forensic Science Society*, 32.

Gudjunsson, G., Clare, I., Rutter, S. and Pearse, J. (1993). *Persons at Risk during Interviews in Police Custody: the identification of vulnerabilities*. Royal Commission on Criminal Justice Research Study No 12. London: HMSO.

Haley, and Swift, (1988). 'PACE and the Social Worker: a step in the right direction?'. *Journal of Social Work Law*, 355.

Hewitt, S.E.K. (1986). *Interviewing Persons with Mental Handicap*. Bath: Hewitt.

Hewson, B. (1993). *Seizure of Confidential Material: PACE special procedure*. London: Butterworths.

Hobbs, R. (1988). *Doing the Business*. Oxford: Clarendon Press.

Hodgson, J. (1994). 'Adding injury to injustice: the suspect at the police station'. *In Justice and Efficiency? The Royal Commission on Criminal Justice*. S. Field and P.A. Thomas (Eds.). Oxford: Blackwell.

Holdaway, S. (1983). *Inside the British Police*. Oxford: Blackwell.

Hollin, C. (1990). *False Confessions*. Report for the Guildford and Woolwich Inquiry. (Unpublished).

Home Office. (1978). *Judges' Rules and Administrative Directions to the Police*. Home Office Circular No. 89/1978. London: HMSO.

Home Office. (1985a). *Arrangements for Local Consultation between the Community and the Police outside London*. Circular 2/1985. London: Home Office.

Home Office. (1985b). *Police and Criminal Evidence Act 1984*. Circular 88/1985. London: Home Office.

Home Office. (1989a). Working Group on the Right of Silence. *Report*. London: Home Office.

Home Office. (1989b). *Police Community Consultative Arrangements under S.106 of the Police and Criminal Evidence Act 1984: report of the internal Home Office review*. Circular 26/1989. London: Home Office.

Home Office. (1989c). *Crime Statistics for the Metropolitan Police District by Ethnic Group, 1987: victims, suspects and those arrested.* Statistical Bulletin 5/89. London: Home Office.

Home Office. (Annually). *Statistics on the Operation of Certain Police Powers under the Police and Criminal Evidence Act, England and Wales.* Statistical Bulletins. London: Home Office.

Home Office. (1992). *Police Bail – Guidance on Interpretation of Subsection 38(1) of the Police and Criminal Evidence Act 1984.* Circular 111/1992. London: Home Office.

Home Office. (1995). *Police Complaints and Discipline England and Wales 1994.* Home Office Statistical Bulletin 13/95. London: Home Office.

Hood, R. (1992). *Race and Sentencing: a study in the Crown Court.* Oxford: Clarendon Press.

Hooke, A. and Knox, J. (1995). *Records of Taped Interview.* Report to the Home Office. Unpublished.

Hughes, G. (1994). 'Talking cop shop? A case-study of police community consultative groups in transition'. *Policing and Society*, (4), 253-270.

Irving, B.L. (1980). *Police Interrogation.* Royal Commission on Criminal Procedure Research Study 1. London: HMSO.

Irving, B.L. and McKenzie, I. (1989). *Police Interrogation: the effects of the Police and Criminal Evidence Act 1984.* London: Police Foundation.

Irving, B. and Dunnighan, C. (1993). *Human Factors in the Quality Control of CID Investigations.* Royal Commission on Criminal Justice Research Study No. 21. London: HMSO.

Jefferson, T. (1993). 'The racism of criminalisation: policing and the reproduction of the criminal other'. In L. Gelsthorpe (ed) *Minority Ethnic Groups in the Criminal Justice System.* Papers presented to the 21st Cropwood Roundtable Conference 1992. Institute of Criminology, University of Cambridge.

Jefferson, T. and Walker, M.A. (1992). 'Ethnic minorities in the criminal justice system'. *Criminal Law Review*, 83-95.

Jones, T., Maclean, B. and Young, J. (1986). *The Islington Crime Survey.* Aldershot: Gower.

Justice. (1994). *Unreliable Evidence?: confessions and the safety of convictions.* London: Justice.

Kay, N. and Quao, S. (1987). 'To be or not to be an appropriate adult'. *Community Care*, no. 688, 20-2.

Knight, R. and Giller, H. (1986). 'Appropriate adults'. *Community Care*, No. 636, 10-11.

Landau, S.F. (1981). *'Juveniles and the Police: who is charged immediately and who is referred to the Juvenile Bureau'.* British Journal of Criminology, 21, 27-46.

Landau, S.F. and Nathan, G. (1983). *'Selecting delinquents for cautioning in the London Metropolitan area'.* British Journal of Criminology, 23, 128-149.

Law Society. (1988). *Advising a Suspect in the Police Station.* London: Law Society. (Second edition.)

Law Society. (1991). *Advising a Suspect in the Police Station.* London: Law Society. (Third edition).

Lidstone, K. (1981). *Magisterial Review of the Pre-Trial Process.* Mimeo. Centre for Criminological and Socio-Legal Studies. University of Sheffield.

Legal Aid Board. (1992). *Duty Solicitor Arrangements.* London: Legal Aid Board.

Leng, R. (1993). *The Right to Silence in Police Interrogation: a study of some of the issues underlying the debate.* Royal Commission on Criminal Justice Research Study No. 10. London: HMSO.

Levi, M. (1993). *The Investigation, Prosecution and Trial of Serious Fraud.* Royal Commission on Criminal Justice Research Study No 14. London: HMSO.

Lidstone, K. (1989). 'The Police and Criminal Evidence (Northern Ireland) Order 1989. 2: Powers of Entry, Search and Seizure'. Northern Ireland Legal Quarterly, 333-362.

Lidstone, K. and Bevan, V. (nd). *Search and Seizure under the Police and Criminal Evidence Act 1984.* A report of research into the police use of search powers provided by the Police and Criminal Evidence Act 1984 funded by the Social Science Research Council. Unpublished. University of Sheffield Faculty of Law.

Littlechild, B. (1994). *Social Workers as Appropriate Adults under PACE 1984.* Birmingham: British Association of Social Workers.

McBarnet, D. (1981). *Conviction.* London: Macmillan.

McConville, M. and Baldwin, J. (1981). *Crime, Courts and Conviction.* Oxford: Oxford University Press.

McConville, M. (1985). 'The legal impact of the Police and Criminal Evidence Bill'. *Issues in Criminal and Legal Psychology*, 21-35.

McConville, M. and Sanders, A. (1989). *Discretion to Charge and to Prosecute.* End of award report to ESRC. Unpublished.

McConville, M., Sanders, A, and Leng, R. (1991). *The case for the Prosecution.* London: Routledge.

McConville, M. (1993). *Corroboration and Confessions: the impact of a rule requiring that no conviction can be sustained on the basis of confession evidence alone.* Royal Commission on Criminal Justice Research Study No. 13. London: HMSO.

McConville, M. and Hodgson, J, with the assistance of Jackson, M. and Macrae, E. (1993). *Custodial Legal Advice and the Right to Silence.* Royal Commission on Criminal Justice Research Study No. 16. London: HMSO.

McConville, M., Hodgson, J., Bridges, L. and Pavlovic, A. (1994). *Standing Accused: the organisation and practices of criminal defence lawyers in Britain.* Oxford: Clarendon Press.

McKenzie, I.K. and Irving, B. (1988). 'The right to silence'. *Policing*, 4, 88-105.

McKenzie, I., Morgan, R. and Reiner, R. (1990). 'Helping the police with their enquiries: the necessity principle and voluntary attendance at the police station'. *Criminal Law Review*, pp. 22-33.

Mackay, P. (1988). *Changes in Custody Practice since the Introduction of the Police and Criminal Evidence Act 1984.* Report submitted to the Police Requirements Support Unit, Home Office. (Unpublished).

Macleod, J.F. (1991). *The Processing of Persons Suspected of Crime: Tape-recording and other Issues.* Ph.D. dissertation submitted at the University of Cambridge. (Unpublished).

Maguire, M. (1988). 'Effects of the 'P.A.C.E' provisions on detention and questioning: some preliminary findings'. *British Journal of Criminology*, 28(1), pp. 19-43.

Maguire, M. and Corbett, C. (1989). 'Patterns and profiles of complaints against the police'. In Morgan, R. and Smith, D.J. (eds). *Coming to Terms with Policing*. London: Routledge.

Maguire, M. and Corbett, C. (1991). *A Study of the Police Complaints System*. London: HMSO.

Maguire, M., Noaks, L., Hobbs, R. and Brearley, N. (1992). *Assessing Investigative Performance*. School of Social and Administrative Studies, University of Wales, College of Cardiff Occasional Paper.

Maguire, M. and Norris, C. (1992). *The Conduct and Supervision of Criminal Investigations*. Royal Commission on Criminal Justice Research Study No. 5. London: HMSO.

Maguire, M. and Norris, C. (1994) 'Police investigations: practice and malpractice'. *In Justice and Efficiency? The Royal Commission on Criminal Justice*. S. Field and P.A. Thomas (Eds.). Oxford: Blackwell.

Mawby, R.I. (1979). *Policing the City*. Farnborough: Saxon House.

Metropolitan Police. (1985). *The Principles of Policing and Guidance for Professional Behaviour*. London: Metropolitan Police.

Mitchell, B. (1983). *'Confessions and police interrogation of suspects'*. Criminal Law Review, 596.

Morgan, P. and Pearce, R. (1988). *Remand Decisions in Brighton and Bournemouth*. Research and Planning Unit Paper 53. London: Home Office.

Morgan, R. and Maggs, C. (1985). *Setting the PACE: Police Community Consultation Arrangements in England and Wales*. University of Bath: Bath Social Policy Paper No. 4.

Morgan, R. (1986). 'Police consultative groups: the implications for the governance of the police'. *Political Quarterly*, January.

Morgan, R. (1987). 'The local determinants of policing policy'. In Willmott, P. (ed). *Policing and the Community*. London: Policy Studies Institute Discussion Paper No. 16.

Morgan, R. (1992). 'Talking about policing'. In Downes, D. (ed.) *Unravelling Criminal Justice*. London: Macmillan.

Morgan, R., Reiner, R. and McKenzie, I.K. (1991). *Police Powers and Police: a study of the work of custody officers*. Full final report to the ESRC. Unpublished.

Morris, P. (1980). *Police Interrogation: review of literature*. Royal Commission on Criminal Procedure Research Study No.3. London: HMSO.

Mortimer, A. (1994). 'Asking the right questions'. *Policing*, vol.10, no.2, Summer.

Moston, S. (1991). 'Assessing the credibility of statements'. In Bull, R., Momon, A., Moston, S., Moston, T. and Williamson, T. *Investigative Interviewing: Volume 1*. Unpublished.

Moston, S., Stephenson, G. and Williamson, T. (1990). *Police Interrogation Styles and Suspect Behaviour*. Final report to the Police Requirements Support Unit: University of Kent, Institute of Social and Applied Psychology. Unpublished.

Moston, S., Stephenson, G. and Williamson, T. (1992). 'The incidence, antecedents and consequences of suspects' use of the right to silence. *Criminal Behaviour and Mental Health*.

Moston, S. and Stephenson, G. (1993). *The Questioning and Interviewing of Suspects outside the Police Station*. Royal Commission on Criminal Justice Research Study No. 22. London: HMSO.

Newburn, T., Brown, D., Crisp, D. and Dewhurst, P. (1990). *Tackling Public Disorder: an exploratory study of the use of ss. 2-5 of the Public Order Act 1986*. Report to the Home Office. Unpublished.

Norris, C., Fielding, N., Kemp, C. and Fielding, J. (1993). 'The status of demeanour: an analysis of the influence of social status on being stopped by the police'. Paper prepared for the British Criminology Conference, University of Wales, Cardiff, July 28-August 1, 1993. Unpublished.

O'Reilly, G.W. (1994). 'England limits the right to silence and moves towards an inquisitorial system of justice'. *Journal of Criminal Law and Criminology*, Vol.85, No.2, pp.402-452.

Painter, K., Lea, J., Woodhouse, T. and Young, J. (1989). *Hammersmith and Fulham Crime and Police Survey, 1988*. Centre for Criminology: Middlesex Polytechnic.

Parker, C. (1992). *Confessions and the Mentally Vulnerable Suspect.* Thesis submitted for L.L.M. in Human Rights and Civil Liberties. Unpublished.

Phillips, C. and Brown, D., with the assistance of Goodrich, P. and James, Z. (forthcoming). *Entry into the Criminal Justice System: a survey of police arrests and their outcomes.* Home Office Research Study. London: HMSO.

Police Complaints Authority. (1995a). *PCA 10: Police Complaints Authority - the first ten years.* London: HMSO.

Police Complaints Authority. (1995b). *Annual Report.* London: HMSO.

Police Complaints Board. (1980). *Triennial Review Report.* London: HMSO.

Police Complaints Board. (1983). *Triennial Review Report.* London: HMSO.

Price, C. and Caplan, J. *The Confait Confessions.* London: Marian Boyars.

Reiner, R. (1985). *The Politics of the Police.* Brighton: Wheatsheaf.

Reiner, R. (1993). 'Race, crime and justice: models of interpretation'. In L. Gelsthorpe (ed) *Minority Ethnic Groups in the Criminal Justice System.* Papers presented to the 21st Cropwood Roundtable Conference 1992. Institute of Criminology, University of Cambridge.

Roberston, G. (1992). *The Role of Police Surgeons.* Royal Commission on Criminal Justice Research Study No. 6. London: HMSO.

Robertson, G., Gibb, R. and Pearson, R. (1995). *'Drunkeness among police detainees'.* Addiction, 90(6), 793-803.

Roberston, G., Pearson, R. and Gibb, R. (1995). *Entry of Mentally Ill People to the Criminal Justice System.* Final Report to Home Office Research and Planning Unit. Unpublished.

Royal Commission on Criminal Procedure. (1981). Chairman: Sir Cyril Philips. *Report.* Cmnd. 8092. London: HMSO.

Royal Commission on Criminal Procedure. (1981a). Chairman: Sir Cyril Philips. *The Investigation and Prosecution of Criminal Offences in England and Wales: the Law and Procedure.* Cmnd. 8092-1. London: HMSO.

Royal Commission on Criminal Justice. (1993). Chairman: Viscount Runciman of Doxford CBE FBA. Cm. 2263. *Report.* London: HMSO.

Royal Commission on the Police. (1962). *Report.* Cmnd. 1728. London: HMSO.

Sanders, A. (1988). 'Rights, remedies and the Police and Criminal Evidence Act'. *Criminal Law Review*, 802-812.

Sanders, A., Bridges, L., Mulvaney, A. and Crozier, G. (1989). *Advice and Assistance at Police Stations and the 24 hour Duty Solicitor Scheme.* London: Lord Chancellor's Department.

Scarman. (1981). *The Brixton Disorders 10-12 April, 1981.* Report on an inquiry by the Rt. Hon. Lord Scarman, OBE. Cmnd. 8427. London: HMSO.

Sigurdsson, J.F. and Gudjunsson, G.H. (1994). 'Alcohol and drug intoxication during police interrogation and the reasons why suspects confess to the police'. *Addiction*, 89, pp.985-997.

Skogan, W. (1990). *The Police and Public in England and Wales.* Home Office Research Study No. 117. London: HMSO.

Skogan, W. (1994). *Contacts between Police and Public: findings from the 1992 British Crime Survey.* Home Office Research Study No.134. London: HMSO.

Smith, D and Gray, J. (1985). *Police and People in London: the PSI report.* Aldershot: Gower.

Smith, D. J. (1986). 'The framework of law and policing practice'. In Benyon, J. and Bourn, C. (eds). *The Police: powers, procedures and proprieties.* Oxford: Pergamon.

Softley, P., with the assistance of Brown, D., Forde, B., Mair, G. and Moxon, D. (1980). *Police Interrogation: an observational study in four police stations.* Home Office Research Study No. 61. London: HMSO.

Southgate, P. and Ekblom, P. (1984). *Contacts between Police and Public: findings from the British Crime Survey.* Home Office Research Study No. 77. London: HMSO.

Stevens, P. and Willis, C.F. (1979). *Race, Crime and Arrests.* Home Office Research Study No.58. London: HMSO.

Stockdale, J. (1993). *Management and Supervision of Police Interviews.* Police Research Series: Paper No. 5. London: Home Office Police Department.

Stone, R. (1986). 'Police powers after the Act'. In Benyon, J. and Bourn, C. (eds). *The Police: Powers, Procedures and Proprieties.* Oxford: Pergamon.

Thomas, T. (1988). 'The Police and Criminal Evidence Act 1984: the social work role'. *The Howard Journal of Criminal Justice,* Vol. 27, No. 4, pp. 256-265.

Thomas, T. (1994). *The Police and Social Workers.* Aldershot: Arena.

Thornton, G.L. (1989). *The Role of the Criminal Investigation Department: Present Performance and Future prospects.* M.A. thesis submitted to University of Manchester, Faculty of Social and Economic Studies. (Unpublished).

Tuck, M. and Southgate, P. (1981). *Ethnic minorities, crime and policing: a survey of the experiences of West Indians and Whites.* Home Office Reseaarch Study No.70. London: HMSO.

Tully, B. and Cahill, D. (1984). *Police Interviewing of the Mentally Handicapped: an Experimental Study.* London: Police Foundation.

Vennard, J. with the assistance of Karen Williams. (1980). *Contested Trials in Magistrates' Courts: the case for the prosecution.* Royal Commission on Criminal Procedure Research Study No.6. London: HMSO.

Walker, M.A., Jefferson, T. and Seneviratne, M. (1990). *Ethnic Minorities, Young People and the Criminal Justice System.* (Main report.) Centre for Criminological and Socio-Legal Studies, University of Sheffield.

Walkley, J. (1987). *Police Interrogation.* London: Police Review Publishing Company.

Williamson, T.M. (1990). *Strategic Changes in Police Interrogation: an examination of police and suspect behaviour in the Metropolitan Police in order to determine the effects of new legislation, technology and organisational policies.* PhD thesis: Faculty of Social Science, University of Kent at Canterbury. Unpublished.

Williamson, T.M. (1990a). 'Are nice cops winning? Trends in police questioning'. Paper presented to the British Psychological Society conference. Unpublished.

Willis, C. F. (1983). *The Use, Effectiveness and Impact of Police Stop and Search Powers.* Research and Planning Unit Paper 15. London: Home Office.

Willis, C.F. (1984). *The Tape-recording of Police Interviews with Suspects: an interim report.* Home Office Research Study No.82. London: HMSO.

Willis, C.F., Macleod, J. and Naish, P. (1988). *The tape-recording of Police Interviews with Suspects: a second interim report.* Home Office Research Study No. 97. London: HMSO.

Young, W. (1987). *An Evaluation of Part IV of the Police and Criminal Evidence Act 1984 Concerning Arrested Persons and its Effect upon Police Performance.* Dissertation submitted for M.Sc. at Teesside Polytechnic. Unpublished.

Young, M. (1991). *An Inside Job: Policing and Police Culture in Britain.* Oxford; Clarendon Press.

Young, J. (1994). *Policing the Streets: stops and search in North London.* Centre for Criminology, Middlesex University.

Zander, M. (1972). 'Access to a solicitor in the police station'. *Criminal Law Review,* 342-350.

Zander, M. (1979). 'The investigation of crime: a study of contested cases at the Old Bailey'. *Criminal Law Review,* 203.

Zander, M. (1990). *The Police and Criminal Evidence Act 1984.* London: Sweet and Maxwell.

Zander, M. and Henderson, P. (1993). *Crown Court Study.* Royal Commission on Criminal Justice Research Study No. 19. London: HMSO.

Zuckerman, A.A.S. (1989). 'Trial by unfair means – the report of the Working Group on the Right of Silence'. *Criminal Law Review,* 855-865.

Publications

List of research publications

A list of research reports for the last three years is provided below. A **full** list of publications is available on request from the Research and Statistics Directorate Information & Publications Group.

Home Office Research Studies (HORS)

133. **Intensive Probation in England and Wales: an evaluation.** George Mair, Charles Lloyd, Claire Nee and Rae Sibbett. 1994. xiv + 143pp. (0 11 341114 6).

134. **Contacts between Police and Public: findings from the 1992 British Crime Survey.** Wesley G Skogan. 1995. ix + 93pp. (0 11 341115 4).

135. **Policing low-level disorder: Police use of Section 5 of the Public Order Act 1986.** David Brown and Tom Ellis. 1994. ix + 69pp. (0 11 341116 2).

136. **Explaining reconviction rates: A critical analysis.** Charles Lloyd, George Mair and Mike Hough. 1995. xiv + 103pp. (0 11 341117 0).

137. **Case Screening by the Crown Prosecution Service: How and why cases are terminated.** Debbie Crisp and David Moxon. 1995. viii + 66pp. (0 11 341137 5).

138. **Public Interest Case Assessment Schemes.** Debbie Crisp, Claire Whittaker and Jessica Harris. 1995. x + 58pp. (0 11 341139 1).

139. **Policing domestic violence in the 1990s.** Sharon Grace. 1995. x + 74pp. (0 11 341140 5).

140. **Young people, victimisation and the police: British Crime Survey findings on experiences and attitudes of 12 to 15 year olds.** Natalie Aye Maung. xii + 140pp.

141. **The Settlement of refugees in Britain.** Jenny Carey-Wood, Karen Duke, Valerie Karn and Tony Marshall. 1995. xii + 133pp. (0 11 341145 6).

142. **Vietnamese Refugees since 1982.** Karen Duke and Tony Marshall. 1995. x + 62pp. (0 11 341147 2).

143. **The Parish Special Constables Scheme.** Peter Southgate, Tom Bucke and Carole Byron. 1995. x + 59pp. (1 85893 458 3).

144. **Measuring the Satisfaction of the Courts with the Probation Service.** Chris May. 1995. x + 76pp. (1 85893 483 4).

145. **Young people and crime.** John Graham and Benjamin Bowling. 1995. 142pp. (1 85893 551 2).

146. **Crime against retail and manufacturing premises: findings from the 1994 Commercial Victimisation Survey.** Catriona Mirrlees-Black and Alec Ross. 1995. xi + 110pp. (1 85893 554 7).

147. **Anxiety about crime: findings from the 1994 British Crime Survey.** Michael Hough. 1995. viii + 92pp. (1 85893 553 9).

148. **The ILPS Methadone Prescribing Project.** Rae Sibbitt. 1996. viii + 69pp. (1 85893 485 0).

149. **To scare straight or educate? The British experience of day visits to prison for young people.** Charles Lloyd. 1996. xi + 60pp. (1 85893 643 5).

150. **Predicting reoffending for Discretionary Conditional Release.** John B Copas, Peter Marshall and Roger Tarling. 1996. vii + 49pp. (1 85893 576 8).

151. **Drug misuse declared: results of the 1994 British Crime Survey.** Malcolm Ramsay and Andrew Percy. 1996. xv + 131pp. (1 85893 628 4).

152. **An Evaluation of the Introduction and Operation of the Youth Court.** David O'Mahony and Kevin Haines. 1996. viii + 70pp. (1 85893 5792).

153. **Fitting supervision to offenders: assessment and allocation decisions in the Probation Service.** Ros Burnett. 1996. xi + 99pp. (1 85893 599 7).

154. **Ethnic minorities: victimisation and racial harassment. Findings from the 1988 and 1992 British Crime Surveys.** Marian FitzGerald and Chris Hale. 1996. xi + 97pp. (1 85893 6039).

156. **Automatic Conditional Release: the first two years.** Mike Maguire, Brigitte Peroud and Peter Raynor. 1996. x + 114pp. (1 85893 659 4).

157. **Testing obscenity: an international comparison of laws and controls relating to obscene material.** Sharon Grace. 1996. ix + 46pp. (1 85893 672 1).

158. **Enforcing community sentences: supervisors' perspectives on ensuring complliance and dealing with breach.** Tom Ellis, Carol Hedderman and Ed Mortimer. 1996. x + 81 pp. (1 85893 691 8).

160. **Implementing crime prevention schemes in a multi-agency setting: aspects of process in the Safer Cities programme.** Mike Sutton. 1996. x + 53pp. (1 85893 691 8).

161. **Reducing criminality among young people: a sample of relevant programmes in the United Kingdom.** David Utting. 1996. vi + 112pp. (1 85893 744 2).

163. **Curfew orders with electronic monitoring: an evaluation of the first twelve months of the trials in Greater Manchester, Norfolk and Berkshire, 1995–1996.** George Mair and Ed Mortimer. 1996. x + 50 pp. (1 85893 765 5).

Home Office Research Studies 159 and 162 are not yet published.

Research and Planning Unit Papers (RPUP)

81. **The welfare needs of unconvicted prisoners.** Diane Caddle and Sheila White. 1994.

82. **Racially motivated crime: a British Crime Survey analysis.** Natalie Aye Maung and Catriona Mirrlees-Black. 1994.

83. **Mathematical models for forecasting Passport demand.** Andy Jones and John MacLeod. 1994.

84. **The theft of firearms**. John Corkery. 1994.

85. **Equal opportunities and the Fire Service.** Tom Bucke. 1994.

86. **Drug Education Amongst Teenagers: a 1992 British Crime Survey Analysis.** Lizanne Dowds and Judith Redfern. 1995.

87. **Group 4 Prisoner Escort Service: a survey of customer satisfaction.** Claire Nee. 1994.

88. **Special Considerations: Issues for the Management and Organisation of the Volunteer Police.** Catriona Mirrlees-Black and Carole Byron. 1995.

89. **Self-reported drug misuse in England and Wales: findings from the 1992 British Crime Survey.** Joy Mott and Catriona Mirrlees-Black. 1995.

90. **Improving bail decisions: the bail process project, phase 1.** John Burrows, Paul Henderson and Patricia Morgan. 1995.

91. **Practitioners' views of the Criminal Justice Act: a survey of criminal justice agencies.** George Mair and Chris May. 1995.

92. **Obscene, threatening and other troublesome telephone calls to women in England and Wales: 1982-1992.** Wendy Buck, Michael Chatterton and Ken Pease. 1995.

93. **A survey of the prisoner escort and custody service provided by Group 4 and by Securicor Custodial Services.** Diane Caddle. 1995.

Research Findings

8. **Findings from the International Crime Survey.** Pat Mayhew. 1994.

9 **Fear of Crime: Findings from the 1992 British Crime Survey.** Catriona Mirrlees-Black and Natalie Aye Maung. 1994.

10. **Does the Criminal Justice system treat men and women differently?** Carol Hedderman and Mike Hough. 1994.

11. **Participation in Neighbourhood Watch: Findings from the 1992 British Crime Survey.** Lizanne Dowds and Pat Mayhew. 1994.

12. **Explaining Reconviction Rates: A Critical Analysis.** Charles

Lloyd, George Mair and Mike Hough. 1995.

13. **Equal opportunities and the Fire Service.** Tom Bucke. 1994.

14. **Trends in Crime: Findings from the 1994 British Crime Survey.** Pat Mayhew, Catriona Mirrlees-Black and Natalie Aye Maung. 1994.

15. **Intensive Probation in England and Wales: an evaluation.** George Mair, Charles Lloyd, Claire Nee and Rae Sibbett. 1995.

16. **The settlement of refugees in Britain.** Jenny Carey-Wood, Karen Duke, Valerie Karn and Tony Marshall. 1995.

17. **Young people, victimisation and the police: British Crime Survey findings on experiences and attitudes of 12 to 15 year olds.** Natalie Aye Maung.

18. **Vietnamese Refugees since 1982.** Karen Duke and Tony Marshall. 1995.

19. **Supervision of Restricted Patients in the Community.** Suzanne Dell and Adrian Grounds. 1995.

20. **Videotaping children's evidence: an evaluation.** Graham Davies, Clare Wilson, Rebecca Mitchell and John Milsom. 1995.

21. **The mentally disordered and the police.** Graham Robertson, Richard Pearson and Robert Gibb. 1995.

22. **Preparing records of taped interviews.** Andrew Hooke and Jim Knox. 1995.

23. **Obscene, threating and other troublesome telephone calls to women: Findings from the British Crime Survey.** Wendy Buck, Michael Chatterton and Ken Pease. 1995.

24. **Young people and crime.** John Graham and Ben Bowling. 1995.

25. **Anxiety about crime: Findings from the 1994 British Crime Survey.** Michael Hough. 1995.

26. **Crime against retail premises in 1993.** Catriona Mirrlees-Black and Alec Ross. 1995.

27.   **Crime against manufacturing premises in 1993.** Catriona Mirrlees-Black and Alec Ross. 1995.

28.   **Policing and the public: findings from the 1994 British Crime Survey.** Tom Bucke. 1995.

29.   **The Child Witness Pack – An Evaluation.** Joyce Plotnikoff and Richard Woolfson. 1995.

30.   **To scare straight or educate? The British experience of day visits to prison for young people.** Charles Lloyd. 1996.

31.   **The ADT drug treatment programme at HMP Downview - a preliminary evaluation.** Elaine Player and Carol Martin. 1996.

32.   **Wolds remand prison - an evaluation.** Keith Bottomley, Adrian James, Emma Clare and Alison Liebling. 1996.

33.   **Drugs misuse declared: results of the 1994 British Crime Survey.** Malcolm Ramsay and Andrew Percy. 1996.

34.   **Crack cocaine and drugs-crime careers.** Howard Parker and Tim Bottomley. 1996.

35.   **Imprisonment for Fine Default.**David Moxon and Claire Whittaker. 1996.

36.   **Fine Impositions and Enforcement Following the Criminal Justice Act 1993.**Elizabeth Charman, Bryan Gibson, Terry Honess and Rod Morgan. 1996.

37.   **Victimisation in prisons.** Ian O'Donnell and Kimmett Edgar. 1996.

39.   **Ethnic minorities, victimisation and racial harassment.** Marian FitzGerald and Chris Hale. 1996.

40.   **Evaluating Joint Performance Management Between the Police and the Crown Prosecution Service.** Andrew Hooke, Jim Knox and David Portas. 1996.

41.   **Public attitudes to drug-related crime.** Sharon Grace. 1996.

42.   **Domestic burglary schemes in the Safer Cities programme.** Paul Ekblom, Ho Law and Mike Sutton. 1996.

43. **Pakistani women's experience of domestic violence in Great Britain.** Salma Choudry. 1996.

44 **Witnesses with learning disabilities.** Andrew Sanders, Jane Creaton, Sophia Bird and Leanne Weber. 1997.

45. **Does treating sex offenders reduce reoffending?** Carol Hedderman and Darren Sugg. 1996.

46. **Re-education programmes for violent men - an evaluation.** Russell Dobash, Rebecca Emerson Dobash, Kate Cavanagh and Ruth Lewis. 1996.

47. **Sentencing without a pre--sentence report.** Nigel Charles, Claire Whittaker and Caroline Ball. 1997.

Research Finding No. 38 not yet published.

Research Bulletin

The Research Bulletin is published each year and contains short articles on recent research.

Occasional Papers

Measurement of caseload weightings associated with the Children Act. Richard J. Gadsden and Graham J. Worsdale. 1994. (Available from the RSD Information Section.)

Managing difficult prisoners: The Lincoln and Hull special units. Professor Keith Bottomley, Professor Norman Jepson, Mr Kenneth Elliott and Dr Jeremy Coid. 1994. (Available from RSD Information Section.)

The Nacro diversion initiative for mentally disturbed offenders: an account and an evaluation. Home Office, NACRO and Mental Health Foundation. 1994. (Available from RSD Information Section.)

Probation Motor Projects in England and Wales. J P Martin and Douglas Martin. 1994.

Videotaping children's evidence: an evaluation. Graham Davies, Clare Wilson, Rebecca Mitchell and John Milsom. 1995.

Managing the needs of female prisoners. Allison Morris, Chris Wilkinson, Andrea Tisi, Jane Woodrow and Ann Rockley. 1995.

Local information points for volunteers. Michael Locke, Nick Richards, Lorraine Down, Jon Griffish and Roger Worgan. 1995.

Requests for Publications

Home Office Research Studies from 143 onwards, *Research and Planning Unit Papers, Research Findings and Research Bulletins* are available on request from:

Research and Statistics Directorate
Information and Publications Group
Room 278, 50 Queen Anne's Gate
London
SW1H 9AT
Telephone: 0171-273 2084 (answerphone)

Internet: http/www.open.gov.uk/home_off/rsdhome.htm
E-mail: rsd.ha apollo @ gtnet.gov.uk.

Occasional Papers can be purchased from:
Home Office
Publications Unit
50 Queen Anne's Gate
London SW1H 9AT
Telephone: 0171 273 2302

Home Office Research Studies prior to 143 can be purchased from:

HMSO Publications Centre

(Mail, fax and telephone orders only)
PO Box 276, London SW8 5DT
Telephone orders: 0171-873 9090
General enquiries: 0171-873 0011
(queuing system in operation for both numbers)
Fax orders: 0171-873 8200

*And also from **HMSO Bookshops**.*